*Barbarous Dissonance and Images of Voice in Milton's Epics*

Elizabeth Sauer brings a new perspective to Milton scholarship through her examination of the relative status and authority of the multiple narrative voices in *Paradise Lost* and *Paradise Regained*. She argues that Milton's epics accommodate a variety of interpretive voices, episodes, and dramatic and discursive exchanges that resist the monological containment of the poems' dominant narratives.

Sauer investigates the texts' discursive practices and the politics of their orchestration of voice, exploring the ways in which Milton's multivocal poems interrogated dominant structures of authority in the seventeenth century and constructed in their place a community of voices characterized by dissonances. She incorporates different critical responses to Milton's texts into her argument as a way of contextualizing her own historically engaged approach.

By injecting concepts such as multiple narrators and genres, open forms, strategic deferrals, and the exchanges between the poetic voices and discourses of the early modern period, Sauer tells us something about how the poems spoke to their own time as well as how they may be recuperated to speak to ours.

ELIZABETH SAUER is associate professor of English, Brock University.

# Barbarous Dissonance and Images of Voice in Milton's Epics

ELIZABETH SAUER

McGill-Queen's University Press
Montreal & Kingston • London • Buffalo

© McGill-Queen's University Press 1996
ISBN 0-7735-1428-7

Legal deposit fourth quarter 1996
Bibliothèque nationale du Québec

Printed in Canada on acid-free paper

This book has been published with the help of a grant from the Humanities and Social Science Federation of Canada, using funds provided by the Social Sciences and Humanities Research Council of Canada. Funding has also been received from Brock University.

McGill-Queen's University Press is grateful to the Canada Council for support of its publishing program.

**Canadian Cataloguing in Publication Data**

Sauer, Elizabeth, 1964–
  Barbarous dissonance and images of voice in Milton's epics
  Includes bibliographical references and index.
  ISBN 0-7735-1428-7
  1. Milton, John, 1608–1674, Paradise lost. 2. Milton, John, 1608–1674, Paradise regained. 3. Narration (rhetoric). I. Title.
  PR3588.S38 1996     821'.4     C96-900477-X

Typeset in Palatino 10/12
by Chris McDonell, Hawkline Graphics.

*For my parents, Anneliese and Albert,*
*for giving me their language and the opportunities and*
*tireless support to develop my own;*
*and for my brother, Albert*

# Contents

Acknowledgments ix

Introduction 3

1 The Voices and Politics of Nimrod 14

2 Critical Interventions 35

3 "I now must change / Those notes to Tragic": The Sad Task of Raphael, Satan, and the Poet-Narrator 62

4 The Gendered Hierarchy of Discourse 87

5 "Learning to Curse": Colonialism and Censorship in Paradise 111

6 The Voices of Nebuchadnezzar in *Paradise Regained* 136

Conclusion 160

Notes 163

Works Cited 191

Index 209

# Acknowledgments

I am especially indebted to Balachandra Rajan and Elizabeth Harvey, who first challenged me to investigate the subject of voice. From their different vantage points they expertly criticized various drafts of this book, and have as well urged numerous other scholars to analyse and reinvent the conversations with the voices of early modern English literature and culture.

I benefited from many fine critical studies on Milton and on the literary and political discourses of his time, particularly those of Stevie Davies, Balachandra Rajan, Annabel Patterson, Marshall Grossman, Mary Nyquist, and Christopher Hill. My written and verbal exchanges with Brian Patton, Dale Churchward, Marta Straznicky, Paul Stevens, Monika Lee, Teresa Hubel, Jane McLeod, and Susan Spearey, who all read parts of the manuscript, as well as with the students of my seventeenth-century and Restoration literature classes, sustained me through the multiple stages of writing this book. I also acknowledge the significant contribution of my assistants, Colleen Pielechaty and Marcus Hadley, who conscientiously aided me in my research and in editing the manuscript.

Doctoral fellowships and a research grant from the Social Sciences and Humanities Research Council of Canada (1992–95) provided funding for my research in Canada, the United States, and England, and I extend my gratitude to the Council. I also owe a considerable debt to the readers from the Canadian Federation for the Humanities and McGill-Queen's University Press for their insightful, incisive evaluations of my manuscript. Special thanks go to Roger Martin at McGill-Queen's for his astuteness and his energetic support in seeing this work go to press.

For the encouragement I received from my colleagues, particularly in the Department of English Language and Literature, I am grateful. A grant from Brock University helped to defray the cost of publishing this book, and I thank the university for its generosity in securing this funding.

Permissions to incorporate previously published material have been granted by the publishers of *Renaissance and Reformation, English Studies in Canada,* the *Ben Jonson Journal,* and *Agonistics: Arenas of Creative Contest* (SUNY Press).

*Barbarous Dissonance and Images of Voice in Milton's Epics*

# Introduction

> There may be four voices. There may be, perhaps, only two. I say this to indicate the tentative nature of my enquiry.
> T.S. Eliot, *The Three Voices of Poetry*

> Give me the liberty to know, to utter and to argue freely according to conscience, above all liberties.
> John Milton, *Areopagitica*

## 1 THE EVOLUTION OF VOICE

This book examines the relative status and authority of the multiple narrative voices in *Paradise Lost* and *Paradise Regained* within interrelated socio-political, linguistic, and narratological contexts. Both epics accommodate a variety of interpretive voices, episodes, and dramatic and discursive exchanges that resist the monological containment of the poems' dominant narratives. Through the inclusion of the multiple, even "unauthorized" voices and creation narratives, the poems are brought into a constructive tension with the Genesis story and its received biblical and literary traditions, as well as with accounts of England's own tragic history. In presenting their individual creation stories, the narrators of both texts renegotiate the terms of their self-definition as speakers and their positions of compliance or resistance in relation to the other narrators, as well as to the other "voices" of seventeenth-century history and culture.[1]

Though products of the late seventeenth century, Milton's multivocal texts speak to the contemporary reader, who becomes engaged in comparing and evaluating the poetic and extra-literary voices the epics inscribe. In "Defamiliarizing *Paradise Lost*" Balachandra Rajan contends that the literary strategy of including multiple narrative perspectives that disrupt the monological function of the official narrative voice has not received sufficient attention in critical studies of the poem. The strong claims to totalization in the poem made by Miltonists of the 1960s and 1970s, who seek to resolve tensions or difference in the text by creating a univocal, ubiquitous poet-narrator, have been challenged in the last two decades in different ways by such critics as William Kerrigan, Jonathan Goldberg, Barbara Lewalski, and Kathleen Swaim, as well as by Gordon Teskey, who observes that "few characters in non-dramatic literature appear as free as Milton's to choose their own story" (11). Burton Weber concludes that Donald F. Bouchard has written the definitive criticism on the subject by treating the question of point of view in *Paradise Lost* "so astonishingly that the theme need never be touched on again" ("Point-of-View" 278). Bouchard's structuralist reading, however, does not address the interweaving of the texts' multiple interpretive voices or the ways in which extra-literary discourses inform the representation of the poems' diverse narratives. In my analysis of *Paradise Lost*, *Paradise Regained*, and the history of the epics' agonistic creation, I demonstrate the relevance of these concerns.

The strategies of reading *Paradise Lost* into univocality have been challenged even since its earliest reception by the contention that the poem is at odds with itself. Throughout this study I examine different responses by early literary critics of Milton as a way of contextualizing my own historically engaged approach. Milton's reputation as the "Goos-quill Champion" of the "Rumpers" in the period of tumultuous pamphleteering on the eve of the Restoration tainted the reception of his epics. Writers of the neoclassical, Tory-dominated Restoration period and eighteenth century, from John Dryden to Samuel Johnson, complained that Milton's poems displayed an inconsistency of poetic greatness alongside political culpability,[2] and even cast the poet-revolutionary as a contemporary Nimrod responsible for the confusion of tongues. Critics denounced Milton's "Babylonish Dialect" and remarked disapprovingly on the incongruity of the voices in *Paradise Lost*, an issue I address in part 1 of chapter 2. Johnson, who in the *Lives of the English Poets* claims that Milton "wrote no language" (1:190–1), does in fact commend the poet for his innovative art of narration, for the texture of the fable, the variation of incidents, the interposition of dialogue, and the stratagems that surprise and enchain attention in *Paradise Lost*. However, Johnson ultimately disarms the poem, glossing over the problematic interplay of voice (1:173–9). Shortly thereafter, these tensions were restored to the epic when Romantic poets, who admired Milton as a poet-revolutionary, celebrated the grandeur and tragic heroism of Satan in *Paradise Lost*, while appropriating Milton's writings to convey hybrid literary and political viewpoints in their own epics.[3] Each interpretation transforms the received literary tradition, which in turn informs our response to

*Paradise Lost* and to the interaction of poetic voices and extra-poetic discourses in the text.

By comparing some critical responses from the 1960s and 1970s to the question of voice in *Paradise Lost*, we discover a range of readings that challenge the unifying imperative of any individual studies. Most Miltonists of this period attributed to the poet-narrator a privileged status and identified this voice with Milton's. By isolating the poem from a socio-political context and foregrounding the authority of the dominant narrative voice, critics developed a reading of the epic as a unified whole.[4] The voice of the bard, the presence of the poet, Louis Lohr Martz announces in *The Paradise Within*, is "indeed everywhere in the poem, advising, exhorting, warning, praising, denouncing, lamenting, promising, judging, in all ways guiding us ... by his strong evaluative comments" (107). Martz anticipates the approach developed by Stanley Fish, who, in his early study of *Paradise Lost*, declares that the historical reality of the epic genre requires the reader to identify the narrator as "an authority who is a natural ally against the difficulties of the poem" (*Surprised by Sin* 47). By privileging one reading of the poem, Fish lends as much authority to the narrator as Anne D. Ferry does in *Milton's Epic Voice: The Narrator in* Paradise Lost. In both cases the critics' interpretation of the monological function of the detached speaker, in the circle of whose vision everything in the poem is contained (Ferry 179), reinforces their claims to totalization. The epic avoids the more familiar language and daily speech of the novel and establishes a formal rather than social relationship between the speaker and both the characters and readers (Ferry 180); cut off by his blindness "from the chearful waies of men," the omniscient voice controls the allegedly self-contained poem and interprets the world without being immersed in the world he interprets. William Riggs in *The Christian Poet in Paradise Lost* likewise argues for the Miltonic presence in the language, tone, and structure of the epic. Though he is justified in criticizing the artificial distinctions made by Ferry to characterize the stylistic uniqueness of the speakers, Riggs simply uses the presence of the other voices to confirm the poet-narrator's dominance. Thus he maintains, for example, that angels do not speak a different language from that of the inspired epic poet (102); in fact they serve merely as a chorus in the poem.

The dialogic nature of the authorial voice is examined by contemporary critics, including William Kerrigan, who develops a powerful Freudian reading of the poem in *The Sacred Complex: On the Psychogenesis of Paradise Lost*, and by Jonathan Goldberg, who in *Voice Terminal Echo: Postmodernism and English Renaissance Texts*, offers a poststructuralist interpretation of the intertextual relationship between the Miltonic voice and written speech. Goldberg explains that the text renders the author speechless and provides him with a voice in the "now" that defines his place in history and in literary history (124–5). The loss of voice and the anonymity of the written "I," which results from the darkness and blankness in which the author writes, paradoxically allow the inscribed voice and the images of voice (133) to be heard in the text. Applying a more traditional critical approach, Barbara Lewalski in *Paradise Lost and the Rhetoric of Literary Form* explores the interaction of the poem's narrative voices in reference to its multiple genres, while Kathleen Swaim, in *Before and After the Fall*, examines the narrative strategies and pedagogical procedures of Raphael and Michael in the context of Platonic and Aristotelian philosophy and seventeenth-century biblical hermeneutics.[5] Marshall Grossman's *"Authors to Themselves": Milton and the Revelation of History*, which analyses the performance of the individual as a historical actor in *Paradise Lost* from a psychoanalytic and narratological perspective, bears some resemblance to my own study in terms of its critical approach, though I am less concerned with the historicizing of selfhood than with the orchestration of voices in literary, linguistic, and extra-literary contexts.

In this study the terms "voice" and "images of voice" – *imago/imago vocis*[6] – have various definitions for me that multiplied as my investigation proceeded. I have, therefore, artificially though necessarily separated the definitions into three interrelated contexts: socio-political, linguistic, and narratological. Voice is an expression created by utterance or allusion, including intertextual allusion. Voices are marked by the fall into language – the symbolic order – and into history; and yet, at the same time, the diverse voices and episodes that make up all literary and historical texts challenge the dominant ideology by disrupting the narrative imperium and the historical continuum. Each voice is informed by a particular expression of will and consciousness and has its own overtones (Bakhtin, *Imagination* 434); moreover, each voice has a political function inside as well as outside the text – another artificial distinction – of intervening in a given context and of offering a point of view or articulating a perception, and yet no speaker is autonomous. In a social context, the solitary speaker participates in a collective expression that constitutes the field of human relations and the multivocal texts.

The range of contemporary critical treatments of voice has expanded considerably since T.S. Eliot announced in *The Three Voices of Poetry*: "all that matters is, that in the end the voices should be heard in harmony: and, as I have said, I doubt whether in any real poem only one voice is audible" (23).[7] Structuralists also attribute to voice an authoritative status by dissociating speech from writing. With the privilege granted to speech in the theory of Ferdinand de Saussure, voice becomes an image of truth and authenticity, a source of self-present living speech that offers the possibility for transparent understanding, thus providing a contrast to the lifeless emanations of writing. However, writing actually destroys the ideal of pure self-presence; by sacrificing authority to "the vagaries and whims of textual 'dissemination,'" writing resists the "traditional view that associates truth with self-presence and the 'natural' language wherein it finds expression" (Norris 28).[8] In "The Weaving of Voices" Roland Barthes explains that the text is produced through utterances – the convergence of various codes and voices that he identifies. Alongside each utterance, one might say that "off-stage voices" can be heard. In their interweaving the voices (whose origin is "lost" in the vast perspective of the *already written*) de-originate the utterance (*S/Z* 21). Barthes declares that writing involves the destruction of every voice, origin, and of the author's own identity, thereby allowing only language to speak. The reader of the text, who is without history, merely holds together all the text's traces (*Image-Music-Text* 142–8). The depriviliging of utterance by writing is reinforced by the Derridian proposition that writing is actually the precondition for language. The textualized, dialogized voices exist prior to speech and disrupt the "natural bond" between sense and sound.

This poststructuralist model of the inscription of voice and the deorigination of the already present voices textualizes the socio-historical evolution of voice and is, therefore, politically dangerous. The multiple voices and diverse languages at work in every linguistic community, of which M.M. Bakhtin in particular has made us aware, develop out of collective expressions – literary, linguistic, historical, and social – which they help to define and by which they are encoded. Defined in a Bakhtinian context as the power to influence and shape thought and opinion through language, authority is dispersed among multiple voices rather than contained in a singular dominant voice. If the embodiment of power in society is socio-political action, then its equivalent in poetry is voice, dramatic exchange, and narrative intervention. The appropriation of voices[9] and the suppression of the political and gender differences of the speakers are significant issues which I will address in examining Milton's response to censorship practices.

In *An Apology against a Pamphlet* Milton describes the exemplary author in terms of a poem: "he who would not be frustrate of his hope to write well hereafter in laudable things, ought him selfe to bee a true Poem, that is, a composition, and patterne of the best and honourablest things" (*Prose* 1:890). In challenging censorship laws, Milton in the *Areopagitica* defends books as living things and compares, in turn, the human experience of the world to the reading of a text: "What ever thing we hear or see, sitting, walking, travelling, or conversing may be fitly call'd our book, and is of the same effect that writings are" (*Prose* 2:528). Paul Ricoeur observes similarly that "human action is in many ways a quasi-text. It is exteriorized in a manner comparable to the fixation characteristic of writing" (*Philosophy* 160).[10] The art of critical reading is the means for interpreting and historicizing both human action and the world as text, a metaphor with a "venerable history" (Eco 23).[11] Ricoeur goes on to discuss the eventual detachment of the action from the actor and of the written text from the author when act and text are "freed from the initial conditions of [their] production" and reinscribed in new historical and social contexts. Examined in isolation from its author – or from authorial intention[12] – the text is opened up to the interpretations of an "indefinite series of possible 'readers.' The judges are not contemporaries, but subsequent history" (161).

The proposed separation of the text from its author or the circumstances of its production merely, however, replaces one form of contingency with another. Though the text speaks in the voice of the reader, the reader at the same time participates in an exchange with the text and thereby with current and past discourses that in turn resist the projection of self-interested demands upon them. The dissociation of the text from the multiple discourses it inscribes inevitably proves futile. The multivocal, multigenre poem *Paradise Lost*, then, should be analysed as a text that not only presents verbal contests among the narrative voices but also engages in dialogism: *Paradise Lost* "dialogues with the other 'voices' of the culture, by referring to them intertextually and also constructing, for the participants in this dialogue, positions of compliance or resistance with respect to those other 'voices'" (Kress 234). "Reality" is constructed in the creation of the fictional world that is situated within the larger narrative of history, thus establishing an ongoing conversation between literary and extra-literary voices. In examining the images of voice in *Paradise Lost*, we become aware not only of the poet-narrator's own dialogized voice and of the different speakers in the poem but also of the language of dissonance and multivocality that informs the text.

Critics expressing discontent with early New Historicist assumptions about literature's production of "social work"[13] continue to defend the relevance of cultural, political, and individual interpretive practices. At the same time, they offer alternative ways of applying these interconnected approaches to the literary text – the primary site of tension – to which they redirect the focus of critical analysis (Pechter 301–2). Rather than attempting to assess literature's impact on society, I investigate the text's own discursive practices and the politics of its orchestration of voice. I also identify ways in which Milton's multivocal poems interrogate dominant structures of authority in the seventeenth century, developing in their place a community of voices characterized by dissonances that work towards a world-transforming counterpoint, one that is always just about to be achieved.

## 2 THE NARRATIVE STRUCTURE

The many Renaissance and seventeenth-century histories of Nimrod and the fall of Babel provide literary and political contexts for examining the interplay of voice and discourses of multivocality. In an extra-literary context, monarchists of the seventeenth century appropriated the symbolic tower of Babel to characterize the multiplicity of sects, the revolutionary movement, and the many-headed monster of democracy – Spenser's Blatant Beast. The cacophonous voices resounded in a society in which public opinion was gaining more recognition[14] and pamphlet literature, religious sects, and political factions proliferated. Milton added his voice to the historical conversations[15] through his appeals for republicanism in his political pamphlets and through the orchestration of narrative voices in his literary texts. In *Paradise Lost* and *Paradise Regained* he included multiple interpretive voices and thereby conditioned in the Restoration years the imaginative possibility for further intervention in the authorized conversations outside the poem. Instead of advocating a return to an original language or a former state of edenic innocence, the poet offered a portrait of a multivocal community as a creative ferment for the re-formation of the nation.[16]

In chapter 1 I contextualize the political representation of voice in the history of Nimrod in book 12 of *Paradise Lost* by examining at length the received tradition of the account. Milton develops his own politicized poetic reading of the story of Babel in which he includes the unnamed Nimrod, the postlapsarian world's first monarch, who declares his dissatisfaction with "fair equality, fraternal state" (12.26). In the second half of the chapter I characterize some alternative and prospective governmental models that Milton designs in the epic to displace the "Empire tyrannous." The complex movement that I trace in chapter 1 from Babel to Pentecost – a recuperative linguistic response to the Confusion[17] – provides an outline of the structure of all the double-formed chapters in this study. I begin each chapter by examining representations of monovocality, censorship, and confusion; as I demonstrate in a discussion of the Nimrod-Bacchus relationship in chapter 3, Milton links tyranny with cacophony and connects the solitary, "negative voice" of monarchy (*Prose, Eikonoklastes* 3:501, 3:579) with "the barbarous dissonance" (7.32) both of the royalist pamphleteers and the "miscellaneous rabble" (*Poems,* PR 3.50). In each chapter I also identify strategies adopted by the poet to order the confusion and to create a community of voices that remains for Milton a conceptual rather than a real possibility.

Milton's story of Babel offers a critical reading not only of the history of polity but also of the evolution of language. In chapter 2 I examine linguistic developments as well as constructions of historical narratives in a seventeenth-century and a contemporary context in order to provide two interrelated frames of reference for my discussion of the poems' multiple speakers in the subsequent chapters. While the biblical story of Babel provided medieval and Renaissance writers with a widely accepted account of the fall into linguistic confusion, explanations for the confusion of tongues multiplied: in the seventeenth century decentralization, political and religious crises, economic changes, scientific discoveries, and print-capitalism challenged the reign of the dominant discourse – the civilized language. After identifying some counter-etiologies to Babel invented by seventeenth-century writers and philologists, I consider how Milton offers diverse explanations for the fragmentation of truth and demonstrates the difficulty of communicating meaning in a flawed medium.

In the second half of chapter 2 I focus on the possibilities for historical intervention. Throughout the seventeenth century historical writings were appropriated and censored by monarchists and church officials alike; Joseph Hall, for example, declared in *An Humble Remonstrance to the High Court of Parliament*: "Since, if Antiquity may be the rule, the civill Politie hath sometimes varied, the sacred [episcopal authority] never" (8). The tight control of history by the authorities discouraged Milton's efforts at facilitating dialogue and provoked his attempt to challenge the master narratives of state and church history. Adding his voice to the anti-monarchical and anti-prelatic movements, Milton denounces all those who uphold "the right of the past to control the present" (Masson 2:242), and he insists on the need to divorce the multivocal drama of the past from "the carnal supportment of tradition" (*Prose* 1:827). Milton constantly redefines his relationship to the nation's history; using a paradoxical discourse to knit together the historical episodes with an emerging vision of Providence, the poet-revolutionary reemplots[18] the drama of his personal failure and of England's tragic history in order to work through the experiences of defeat. Throughout the epic and particularly in the final two books, the poet examines the voices and structural mechanisms that make up the poem and the narrative of history. Milton also offers possibilities for the recuperation of linguistic ambiguity and the reemplotment of the historical tragedy.

In presenting their oral histories, the different speakers in *Paradise Lost* interrogate the official biblical, historical, and poetic narratives while also exposing the constructed nature of their own genesis stories. Moreover, the different creation accounts and tragic narratives betray the heightened self-awareness of the speakers, which is manifested in soliloquy – the discourse of the divided self, of which the multivocal poem is intensely distrustful. The soliloquy is also the site of agonistic strife between various voices and discourses inscribed in the poem. In chapter 3 I first examine the narration of tragic events that constitutes Raphael's "Sad task," and then focus on the monological speeches and verbal contests between two of the poem's authoritative voices. Despite the apparent opposition between Satan and the inspired narrator, *Paradise Lost* in fact is sustained by primal ambivalence, *kairos*, or "image of voice" (Bloom, *Agon* 38), produced by the struggle between the epic poets. The word-play and wandering signification denied by the classical orator threaten the primary speaker, who becomes conscious of the dialogized nature of his own voice as well as the other viewpoints in and outside the official narrative. After studying the related discourses and narrative strategies of Satan and the primary speaker, I briefly analyse the politics of the poet-narrator's relationship to the epic's other interpretive voices.

I begin chapter 4 by discussing Milton's representation of voice in relation to seventeenth-century debates about government and gender politics.[19] In satirizing political corruption and civil unruliness in the early Restoration years, Milton employs the tradition of the Renaissance literature on prodigy, which reinforced hierarchical gender relations and relegated women to the private sphere by feminizing confusion and tyranny. The first part of this chapter, "The Gendered Hierarchy of Discourse," focuses on interconnected discourses of political anarchy, gender inversion, and monstrous births in Sin's creation story in book 2 of *Paradise Lost*, which I interpret as an intertextual account that is both strategically distanced from and simultaneously freighted with topical concerns. The classical myths, Renaissance allegories, and seventeenth-century popular culture and political satires that inform Milton's account of Sin associate the disintegration of political and civil order with the violation by women of traditional social, marital, and maternal roles. The description of Eve in the poem does not redeem the portrait of the "double-form'd" Sin; in fact, Milton portrays his primary female character at best as a secondary antihero in the epic. Moreover, the poet appropriates both her voice and creation story, represented by Adam's possession and rupturing of the lyrical space that Eve constructs in delivering her historical narrative. Finally, as I discuss in chapter 5, Milton assigns Adam rather than Eve an important role in the unfolding of Michael's prophetic vision of human history.

Having examined the interpretive voices and the creation stories individually in the previous chapters, I begin chapter 5 by adopting a poetic-ecological metaphor to characterize the development of meaning and the interrelationship of the poem's different speakers. The Fall, I argue, results from the censorship of voices, conversation, and of "superfluity" and wildness in the garden that Satan violates and colonizes.[20] The gradual restoration of dialogue eventually allows Adam and Eve to reemplot their tragic fall and that of the "woeful Race" they conceive (9.984). In part 2 of this chapter I focus on the revelations and double-voiced narrative of books 11 and 12 respectively in examining Michael's resistance to Adam's literalization of postlapsarian history and his reemplotment of the ravished nation's tragic history. The development of a meta-narrative of history is an act of censorship, one challenged by the recasting of events in a paradoxical – "(pure of any *doxa*)" – discourse (Barthes, *Sade* 126). In the final books of the epic the angelic narrator adopts a paradoxical, prophetic discourse to interweave the historical narrative with an emerging vision of Providence and thereby to recast Adam's personal defeat and the tragedy of human history. Though Adam's role in the final act appears to be insignificant, he is responsible, I demonstrate, for the individual stories of social outcasts and unsung heroes in Michael's prophecy, which constitute the history of the imagined political community and the postlapsarian Eden of the future.

My examination of the staged debates in *Paradise Regained* offers an effective conclusion for this study because it affords an opportunity to address the relationship of verbal expression, political engagement, and historical progress in a poem that has traditionally been labelled undramatic and has been read as an allegory of Milton's post-revolutionary resignation to quietism.[21] Certainly the poem's format appears hostile to multivocality since, with the exception of the prophetic voices of the fishermen and Mary, it consists of a debate between two principal speakers. However, in this study I suggest that the Son's prophetic and paradoxical discourse objects throughout to the oppressive homogeneity of the opposing discourse. Moreover, I demonstrate that the debate in which Satan and the Son engage is not a substitute for political engagement; rather, the verbal combat relocates, without confining, that engagement in language – a highly dramatic and prophetic language in which the speakers compete for dominance. In part 2 I argue that Satan's fall from the temple pinnacle – Nebuchadnezzar's reconstructed tower of Babel in *Paradise Regained* – represents the silencing of the monological, negating voice and, as Milton suggests in *Eikonoklastes*, the symbolic end of monarchy itself (*Prose* 3:405).

Even when examining the voices and focalizers of the poems or when quoting directly, the literary critic inevitably engages in focalization herself by lending a (number of) perspective(s) to the analysed texts.[22] Nevertheless, I maintain throughout this study that there are a variety of voices, discourses, and manners of orchestrating voices that are characteristically Miltonic and yet present in spite of their author. I argue furthermore that the poems convey the desire for multiple voices within society and yet offer themselves as something more than mediators between art and society: they engage the conversations about events and issues outside themselves through the interplay of literary and extra-literary voices. In examining Milton's poems and their reception, we discover how literature encodes cultural and political discourses about multivocality. We become aware in turn of how we orchestrate as well as censor the many voices and episodes that make up our own culture and history. The accommodation of multiple voices in Milton's epics teaches us about dialogism while exhibiting the dialectical relationship between the desire for plurality and the ever unfulfilled need for consensus. This study of diverse voices, narratives, and counter-narratives in the epics and the range of issues they address that speak with reticence on politics and history approaches the poems as controversial texts, which interrogate dominant structures of belief while establishing the conditions for intervention in a culturally or politically censored environment.

# 1 The Voices and Politics of Nimrod

> one shall rise
> Of proud ambitious heart, who not content
> With fair equality, fraternal state,
> Will arrogate Dominion undeserv'd
> Over his brethren, and quite dispossess
> Concord and law of Nature from the Earth;
> Hunting (and Men not Beasts shall be his game)
> With War and hostile snare such as refuse
> Subjection to his Empire tyrannous:
> A mighty Hunter thence he shall be styl'd
> Before the Lord, as in despite of Heav'n,
> Or from Heav'n claiming second Sovranty;
> And from Rebellion shall derive his name,
> Though of Rebellion others he accuse.  *Paradise Lost* book 12

The restoration of the monarchy in 1660 led again to the suppression of public opinion, debate, and participation in political conversations. Disempowered and disillusioned by the turn of events, the remaining republicans sought alternatives to direct political involvement. A victim of the royalists' return, Milton chose to compose an epic for the nation in which he recounted England's tragic history and also proposed the establishment of a commonwealth to replace the "Empire tyrannous" (12.32) constructed by the monarchy.

In *Paradise Lost* Milton invites a political reading of the story of Babel by including the unnamed Nimrod in the account. Francis Blackburne claims that the Nimrod passage has "always been supposed to allude to [Milton's] own time" (2:625). Milton represents Nimrod in the epic as the postlapsarian world's first monarch, who declares his dissatisfaction with "fair equality, fraternal state" (12.26) and who, by imposing a self-serving unification on the pastoral society, becomes responsible for the confusion of tongues. In attempting to make a name for themselves by building the tower, Nimrod and his crew remain, ironically, nameless and powerless. Babble resounds through time, and the unfinished tower becomes a symbol for the tyrant's political failure. In place of Nimrod's empire the poet-revolutionary proposes the development of a republican government, national consciousness, and a multivocal society – created in part through the dissemination of language; he thereby maintains that multifaceted truths and divergent points of view should be expected and tolerated rather than regarded as regrettable lapses from the one standard of rectitude. In this chapter, then, I first examine discursively linked debates in the seventeenth-century about kingship, popular and political representation, and social formation by investigating the representation of voice in Milton's book 12 history of Nimrod and in various other accounts of the fall of Babel written by Milton's predecessors and contemporaries. In part 2 I characterize some of the alternative models of authority and prospective state and church governments that Milton offers in place of the tyrannical empire of his own day.

## 1 THE "EMPIRE TYRANNOUS"

The political pamphlet literature of the Civil War years identified the voices of the populace with the confusion of tongues. The liberties taken by commoners – apprentices, street vendors, and even women – who not only presumed to have diverse opinions on religion and politics but actually to voice them in public, all claiming possession of the truth, fuelled the rebellion against the established authorities, which would lead to the regicide. According to "The Rebellion" or "The Anarchie, or The Blessed Reformation since 1640," as this ballad is later renamed,[1] the babble that issues from the many voices of the Round-headed beast contributes to the fragmentation of meaning and the disintegration of political unity, which "with good Monarchy / Begin[s] and end[s] in one" (V3r):

> Now, thanks to the Powers below,
> We have even done our do,
> The Mytre is down, and so is the Crown,
> And with them the Corronet too:
> All is now the Peoples, and then
> What is theirs is ours we know;
> There is no such thing as a Bishop or K–
> Or Peer, but in name or show;
> Come Clowns, and come Boys, Come Hoberdehoys,
> Come Females of each degree,
> Stretch out your throats, bring in your Votes,
> And make good the Anarchy;
> Then thus it shall be, sayes *Alse*,

Nay, thus it shall be, sayes *Amie*,
Nay, thus it shall go, sayes *Taffie*, I trow,
Nay, thus it shall go, sayes *Jemmy*.

Oh but the truth, good People all, the truth is such a thing.
For it will undo both Church and State too,
And pull out the throat of our King ...

Well, let the truth be whose it will,
There is something else in ours,
Yet this devotion in our Religions
May chance to abate our Powers ...
We are fourscore Religions strong,
Then take your choice, the Major voice
Shall carry't right or wrong;
Then let's have King *Charles*, sayes *George*,
Nay, wee'l have his Son, sayes *Hugh*;
Nay, then let's have none, sayes gabbering *Jone*,
Nay, wee'l be all Kings, sayes *Prue* ....

If then when all is thought their own,
And lyes at their belief,
These popular pates, reap nought but debates
From these many round-headed beast;
Come Royalists then, do you play the men,
And Cavaliers give the word,
And now let's see what you will be,
And whether you can accord;
A health to King *Charles*, sayes *Tom*,
Up with it, sayes *Ralph*, like a man,
God blesse him, sayes *Doll*, and raise him, sayes *Moll*,
And send him his own, sayes *Nan*.

But now for these prudent Wights,
That fit without end, and to none,
And their Committees in Towns and Cities
Fill with confusion. (V2r–3v)

James I himself had insisted in *The True Lawe of free Monarchies* that without the king the people were nothing more than a headless multitude (D4v–5r).[2] John Cleveland's reference to "the rable, that fierce beast of ours" (33) in "On the Archbishop of Canterbury" is characteristic of the royalist rhetoric that identified the Puritan revolution as a democratic and chaotic movement. Democracy is "but the Effect of a crazy Brain" that mixes words and things, Samuel Butler announces in "A Republican" (59). Seventeenth-century political and religious uprisings and the proposed establishment of a commonwealth as a forum for the voices of the people were regarded as direct violations of the established political and natural orders. The divinely sanctioned political and ecclesiastical hierarchies possessed an ontological reality that, according to their respective supporters, rendered them impervious to change and to corruption by republicans and radicals.

Of the innumerable representations of monarchical rule used to defend kingship in Renaissance and seventeenth-century political, philosophical, and literary texts, the Platonic metaphor of the beehive (*Republic* 7.520b) was an especially popular one, which monarchists adopted and republicans in turn defamiliarized. Contrasting the Greek *Aristocratia* with the many-headed monster of the Athenian *Democratia*, Thomas Elyot in *The Book named The Governor* promotes a hierarchical consciousness and defends the aesthetic and natural value of order in the public weal (6). Royalists like Elyot insisted that the ancient form of rule was the most stable because the commonwealth allowed too much liberty; just as there is in nature one principal bee for whom all others labour (7), so must the public weal – the living body made up of sundry estates and degrees of men – be governed by a monarch or a small aristocracy. Elyot borrows his analogy from Erasmus, who in *The Education of a Christian Prince* invokes Seneca to provide an "important example for powerful kings"; Erasmus explains that "although bees are very angry creatures, so much so that they leave their stings in the wound, the king alone has no sting. Nature did not want him to be fierce and seek a revenge which would cost him so dear, and she deprived him of a weapon, leaving his anger ineffective" (225–6).[3] Pro-royalists thereafter continued to use the analogy without greatly altering its significance. Sir Walter Raleigh in *The marrow of historie* declares that "the Bees have their prince" (80), and Izaak Walton in *The Compleat Angler* offers the productive beehive as a political model: Auceps commends "the laborious *Bee*, of whose *Prudence, Policy* and regular Government of their own Commonwealth I might say much, as also of their several kinds, and how useful their honey and wax is both for meat and Medicines to mankind" (182.7–11).

In *A Defence of the People of England* Milton replies to his contemporaries, particularly to humanists like Salmasius, who used the example of the bee to represent and legitimize monarchical government: "'Bees have a king.' Those of Trent, I suppose, as you

[Salmasius] perhaps recall? The others, as you affirm, have republics. You should really give up this nonsense about bees; they belong to the Muses and hate insects like you and, as you see, refute you" (*Prose* 4:428). In book 1 of *Paradise Lost* Milton again appropriates the royalist symbol of the beehive, this time to parody the assembly of devils and, by extension, institutional hierarchies. Employing an epic simile, Milton compares the demonic council – which convenes, ironically, just after Mulciber-Nimrod's construction of Pandemonium – to the noisy swarming bees (768–76). The scene anticipates both the hissing of the devils, who are later transformed into serpents, and the confusion of tongues at the fall of Nimrod's tower of Babel. Not monarchy but rather the commonwealth, in which the leaders serve the public, comes closest to the Christian ideal for Milton. "*Go to the Ant, thou sluggard, saith Solomon; consider her waies, and be wise; which having no prince, ruler, or lord, provides her meat in the summer, and gathers her food in the harvest,*" he recommends in *The Readie and Easie Way* (*Prose* 7:427). Addressing those who think the nation undone without a king, Milton proposes an alternative form of government that he hopes England will adopt in the future. In his commentary on the alternative political structure that nature offers in the form of the ant colony Milton maintains that, far from living in "lawless anarchie," these creatures establish a model for a "frugal and self-governing democratie or Commonwealth; safer and more thriving in the joint providence and counsel of many industrious equals, then under the single domination of one imperious Lord" (*Prose* 7:427).

In contrast to the bee, the emmet, then, provides a model of communality. Raphael's description of the emmet community in *Paradise Lost* presents an example not only of an ideal political arrangement from the past, like the one that existed prior to Nimrod's appearance (12.26), but more importantly one that could be realized in the future. Raphael explains that the emmet is

> provident
> Of future, in small room large heart enclos'd,
> Pattern of just equality *perhaps*
> *Hereafter*, join'd in her popular Tribes
> Of Commonalty. (7.485–9, my emphasis)

Christopher Hill argues that Milton after the Restoration still managed to convey many radical opinions in his later poems despite writing under strict censorship and being himself deeply suspect. In this context the parsimonious emmet serves as a model for just equality in an ideal republic (*World Turned* 399). Milton "covers himself" both by using the *"functionally* ambiguous" word "perhaps" and by giving the account over to the archangel Raphael. The word "Hereafter" is equally significant in so far as deferral or the protraction of history proves to be another contra-censorship strategy and act of political resistance, as I demonstrate in chapter 2.[4]

Appropriating the royalist polemic for his own purposes, Milton identifies the government of the established church and the monarchy with Nimrod's tyranny and Babel's confusion. In reply to the royalist prophecy that God will not "suffer those men long to prosper in their Babel, who build it with the bones and cement it with the blood of their kings" (*Eikon Basilike* 175), Milton in *Of Reformation* accuses the prelates – the merchants of Babylon – and the king, who is later identified as Nimrod and Nebuchadnezzar, of having "built up the *spirituall* BABEL to the heighth of her Abominations" (*Prose* 1:590).[5] The bishops and prelates, who, like the royalists, charged their opponents with the very crimes they themselves committed, are characterized by Milton as predatory animals and hunters, of which Nimrod was the first. Addressing Salmasius in *A Defence of the People of England*, Milton offers a more specific example of hypocrisy: "You call the people 'a beast.' What then are *you*? For neither that Sacred Consistory nor that St. Wolf can set you its master above the people or the populace, nor keep you from being what you are, the foulest of animals! Certainly the prophetic books of Scripture denote the monarchical dominion of great kings by the name and likeness of a raging beast" (*Prose* 4:484). This accusation is echoed in the *Paradise Lost* description of the first postlapsarian totalitarian ruler, the mighty hunter Nimrod, who "from Rebellion shall derive his name, / Though of Rebellion others he accuse" (12.36–7).[6]

Milton's account of the fall of Babel, which he appropriately derives from a number of sources, deviates from the Genesis story through the inclusion of the unnamed Nimrod, the first king (*Prose, Eikonoklastes* 3:598) and tyrant (*Prose, A Defence* 4:473). His usurpation and forcible containment of a postlapsarian people living idyllically leads, ironically, to their dispersion and to the dissemination of language. As he adapts the Genesis commentators' stories of Babel, Milton attributes the fall of Babel to Nimrod directly in accordance with the received Protestant tradition. The account thereby acquires not only a dramatic element but also an added political significance.

The Genesis story of Babel serves primarily as an etiology of the diversity of languages and as a polemic against pride in society. Though his tyranny is suggested, Nimrod, who is mentioned in chapter 10 of Genesis, does not figure in the fall recounted in chapter 11. Before the Renaissance inherited it, however, the Old Testament story was reinterpreted by Philo, Augustine, Gregory, Isidore of Seville, Jerome, Bede, Dante, and Lydgate, among others, who were all indebted to Josephus' politicized reading.[7] In *The Antiquities* Josephus attributes the fall to the proud defiance of the people who declared their autonomy from God and to the coercion of Nimrod, "who excited them to such an affront and contempt of God" (35). Reigning as a tyrant, Nimrod, who is described by Jerome as "the first to seize absolute power over the people, something not known before" (Schmidt 305), succeeds in persuading his followers to defy divine authority by constructing a tower. God in turn punishes them with the confusion of tongues.

Through the later influence of the anti-monarchist Boccaccio, the political emphasis that had first entered Western consciousness through Josephus was strongly reasserted in John Lydgate's *Fall of Princes*. Nimrod, who vainly attempted "to be put in memorie," challenged Fortune by having "wan many a straunge cuntre"; Lydgate continues, "And day be day his power gan encrese, / For which he wolde off his conquest nat cese" (1.1517–19). The political reading, along with the interest in the origin of diverse languages, figuring in Dante but absent in Boccaccio, was adopted by Renaissance writers, including Calvin, Luther, Spenser, Raleigh, Browne, and Milton. They each modified the story to accommodate and promote their own specific political and linguistic statements.[8]

As a monarchist who cautiously distinguishes between kingship and tyranny, Raleigh devotes less attention to Nimrod's dissenting voice in the account of Babel than to the aberrant behaviour of his followers. In rewriting the story, Raleigh makes it polemical and moralistic. The fall becomes an allegory of the decline of the ideal monarchical government through humanity's defiance. The people's freedom is illusory, according to the historian: "licentious disorder (which seemed to promise a libertie upon the first acquaintance) proved, upon a better trial, not less perilous then an indurable bondage" (79). Nimrod, the tyrannical king and the father of the first adulterer and idolator, Belus (83–4), makes his appearance in the story only after the difference between a tyrannical rule and a regal government – one that balances supreme power and common right – is outlined. Raleigh suggests thereby that Nimrod is among the various causes and casualties of humanity's fall rather than the author of rebellion (79–84).

In contrast to Raleigh's detailed cataloguing of the evolution of kingship from the rule of elders in *The marrow of historie*, Milton in book 12 of *Paradise Lost* presents a very different history of polity. Nimrod's autocratic seizure of the pastoral tribal society suggests in Milton's account that the organization of peoples in the postlapsarian world is not divinely determined; the ultimate responsibility for delegating authority and shaping the course of political history lies with humans themselves. In turn, the political structures can justly be criticized for reasons that a divinely sanctioned monarchy or utopian state cannot. The foundation for the construction of an alternative form of government in the commonwealth might then be laid according to a "Pattern of just equality perhaps / Hereafter, join'd in her popular Tribes / Of Commonalty" (7.487–9), as Raphael proposes in the reworked creation story.

When Milton's God imposes order on the formless mass that will constitute earth on the first day of creation, chaos hears his voice, and confusion is transformed and tamed. But in the account of the fall of Babel, God is the one who causes the confusion of tongues among Nimrod's folk:

> [God] in derision sets
> Upon thir Tongues a various Spirit to rase
> Quite out thir Native Language, and instead
> To sow a jangling noise of words unknown:
> Forthwith a hideous gabble rises loud
> Among the Builders.  (12.52–7)

God's implantation of the quarrelsome spirit among the builders, like his act of sending a "spirit of frenzy" to the idolatrous Philistines in *Samson Agonistes* (*Poems*, SA 1675), seems quite out of character with his creative impulses, as does his transformation of Eden into a wasteland at the end of book 11 in *Paradise Lost*. To add insult to injury, Nimrod, like the newly fallen angels, whose names are "blotted out and ras'd / By thir Rebellion" (1.362–3), remains nameless after his fall. The irony is compounded by Nimrod's literal and nominal identification with rebellion, which he hopes to prevent and of which he accuses others. Moreover, the builders' unfinished structure of the tower of Babel – *Babili* in Hebrew meant "gate of the Gods" – is in ridicule renamed "Confusion" (12.62). "As the tongue is the instrument of domination, in it pride was punished," Augustine explains, in his account of Nimrod and the fall into linguistic confusion (*City of God* 2:113). After attempting to "get themselves a name lest far disperst / In foreign Lands thir memory be lost, / Regardless whether good or evil fame" (12.45–7), the builders' addresses to each other are, ironically, "Not understood" (58).

In his *Commentarie ... Upon Genesis* Jean Calvin interprets the efforts of Nimrod's followers to achieve fame: "this is always the way of the world, never to bother about heaven and to look for immortality on earth where everything is transitory" (128). The rebels' attempt to "make a name" – *sem* in Hebrew – is a struggle for immortality or fame that requires them to assemble their forces in one place – *sam* – to penetrate the heavens – the *samayim* (Fokkelman 16–17). The three Hebrew words are connected in meaning and sound in a biblical story that presents, ironically, the fall into linguistic confusion. As Milton later does, Calvin identifies "name" with fame and distinguishes between a secular and a spiritual definition of fame with a particular emphasis that is not to be found in the Genesis account of Babel. Both writers thereby appropriate the story for the purpose of criticizing tyranny and commenting on the vain ambitions of their own age.[9]

God's answer to the builders' attempt to achieve immortality is a miracle, according to the *Art of Logic*: "Languages, both the first one which Adam received in Eden, and those various ones, perhaps derived from the first, which the builders of the tower of Babel suddenly received, were without doubt divinely given" (*Prose* 8:294). The miracle includes the dissemination of languages, a fitting response to the confusion created by the internally divided builders, who, in the search for fame and titles, ignore the call for dispersion and abuse their native tongue. By causing the "jangling noise of words unknown" (12.55), God is again rejoining letter and spirit, name and meaning, as he externalizes the inner turmoil. Michael psychologizes this act after the Nimrod account: "God in Judgment just / Subjects him from without to violent Lords; / Who oft as undeservedly enthral / His outward freedom" (12.92–5).

The scattering of languages in Genesis prefigures a far more significant event in biblical history – Pentecost, a recuperative linguistic response to Babel, with which book 12 of *Paradise Lost* concludes. This time the spirit sent by the Comforter will allow the apostles to "speak all Tongues" (12.501) in order that they might evangelize the nations, thereby reuniting them without imposing an artificial unity, that is, without neutralizing the differences among the people and their languages. When God translates the curse into a blessing, he restores communication but does not reverse the confusion of Babel. Calvin remarks on the paradox of Pentecost in his *Sermon on Pentecost*: "If we seek the reason why there are different languages in the world, we must come to the conclusion that it is on account of a curse from God. Yet here appeared His goodness and fatherly mercy, when the message of life was brought into all tongues. That is how God converted evil into good" (*Selections* 565). According to Calvin, the miracle was performed that all people might partake of the covenant of salvation, which initially belonged only to the Jews. The dispersion of multiple languages becomes, thereby, a way of increasing the number of the elect and, for Calvin, of justifying greater representation in church affairs in his own day. Communication among the members of society, which will be disrupted continually (12.530–9), is facilitated by the dissemination of the Word in different tongues, out of which a multivocal society and a multifaceted truth develop.

In his invocation in *The Divine Weeks* Du Bartas requests the heavenly king to reform the iniquity caused by "Nimrodizing" – the perversion of the Word – and to reverse the effects of political corruption:

> if our courtiers now-*Po*-poysoned phrase;
> Or now-contagion of corrupted dayes,
> Leave anie tract of *Nimrodizing* there;
> O cancell it, that they may every where
> Instead of *Babel*, build *Jerusalem* :
> That lowd my *Muse* may eccho under them. (2.2.2.33–8)

In *Paradise Lost* "Nimrodizing" results in the failure to complete the idolatrous tower; the building is appropriately described by the archangel Michael as "Ridiculous" – "an exquisitely bathetic and derisive polysyllable" (Davies, *Images of Kingship* 33), echoing the confusion. On the base of the unfinished tower in the spiritual Babylon of the prelates, the building of Jerusalem must commence. Ezra 5:8–17 offers one of several histories describing the legendary building of the temple of Jerusalem. The temple of God, whose construction continues indefinitely (5:16), is built with the spoils retrieved from Nebuchadnezzar's Babylon, a city that is destroyed with the creation of Jerusalem.[10]

## 2 "THE FORM OF A COMMONWEALTH"

The various histories of Nimrod in the Renaissance and seventeenth century displace the Genesis account and contribute, ironically, to the proliferation and confusion of the authoritative biblical Word. Milton intervenes in the received tradition I have traced and, in response to his political and personal experience of defeat, rewrites the accounts to justify the establishment of an alternative political community founded on just representation. The commonwealth

Milton designs is a composite construction, built on the foundations of various ancient and contemporary models. At the same time it is a prospective model, whose construction complements both the ongoing process of re-membering the body of Truth and the continuing attempts to orchestrate the numerous voices that compose the nation.

The received Genesis tradition distinguishes between two kinds of unity. The first is a rigid, stifling order desired by the people in resistance to God; it is, as Milton claims in the *Areopagitica*, "the forc't and outward union of cold, and neutrall, and inwardly divided minds" (*Prose* 2:551). The second is a unity-dispersion dialectic, a type of harmony willed by God that permits creativity and diversity. "Bring forth the frute and increase upon the earth," God commands Noah and his sons (Gen. 8:17). Josephus' words are: "God also commanded them to send colonies abroad, for the thorough peopling of the earth, – that they might not raise seditions among themselves, but might cultivate a great part of the earth, and enjoy its fruits after a plentiful manner." The people, however, defiantly refuse to live according to these terms and become suspicious of their freedom, concluding that "being divided asunder, they might the more easily be oppressed" (35). A similar resistance to dispersion is displayed by Nimrod's people in *The Divine Weeks*: "Under a king let's lead our lives; for feare / Least severd thus, in Princes, and in tents, / We be dispearst" (2.2.2.110–12). The people who achieve a self-securing homogeneity by raising the idolatrous tower directly violate the divine mandate for the cultivation of the world.

The construction of the tower and the city of Babylon was no sin in itself, Martin Luther insists, for others had done the same (214); Asschur in Genesis 10:11, for example, built Nineveh because he could no longer live with the ungodly. Just as "God áttributes to place / No sanctity, if none be thither brought" (11.836–7), so does he not abandon – or leave in the dark – those who create in his name, as Milton's epic narrator maintains. The sin of Nimrod's people lies in attaching their own name to the structure they build, thus severing their ties with God. The idolatry of the builders is represented by the unfinished tower in *Paradise Lost,* which Milton in turn uses in a political context to chastise the nation for the unsuccessful construction of the Commonwealth. In *The Readie and Easie Way* he warns his compatriots that their failure to erect the main structure of the Commonwealth – for which the base had been established during the struggle for liberty and religious toleration – would "render [them] a scorn and derision" before all of Europe. What will they say of us, Milton asks, but "Where is this goodly tower of a Commonwealth, which the English boasted they would build to overshaddow kings, and be another *Rome* in the west? The foundation indeed they laid gallantly; but fell into a wors confusion, not of tongues, but of factions, then those at the tower of *Babel*; and have left no memorial of thir work behinde them remaining, but in the common laughter of *Europ*" (*Prose* 7:422–3). Like Milton's history of Nimrod's fall, the account of the construction of the Commonwealth is a composite one. The references to the uncompleted tower and the scoffing laughter of the onlookers are taken not only from the Genesis story of the unfinished tower of Babel but also, as Milton implies, from Luke's Gospel (14:25–33), which describes the foolish builder who laid the foundation for – but failed to complete – the tower he prematurely proposed to build.[11]

Though Milton himself always continued to believe in the justness of the revolt against monarchy, his disillusion with state converts, traitors to the "the good old cause" (*Prose* 7:387) of the Revolution, is apparent when he redirects his criticism at the newly formed anti-republican movement. By 1660 Milton recognized that Oliver Cromwell had for years been breeding predatory bloodhounds (Davies, *Images of Kingship* 45) and that the factions created by the negligent and foolhardy builders of the Commonwealth were even worse than the confusion of the fall of Babel. Milton recontextualizes the images from the account of Babel not only in denouncing the enemies of the republic but also in castigating the treacherous parliamentarians themselves. At the conclusion of *Eikonoklastes* the revolutionary accuses his countrymen, whose barbarousness prevented them from completing the Commonwealth, of idolatry and hypocrisy; having expressed remorse at the regicide, they have become in his eyes an "inconstant, irrational, and Image-doting rabble; [... like a credulous and hapless herd, begott'n to servility, and inchanted with these popular institutes of Tyranny]" (*Prose* 3:601). The attack on the "miscellaneous rabble" is continued by the Son in *Paradise Regained* (*Poems* 3.50).

In *An Apology against a Pamphlet* Milton initially praised Parliament for its ideological firmness and its willingness to hear the grievances from all members of society, "Insomuch that the meanest artizans and labourers, at other times also women, and often the younger sort of servants assembling with their complaints, and that sometimes in a lesse humble guise then for petitioners, have gone with confidence, that neither their meannesse would be rejected, nor their simplicity contemn'd, nor yet their urgency distasted either by the dignity, wisdome, or moderation of that supreme

Senate; nor did they depart unsatisfi'd" (*Prose* 1:926). The recent history of the state and church, however, led Milton both to distrust the voices of the masses and to believe that Babel had not been wholly destroyed. When Milton discovered that the English Revolution was not prepared to sanction divorce or the freedom of the press, he turned on the Presbyterian influence in the Long Parliament. In his poems and treatises written during the Civil War and Interregnum, Milton transforms his countrymen into beasts and declares that the parliamentarians' intolerance and oppression, masked by their feigned cries for liberty, create a rift between meanings and words. They produce the "barbarous noise" (Sonnet 12, 3) of "Owls and Cuckoos, Asses, Apes and Dogs" (4) by embracing what Milton calls in "On the New Forces of Conscience" the "widow'd whore Plurality" (3). Again the poet-revolutionary equates and, as I discuss in chapter 4, feminizes tyranny and confusion.[12]

In 1660 Milton assented to criticism by acknowledging in *The Readie and Easie Way* that Parliament itself was responsible for the failure to complete the Commonwealth:

Tis true indeed, when monarchie was dissolvd, the form of a Commonwealth should have forthwith bin fram'd; and the practice therof immediatly begun; that the people might have soon bin satisfi'd and delighted with the decent order, ease and benefit therof: we had bin then by this time firmly rooted past fear of commotions or mutations, & now flourishing: this care of timely setling a new government instead of y$^e$ old, too much neglected, hath bin our mischief. Yet the cause therof may be ascrib'd with most reason to the frequent disturbances, interruptions and dissolutions which the Parlament hath had partly from the impatient or disaffected people, partly from som ambitious leaders in the Armie; much contrarie, I beleeve, to the mind and approbation of the Armie it self and thir other Commanders, once undeceivd, or in thir own power. Now is the opportunitie, now the very season wherein we may obtain a free Commonwealth and establish it for ever in the land, without difficulty or much delay. (*Prose* 7:430)

Milton was interested in more than criticism and thus did not hesitate to warn Cromwell that the establishment of a just rule in peacetime would be more difficult than winning the war.[13] In *Paradise Lost* Milton offers, along with the example of the meritocracy in the heavenly court, several model political communities. In fact, the episode of King Nimrod's fall into confusion is framed between two versions of broadly republican forms of government. Milton, then, not only condemns the tyrannical empire but offers alternatives in its place. At the same time he presents a history of seventeenth-century polity.

Prior to the appearance of the warrior-king, the pastoral society is organized into familial and tribal divisions and ordered according to paternal rule, thereby constituting what Michael calls a government with "fair equality, fraternal state" (12.26). Michael's description of this ideal postlapsarian society is contrasted sharply with the autocracy of Nimrod, who arrogates "Dominion undeserv'd / Over his brethren" (12.27–8), thus disrupting social concord and violating the laws of God and nature. The "Empire tyrannous" fragments into the numerous factions and voices that it sought to suppress.[14]

In his reaction to the account Adam underscores the sanctity of the fraternal state by recalling the divine mandate of human liberty that constituted exemplary edenic polity:

> He gave us only over Beast, Fish, Fowl
> Dominion absolute; that right we hold
> By his donation; but Man over men
> He made not Lord; such title to himself
> Reserving, human left from human free. (12.67–71)

By placing these words in the mouth of Adam directly, Milton challenges the identification of Adam with the "first monarch of the whole world" made by Milton's contemporaries, including Robert Filmer in *Observations upon Aristotle's Politiques* (Wooton 110). Moreover, Milton goes one step further than the Christian exegetes who identified Nimrod with tyranny when he conveys Christian egalitarian and anti-royalist attitudes through Adam's speeches.[15]

Contrasting the present dictatorship to the prelapsarian government, Adam leaves Michael to describe the emergence of the new nation out of the tyranny of the old. In framing the form of a commonwealth in the account that follows the story of Nimrod, Michael offers not a nostalgic view of a lost world but a portrait of a political community whose future construction is inevitably interrupted by Nimrod's successors. The building commences, nevertheless, first with the strengthening of self-governing reason, which forms the basis for any construction, psychological or material. Liberty of conscience and the right to exercise reason are, conversely, most effectively protected by a free commonwealth.

The subsequent form of government that Michael portrays is one established in the wilderness under Mosaic law (12.223–35). Raleigh in *The marrow of historie* explains that the invention of laws – a recourse taken in a fallen world – followed the reign of kings (80).

Monarchy was in turn preceded by the ideal form of government by wise elders. The evolution from kingship to the government by law under Moses, the twelve tribes of Israel, and the chosen senate is progressive rather than regressive, Milton emphasizes.[16] This senate, along with the people and magistracy, constituted what James Harrington in *The Commonwealth of Oceana* (1656) regarded as the perfect pattern of a government by law and tribal organization rather than by royal power:

If all and every one of the laws of Israel being proposed by God, were not otherwise enacted than by covenant with the people, then that only which was resolved by the people of Israel was their law; and so the result of that commonwealth was in the people. Nor had the people the result only in matter of law, but the power in some cases of judicature; as also the right of levying war, cognizance in matters of religion, and the election of their magistrates, as the judge or dictator, the king, the prince: which functions were exercised by the *Synagoga Magna*, or congregation of Israel, not always in one manner, for sometimes they were performed by the suffrage of the people, *viva voce*, sometimes by lot only, and at others by the ballot, or by a mixture of the lot with suffrage. (47)

Harrington's description of the Israelite commonwealth and of the relationship between the established law and "the people's" right to political representation and self-determination[17] provides the base for the ideal political community he designs. When it became apparent that Cromwell was not inclined to establish an "equal commonwealth," Harrington dedicated *Oceana* to him. Though utopian, *Oceana* served the practical purpose of supplying a design for the kind of political institution that its author hoped would be established in England. Like Harrington, Milton not only designed models of prospective governments on the bases of ancient ones but also proposed in the wake of the Civil War the establishment of a republic on the foundation built by the revolutionaries.[18]

The period between 4 September 1658 to 16 March 1660 was marked by considerable political turmoil, to which the vigorous pamphleteering by the defenders and opponents of the Good Old Cause contributed significantly. Arguing against kingship more vehemently than ever, Milton produced two letters – "A Letter to a Friend Concerning the Ruptures of the Commonwealth" and a letter to Monk – as well as two 1660 editions of *The Readie and Easie Way*.[19] An examination of the royalist pamphlets that mock or attack Milton's political and prophetic treatise is telling, even *foretelling*. The satirical remarks and criticisms by his opponents at the same time betray an uneasiness about Milton's vision for a new commonwealth, as is apparent in such pamphlets as *Be Merry And Wise* (A4v) and throughout George Monk's long-winded response to the tract *Plain English* in *Treason Arraigned*. Milton's arguments are further defamed in *The Dignity of Kingship Asserted* by G.S., who denounces the "unpracticableness of ... [Milton's] fanatique *Statewhymsis*" (H7v), and by the author of *The Censure of the Rota Upon ... The Ready and Easie Way*. Many of the pamphlets identify the "Divorcer" with the political anarchist, and all accuse Milton of contributing to the confusion and disintegration of the nation through his defence of the Commonwealth, the multiheaded, headless Rump, and the "monstrously deformed" churches of religious individualists. In *The Censure* Harrington, the alleged author, reports in an imaginary debate on the charges levied against Milton, who defended "Liberty of Conscience and Christian Liberty" (B2v) through the heretical proposition that "the Church of Christ ought to have no Head upon Earth, but the Monster of many heads, the multitude, who are the onely supream Judges of all matters that concern him" (B2r).

In his attack on the author of *The Readie and Easie Way* Roger L'Estrange, in *No Blinde Guides*, challenges Milton's assumption about the imminent establishment of the free commonwealth: "give me leave to mind you, that you make an *observation* of things *Past*, amount to a *foretelling* of what's to *come*" (3). The royalist censor accuses Milton of idolatry and delusion: "*Under the Reign of God onely their King* you say. This expression, doubtfully implies you a Millenary. Doe you then, really expect to *see* Christ, Reigning upon Earth, even with *those very eyes* you *Lost* (as 'tis reported) *with staring too long, and too sawcily upon the Portraiture of his Vicegerent, to breake the* Image, as your Imprudence Phrases it? (It is generally indeed believed, you never wept them out for this *Losse*.)" (8). The sense of conflict and contradiction that inevitably underlies the utopian project is apparent in Milton's treatise, in which he represents himself, as L'Estrange recognized, not just as a historian but also as a theorist and prophet of revolution. L'Estrange argues that Milton's prediction of the Restoration commonwealth confirms his inability to acknowledge the failure of his millenarian dream. Despite the unrealistic claims about the establishment of a commonwealth, the treatise's emphasis on design and construction betrays the author's awareness that his goal is ultimately unattainable and reveals his desire for empowerment through prophecy. Milton's metaphorical language ruptures the closure of the treatise, which becomes increasingly poetic. The language of prophecy and multivocality is, then, an instrument for resisting censorship, including the kind of censorship that L'Estrange enforces when he connects Milton's personal tragedy with his experience of political defeat.[20]

In his reassessment of civic liberties and popular representation in the later part of the Revolution, Milton himself gradually discovered that individual freedom is too often eroded by coercive relationships and is, in fact, secured only through governmental protection. Milton increasingly feared, as the royalists themselves did, the misguided or abused multitude.[21] To check the rabble of a licentious and unbridled democracy, Milton proposes not the reinstatement of monarchy but the election of meritorious representatives who attain "true nobility by their own industry and virtue." These "worthy people" refer to the middle class, whose members include "the greatest number of men of good sense and knowledge of affairs. Of the rest some are turned from uprightness and from their interest in learning their country's laws by excessive wealth and luxury, and others by want and poverty" (*Prose* 4:471). The restrictions on suffrage would, paradoxically, ensure the liberty of the people by not committing them "to the noise and shouting of a rude multitude, but permitting only those of them who are rightly qualifi'd to nominat as many as they will; and out of that number others of a better breeding, to chuse a less number more judiciously, till after a third or fourth sifting and refining of exactest choice, they only be left chosen who are the due number and seem by most voices the worthiest" (*Prose* 7:442–3).

Milton's refusal to promote the franchise for all and his advocacy of a senate or "perpetual" council seem to be quite at odds with his "democratic principles." Z.S. Fink explains: "the reader will doubtless feel that Milton's discovery that the better part of the people could be taken as standing for the whole even when they were a numerous minority removed whatever genuinely popular elements there may have been in his political theory. The fact, however, that there would appear to be nothing truly democratic about Milton's conception of the people in 1660 must not be permitted to obscure the fact that he saw the better part of the people as constituting the democratic element in his ideal commonwealth" (119). In opposition to the monarchists, Milton insisted that power be granted to the people, and at the same time he proposed that a balance be maintained to preserve due authority on the side of the council.[22] By possessing and relegating all powers and functions necessary to public interest, the council could guarantee the sovereignty of the people and prevent the lapse of the nation into an unchecked democracy. In seventeenth-century England the term democracy was used to identify a range of governments whose power was distributed more broadly than in an aristocracy. Despite the eligibility of a select number of voters, Milton could see the better part of the people as constituting the democratic element in his ideal commonwealth if it were governed by virtuous leaders, and if the mode of choosing representatives was regarded as more important than the proportion of people who participated in the electoral process.[23]

Milton's ideal commonwealth supports a constitution modelled on mixed governments of both state[24] and church from the sixteenth and seventeenth centuries. Analogues between the governments of state and church were in fact common during these periods. Thomas Cartwright, the Elizabethan Puritan leader, had described the true (Presbyterian) church, which resembled the "best commonwealths," as a monarchy, aristocracy, and democracy: "For, in respect of Christ the head, it is a monarchy; and in respect of the ancients and pastors that govern in common and with like authority amongst themselves, it is an aristocraty, or the rule of the best men; and in respect that the people are not secluded but have their interest in church-matters, it is a democraty, or a popular estate. An image whereof appeareth also in the policy of this realm; for as in respect of the queen her majesty, it is a monarchy, so in respect of the most honourable council, it is an aristocraty, and having regard to the parliament, which is assembled of all estates, it is a democraty" (Pearson 142–3). Cartwright characterized this mixed government as a "mean which is to be houlden" between an authoritative monarchy and an unchecked democracy. The Independents established their own church government according to such a model in the seventeenth century but, in doing so, defined the mean quite differently: Presbyterianism had now become one of the extremes.[25]

To counter censorship and institutionalization of religious truths in the seventeenth century, critics of the prelacy, primarily radical sect leaders, proposed various models for church reformation and promoted an ongoing search for truth. In order to justify the establishment of their "congregationall church" – a congregation ruled over by appointed Elders – spokesmen of Independency Thomas Goodwin and Philip Nye in *An Apologeticall Narration* first had to answer to the charge of fanaticism: "And wee did then, and doe here publiquely professe, we beleeve the truth to lye and consist in a *middle way* betwixt that which is falsly charged on us, *Brownisme*; and that which is the contention of these times, the *authoritative Presbyteriall Government* in all the subordinations and proceedings of it" (332). The divorce between church and state in the seventeenth century left the Independents, unlike their predecessors in the previous century, with no contemporary political models for their church: "We had no new Common-wealths to rear, to frame Church-government unto" (311), they maintained, identifying, as Milton would do, Abraham's community of worshippers in the wilderness (313) and the church of the early Christians as their only true patterns.

In his objections to the labels of "Annabaptist," "Antinomian," and "Seeker," which were used indiscriminately – particularly by Thomas Edwards in *Gangraena* – to marginalize him from the community,[26] William Walwyn in *A Whisper in the Eare of Mr. Thomas Edwards* describes his post-pentecostal search for a multifaceted truth:

> mistake me not, I do not esteeme these as names of reproach, no more then to be called Presbyterian or Independent; nor doe I take upon me peremptorily to determine what is truth, and what is error, amongst any of them: all have a possibility of error: I judge all Conscienscious, and to hold their severall judgements upon grounds of scripture ... for though I do fully assent with [those whom you judge seekers] that now in these times there is no such ministry as the Apostles were, endowed with immediate power from on high, by imposition of whose hands, the Holy Ghost was conferred, enabling to speak with tongues, and do miracles, in a most wonderfull manner, and to speake to all men, the infallible word of God: and that convincingly to the Consciences of gain sayers: yet am I not thereby of opinion that we may not make use of those things they have left unto us in the scriptures of the mind and will of God; or that it is not profitable to follow their examples so far as we are able in all things. (330–1)

In the passage Walwyn analyses the name of "seeker" used to defame him, complicating the term by identifying not only its negative but also its many other connotations. Moreover, he reminds his opponents of the original meaning of the word "seeker": "see now what a seeker you have found of me: I once heard you a Christ-Church, which few seekers will do, but never but once, for I was not so blind a seeker, as to seek for Grapes of thornes, or Figges of thistles" (331). Walwyn reveals that, in the pentecostal act of multiplying the significances of "seeker," he can develop a more accurate, certainly more meaningful version of the original. However, because no miracle of Pentecost is possible in a fallen world, he must foreground the process of searching for the truth.

Images and metaphors of the re-membered body of Truth and the reconstructed temple are favourite ones for Milton, who uses them to associate the different quests for political, religious, and also linguistic meaning – my concern in the next chapter. After describing the ongoing assembly of the bodies of the Christian Truth and the Egyptian Osiris in the *Areopagitica*, Milton compares the numerous sects and schisms that constitute the religious community to the "schisms" in the stones and timber that fit together contiguously to make up the house of God on earth: "out of many moderat varieties and brotherly dissimilitudes that are not vastly disproportionall arises the goodly and the gracefull symmetry that commends the whole pile and structure" (*Prose* 2:555). The specifications for the constructed and reconstructed temple of Solomon are outlined in 1 Kings 5–6, as well as in 1 Chronicles 28 and Ezekiel 40–8, also addressed by Milton (*Prose, Reason of Church-Government* 1:756–8). Solomon, who oversees the construction in Kings and Chronicles, is displaced in the Areopagitican account by the people, who continue building indefinitely. In *The Reason of Church-Government* Milton psychologizes the biblical history by referring to God's prescribed delineations for the "rationall temple." This temple is the human soul and the immortal statue of Christ's body, which is his Church "in all her glorious lineaments and proportions" (*Prose* 1:758). Physical structures, then, are encasements for "th' upright heart and pure" (*PL* 1.18) or for inwardly divided minds like Mulciber's. Mulciber, of course, is the architect of Pandemonium, which, anachronistically, "Not *Babylon*, / Nor great *Alcairo* such magnificence / Equall'd in all thir glories" (*PL* 1.717–19).

When Milton inserts Nimrod into the story of Babel and transfers the Babel and bestial imagery from the pro-royalists to the lapsed parliamentarians, he indicates that his criticisms are directed less at existing establishments than at those who corrupt them. He thereby emphasizes the significance of the individual's involvement in existing social and political systems. The failure of the Revolution could be regarded as less devastating and catastrophic if the defeat was attributed to a few individuals rather than to all the participants or to the Cause itself; as Milton announces in *The Readie and Easie Way*, the revolutionaries' actions are characterized by "just and religious deeds, though don by som to covetous and ambitious ends, yet not therefor to be staind with their infamie, or they to asperse the integritie of others" (*Prose* 7:422). Milton criticized the builders of the Commonwealth for their failure to erect it on the already prepared base, and in other instances for the instability of the foundation itself. Now, after the Revolution, he realizes that the foundations themselves must be laid deeper in the minds of individuals in order that they might build more securely.

The socio-political allegory is transformed into a psychological model that urges the reader to conquer the enemy within. Michael explains after the account of Nimrod that corrupt government is the outward sign of right reason obscured by the Fall; the loss of inward liberty deprives people of outward freedom (12.90–101). The relationship between the abuse of reason and the loss of freedom is the subject of a refrain heard throughout Milton's works: "What wise and valiant man would seek to free / These thus degenerate, by themselves enslav'd, / Or could of inward slaves make outward free? (*Poems, PR* 4.143–5). By connecting the two kinds of freedom, Milton suggests that political reform will depend at least as much on individual as collective efforts. The pre-Restoration arguments for social regeneration that Milton develops in treatises including *Of Education* and *The Tenure of Kings and Magistrates* are qualified and reworked in *Paradise Lost* and *Paradise Regained*, when the intervention of singular leaders, who "seem by most voices the worthiest," becomes a precondition for the eventual establishment of the commonwealth as well as the basis from which the collective interest takes effect.

# 2 Critical Interventions

> Metaphors, and senseless and ambiguous words, are like *ignes fatui*; and reasoning upon them is wandering amongst innumerable absurdities; and their end, contention and sedition, or contempt?
> 
> Hobbes, *Leviathan*

> The new cultural and creative consciousness lives in an actively polyglot world. The world becomes a polyglot, once and for all and irreversibly. The period of national languages, coexisting but closed and deaf to each other, comes to an end. Languages throw light on each other: one language can, after all, see itself only in the light of another language. The naïve and stubborn coexistence of "languages" within a given national language also comes to an end – that is, there is no more peaceful co-existence between territorial dialects, social and professional dialects and jargons, literary language, generic languages within literary language, epochs in language and so forth.
> 
> Bakhtin, *The Dialogic Imagination*

> The play of metaphor is an imposing threat to the work of referential security in the way that artistic freedom imperils fascism.
> 
> Appelbaum, *Voice*

> God every morning raines down new expressions into our hearts and, for a variety of circumstances, gives a varietie of words.
> 
> Milton, *Eikonklastes*

Religious crises, political upheaval and decentralization, economic changes, social and scientific discoveries, and print-capitalism contributed to the development of a national consciousness and the formation of a social dynamic based on boundary-oriented and horizontal communities in Western Europe during the Renaissance.[1] The restructuring of the centripetally and hierarchically organized state accompanying the development of the new imagined community challenged the reign of the dominant language that provided "privileged access to ontological truth" (Anderson 40). Bakhtin claims that the changes in European civilization at this time resulted in Europe's emergence from a "socially and culturally deaf semi-patriarchal society" into one of numerous different languages and cultures, which consequently became decisive factors in its life and thought (*Imagination* 11).

Milton's celebration of and, simultaneously, his interest in refining the "native tongue" in England inform his proposals for national development and reform: "not once have we heard of an empire or state not flourishing at least moderately as long as it continued to have pride in its Language, and to cultivate it" (*Prose* 1:330). The cultivation of language is for Milton a civilizing act, involving the removal of barbarous elements that threaten the integrity of the community, just as the Orphic poet resists the "barbarous dissonance" that pervades the text. In this chapter, after first outlining the relationship between socio-political developments and linguistic mutability in the seventeenth century, I consider how *Paradise Lost* offers multiple explanations for the fragmentation of truth and demonstrates the difficulty of constructing and communicating meaning in a flawed medium. Thereafter, I examine the movement from Babel to Pentecost in *Paradise Lost* by addressing three ways in which the poet attempts to recuperate doubleness and confusion: the creation of a multigenre and prophetic text, the development of a stylistics of indirection, and the accommodation of various interpreters in the poem. The interconnected discourses about political, social, and linguistic change combine with the epic's multiple perspectives to free the poem from the fixity of the monological voice and from the institutionalization of truth. All three efforts at recuperation assume, then, that the poem responds to the extra-literary discourses of the seventeenth century and that language bears, in a Bakhtinian context, "traces of reality" that are inscribed in the text through its engagement with these various discourses.

In part 2 of this chapter I change my focus from the processes of speech to the conversations of history in order to examine the complexly configured narrative of history, the encoding of events in plot structures, and the development of critical interventions. The presentation of the "great Argument" in an "answerable style" is facilitated by a community of enlightened readers – the "fit ... though few" – whom Milton enlists to re-member the fragmented Word, to orchestrate the poetic voices, and to reemplot events of the historical tragedy. Like the construction and critical reading of history, the politics of narrative design encourage active participation by soliciting the reader not only to understand the story but to complete it, "to make it fuller, richer, more powerfully ordered, and therefore more hermeneutic" (Brooks 260). As the greatest narrative poet of the seventeenth century, Milton was "as resourceful in his grasp of its poetics as modern theorists like Roland Barthes, Tzvetan Todorov, Gérard Genette, Frank Kermode, and Peter Brooks," Wittreich maintains in his illuminating chapter on narrative strategies in *Interpreting Samson Agonistes* (126). My duplicitous chapter treats the history of linguistic developments and the narratives of providential and human history in some detail because the voices and creation accounts of the poem's multiple speakers, on which I focus in the following chapters, develop in reference to both contexts. The dialectical creation of voice is marked, I will argue, by the fall into language – the symbolic order – and into history.

## 1 AFTER BABEL

*"Let's all-confound their speech"*

Language in the Renaissance was characterized, according to Michel Foucault, by a direct correspondence between words and meanings, a linguistic unity that reinforced the integrity of the represented subject; words were "intimately connected with things; words were believed to be inherent in the script of an ontological discourse (God's Word) that only required reading for the guarantee of their meaning and truth. Words existed inside Being: they reduplicated it; they were its signature; and man's decipherment of language was a direct, whole perception of Being" (Said 284). The Humanists' program, which had at its centre the fashioning of the gentleman and the construction of a social identity, promoted the study of language: the courtly gentleman's rhetorical and oratorical skills testified, in turn, to his civility. Despite Foucault's observation, however, many Renaissance texts exhibit a tenuous relationship between *res* and *verba* as well as a self-consciousness about the failure of the representative power of language. In fact, the very insistence on a direct word-meaning correspondence in many Renaissance texts betrays a referential insecurity. The anxiety over linguistic volatility reflects concerns about social and political disintegration – produced in part by the "Nimrodizing" of the corrupt court, as Du Bartas suggested (2.2.2.33–8), and by the instability of identity that resulted from the foregrounding of inwardness and the resistance to established social roles. Francis Bacon and Milton use the image of the double-formed Scylla to represent the rupture between signified and signifier, which they attribute to the various attempts by royalists and intellectual philosophers to refine language and monopolize truth. Absolutism poses as great a threat to national stability as does linguistic relativity.

In *De Vulgari Eloquentia* Dante describes the effects of the confusion of language that in turn register moral decline and cultural disintegration: "Since therefore every language of ours, except that created by God with the first man, has been restored at our pleasure after the Confusion, which was nothing else but forgetfulness of the former language [Hebrew]; and since man is a most unstable and changeable animal, no human language can be lasting and continuous, but must needs change like other properties of ours, as, for instance, our manners and our dress, according to differences of time and place" (29-30). The breakdown in communication attributed to humanity's disobedience led to the original Fall and the confusion of tongues at Babel in the Old Testament. Alternative causes for the corruption of language identified by philosophers and philologists of the Renaissance both complemented and displaced biblical accounts of linguistic mutability; not only was the truth fragmented, but the explanations for the fragmentation multiplied.[2] Thomas Wilson in *The Arte of Rhetorique* offered social and moral reasons for the loss of the original tongue: "Eloquence first given by God, and after lost *by man, and last repayred* by God agayne" is the title of his preface. God stirred up his faithful, to whom he granted the gift of utterance, to "perswade with reason, all men to societye" (10). George Puttenham in *The Arte of English Poesie* claimed that utterance and language were given by God to humanity for the persuasion of others, which is most effectively accomplished through poetry (8). He outlined various rules to prevent the misuse of rhetoric and poetic language, all the while lamenting the damage done by figures of speech, which created "a certaine doublenesse": "As figures be the instruments of ornament in euery language, so be they also in a sorte abuses or rather trespasses in speech, because they passe the ordinary limits of common vtterance, and be occupied of purpose to deceiue the eare and also the minde, drawing it from plainnesse and simplicitie to a certaine doublenesse whereby our talke is the more guilefull & abusing" (154). The abuses of rhetoric and of figures of speech, including metaphor, allegory, and enigma, might, then, be repaired through the art of poetry, which has the potential to transform and perfect nature and humanity.

While defending the power invested in the poetry to transcend the changeability of nature and to imitate, even participate in, the divine, Renaissance and seventeenth-century writers remained conscious of the ability of language both to cause and to reflect social discord. *The Divine Weeks* describes the disruption of social ties by the curse of the Confusion: "Let's all-confound their speech," Du

Bartas's God declares; "let's make the brother, / The sire, and sonne, not understand each other" (2.2.2.187–8). Ben Jonson, who lamented the loss of the original language and the decline of culture, observed in his *Discoveries* that "Wheresoever, manners, and fashions are corrupted, Language is. It imitates the publicke riot" (8:593). Though originally a divine act, the dissemination of languages is also identified in Milton's *Art of Logic* with the collapse of social order: "But as for words which are derived or compound, either their origins are to be sought in other ancient and now obsolete languages, or because of their age or the usually corrupt pronunciation of the lower classes they are so changed and from the practice of incorrect writing are as it were so far obliterated that a true notation of words is very rarely to be had" (*Prose* 8:294).

The abuse of language and rhetoric in turn contributes to political disintegration. Thomas Hobbes contended that the rhetorical strategy of arguing two sides simultaneously – *in utramque partem* – was not a sign of rhetorical possibility, as the humanists maintained, but rather of logical scandal and, in fact, a cause of civil war. His recommendation in "Of Speech" for the purgation of speech and language through the precise use of definitions and the abandonment of all rhetoric (except his own rhetoric of science) complements his proposed implementation of the "law of contradiction" in the form of a commonwealth. The development of his great Leviathan demands the surrender of all individual judgment, authority, and will to the sovereign power. It necessitates, accordingly, the conferring of all political power to an assembly that speaks with a single voice. A plurality of tongues is, like individual expression, synonymous with madness and leads to war. Even the potential for difference, opposition, the clash of voice against voice, or contradiction is politically subversive according to Hobbes. The extreme measures taken by the Leviathan to avert confusion are, however, tyrannical.

While Milton would eventually attribute the fall of Babel to Nimrod's attempt to control the native language absolutely, Hobbes explained the Confusion in terms of the resistance to authority by the rebellious multitudes: "But all this language gotten and augmented by Adam and his posterity, was again lost at the Tower of Babel, when, by the hand of God, every man was stricken, for his rebellion, with an oblivion of his former language" (4.141). No linguistic *felix culpa* or Pentecost is possible for Hobbes. Society can only try to recover a common language or conversation, one that Milton would identify with the reconstruction of the original tower. To characterize any breech or disruption of the conversation as seditious suggests that the conversation is subject to the control of the sovereign, "the soul of the commonwealth" (21.202) – Hobbes's unnamed King Nimrod in *Leviathan*.

The censorship of conversations proposed in the Hobbesian commonwealth and Charles's staged parliamentary debates offer two seventeenth-century examples of the appropriation of voice and of discourses of multivocality for political purposes. Hobbes announces in *Leviathan* that the prevention of confusion and war is achieved through the (re)alignment of signifier and signified, as well as through "conversation" – "people keeping company with one another": "But the most noble and profitable invention of all other, was that of *speech*, consisting of *names* or *appellations*, and their connection; whereby men register their thoughts, recall them when they are past, and also declare them one to another for mutual utility and conversation; without which there had been amongst men neither commonwealth, nor society, nor contract, nor peace, no more than amongst lions, bears, and wolves" (4.140–1). In the *Leviathan* everyone speaks, but all in the same tongue. Dissent is not tolerated: all must participate in the "conversation" regulated by the state at the expense of the individual voice.

In his account of the corruption of the English language in *The History of the Royal Society of London*, Thomas Sprat provides alternative explanations for the flux and mixing of individual languages. From the time of Henry VIII, he explains,

down to the beginning of our late *Civil Wars*, it was still fashioning, and beautifying it self. In the Wars themselves (which is a time, wherein all Languages use, if ever, to increase by extraordinary degrees; for in such busie, and active times, there arise more new thoughts of men, which must be signifi'd, and varied by new expressions) then I say, it receiv'd many fantastical terms, which were introduc'd by our *Religious Sects*; and many outlandish phrases, which several *Writers* and *Translators*, in that great hurry, brought in, and made free as they pleas'd, and with all it was inlarg'd by many sound, and necessary Forms, and Idioms, which it before wanted. (42)

Pedantry, scholasticism, figures of speech, and vain knowledge feed the confusion. The foreign elements, including figures of speech – "this vicious abundance of *Phrase*, this trick of *Metaphors*" – produce "this volubility of *Tongue*, which makes so great a noise in the World" (112). The maintenance of the kind of "civil Society" that the Royal Society advocated necessitated, then, the refinement of the "impurities" of language – introduced by the "Impuritans" (Wedgwood 91) – as well as the establishment of an "*Impartial Court of Eloquence*, according to whose Censure, all Books, or Authors should either stand or fall" (43). Figures of speech obstruct the advancement of knowledge, causing language to degenerate into "the feeblest of instruments – far more untrustworthy than a silvan pipe – preferably to be dispensed with altogether if possible" (Steadman 1).[3] Sprat not only recommends the correction of linguistic abuses and the censorship of texts, but also promotes the writing of an official "Principal Work" in which to record "the Glory of this Age" (43). He justifies his proposal in political terms by arguing that the compilation of a *"History* of our *Civil Wars"* that presented "a full view of the miseries, that attended rebellion" would guarantee, as it had in Augustus's time, the obedience of the subjects to the ruler and the nation (44).

The new multivocal nation, whose plurality of voices Sprat and his like-minded contemporaries feared, was built on the base of the former state, which had privileged the Latin language. The collapse of the hegemony of Latin was followed by the adulteration of the languages that superseded it, including English. In *An Essay Towards a Real Character, And a Philosophical Language* Bishop John Wilkins, under the auspices of the Royal Society he helped to found, provided a Renaissance counter-etiology to the fall of Babel by explaining the variations in the dominant languages in social and political terms:

Besides the common fate and corruption to which Languages as well as all other humane things are subject, there are many other particular causes which may occasion such a change: The mixture with other Nations in Commerce; Marriages in Regal Families which doth usually bring some common words into a Court of fashion; that affection incident to some eminent men in all ages, of coining new words, and altering the common forms of speech, for greater elegance; the necessity of making other words, according as new things and inventions are discovered. Besides, the Laws of forein Conquests usually extend to Letters and Speech as well as Territories; the Victor commonly endeavouring to propagate his own Language as farre as his Dominions; which is the reason why the *Greek* and *Latin* are so universally known. And when a Nation is overspread with several Colonies of foreigners, though this do not alwaies prevail to *abolish* the former Language, yet if they make any long abode, this must needs make such a considerable *change* and *mixture* of speech as will very much alter it from its original Purity. (6)

Migration, war, political instability, epistemological crises, sectarianism, and commercial intercourse as well as colonization account in part for the variety of tongues that replaced those of the Confusion. While the language of the new colony is inevitably appropriated, language acts as a palimpsest; the mixture of tongues greets both the colonist and the colonizer despite the power differential.[4]

Linguistic mutability was, then, a source of considerable anxiety for various seventeenth-century writers besides Hobbes, Sprat, and Wilkins. Robert Boyle, Robert Hooke, Cave Beck, George Dalgarno, Francis Lodowick, John Locke, and Isaac Newton, among others, expressed concern about the flux of meaning and volatility of language that accompanied social and political upheaval. As the seventeenth-century study of linguistic developments became increasingly self-conscious and critical, the language reformers, mainly Royal Society members, adopted in imitation of their precursors, including Francis Bacon, the methods of the scientists and philologists of the period. Through linguistic analysis, the study of stylistics, the creation of hierarchical schemes of classification, the attempted suppression of the historicity of discourse, and the development of a "universal character," the philologists explored the possibilities for restoring the original language. The power invested in the Renaissance poet to repair the effects of the Confusion was, then, transferred in the seventeenth century to the philologist and natural philosopher. Wilkins himself produced the most comprehensive proposal for the restoration of what he called in *Mercury: or the Secret and Swift Messenger* a "universal character," which would effectively spread and promote the arts and sciences (106) and return humanity to a state of linguistic innocence. The regulation of this language by the Royal Society, he maintains in *An Essay Towards a Real Character*, is the next best solution to Pentecost itself, "the Gift of Miracles" (1br). These efforts at reversing the effects of Babel exposed an underlying political agenda: "After a divisive civil war characterized by a breakdown of censorship and a cacophony of voices struggling to articulate the rights of various factions, the ideological appeal of universal language schemes lies in the images of unity and structure they deploy; these images, like that of '*Babel* revers'd,' function as a kind of second-order typology to buttress (after 1660) the ideology of restoration, the metaphysics of a providential order" (Markley 72).[5]

While many of their contemporaries were lamenting the fall into linguistic, socio-political, and epistemological ambiguity, and were attempting in response to invent or return to an Adamic language, John Donne, Sir Thomas Browne, and Milton, among others, were at the same time attracted to paradox, the play of signification, and a Janus-faced truth created in reference to a pluralistic society.[6]

Milton mediates between an attraction to the natural language identified in the *Art of Logic* (*Prose* 8:294) and word-play, for which he was mocked by Restoration and eighteenth-century commentators. Hobbes and his contemporaries identified individual expression, linguistic mutability, and referential insecurity with barbarism and insanity. The resistance to historical objectivity, monovocality, and traditional ways of conveying meaning constitutes an act of revolution: "the revolutionary, most feared in the sovereign kingdom of speech, wears the identity of the madman. He alone breaks the cognitive hold on the breath and glottis, liberates inarticulate and brutish sounds from his body, and negates the civil state at its origin. His attack on the signifier-signified relation is the most significant antipolitical act. Its effect is to retrieve the world from the political history" (Appelbaum 57–8). Milton was cast as a contemporary Nimrod who reconstructed Babel through his writings. In the confusion of the tumultuous pamphleteering on the eve of the Restoration, Milton, who was identified in *The Character of the Rump* as the "Goos-quill Champion" of the Rump and "an old Heretick both in Religion and Manners" (A2v), was accused of betraying his country and perverting his native language by defending the rabble. Critics from the Restoration period characterized his verbal and written statements as the politically subversive expressions of a madman. Criticism was also directed at Milton's verse, particularly the epic poems; Dryden complained about his excessive use of "antiquated words," a fault as great as the practice of "unnecessary coinage" (13:20, 21). In his account of the defects in Milton's language Joseph Addison likewise mentioned the poet's overreliance on "old Words, Transpositions, and Foreign Idioms." Addison qualified this observation by admitting that the native tongue itself was at fault for failing to provide the poet with an adequate medium for his sublime thoughts; thus "Our Language sunk under him" (48). Leonard Welsted complained that Milton's style was that of "a second *Babel*, or Confusion of all Languages" (ix). John Clarke criticized Milton both for allowing the demons in *Paradise Lost* to "pour forth one blasphemous Harangue after another, without any Interruption or Correction" (205) and for his "unpardonable Boldness" and "blasphemy" in introducing God and the Son as actors in the epic. Voltaire promised not to "dwell upon some small Errors of *Milton*," including his "preposterous and aukward Jests, his Puns, his too familiar Expressions so inconsistent with the Elevation of his Genius and of his Subject" (138). More relevant is Voltaire's observation that Milton, in describing the setting for the Parliament of Devils, seemed "to delight in building his *Pandaemonium* in *Doric*

Order with Freeze and Cornice, and a Roof of Gold" (138). Samuel Johnson quoted Butler's characterization of Spenser's "Babylonish Dialect" to criticize Milton's verse, though he also admitted to finding "grace in its deformity" (1:191). Like Clarke, Johnson numbered himself among the critics who faulted Milton for the incongruity of voices in *Paradise Lost* (1:173–9).

### "Functional ambiguities"

Not all of Milton's early critics denounced the poet's language as "hideous gabble"; Francis Peck, for example, borrowed from Jonathan Richardson's *Explanatory Notes and Remarks* (cxlii) in his commendation of the experimental, multilingual quality of Miltonic language: "MILTON's language is *English*, but 'tis MILTON's *English*; 'tis *Latin*, 'tis *Greek* ENGLISH. Not only the words, the phraseology, the transpositions, but the antient idiom is seen in all he writes" (64). Miltonic language is, paradoxically, "*greek'd* & *latiniz'd*, & made as uncommon & expressive as our tongue could be, & yet intelligible to us for whom he wrote" (66). In recalling this passage from Richardson as printed in T. Birch's second edition of Milton's prose, Blackburne entertains the possibility that it is politically charged: it "might justly be applied to the prose-works, though probably (for it is a little dubious) only meant as a character of Milton's poetry" (1:139). Following the quotation, he raises the issue of the editors' intentions again: "whether Mr. Richardson designed to characterize the prose of the poetic Milton, or *both*, we know what he means. And if Dr. Birch brought these passages to do honour to *both*, we are obliged to him; and we, in our turn, will honour him, as an approver of Milton's prose-works" (140). Before examining Milton's various attempts at recuperating the dissonance that registers in his major epic, I might note that the charges of eighteenth-century critics against Milton's Nimrodizing contrast with the common accusation levelled against him by twentieth-century critics and theorists – that of formalism. The difference in the charges testifies to the ideologically freighted nature of the critics' own positions and, in the case of the latter, to a common desire to read *Paradise Lost* into univocality and to deny its multilanguage-conscious nature.

Undeniably epic discourse remains infinitely far removed from the discourse of a contemporary addressing a contemporary or a man speaking to men. The representation of the history of a people in the early epic required impersonality in the poet, who served the one project of further unifying and suppressing difference in the languages of social groups and generations (Bakhtin, *Imagination* 271). In her reading of the lofty epic style of *Paradise Lost* Leslie

Brisman argues that the conversational mode itself – which comforts by imitating human discourse – is sacrificed for the higher mode in the poem: "Conversation is the mode of antihierarchic equality, but in an epic equality does not stand a chance. Milton writes with 'answerable style,' answerable to his high argument and therefore necessarily above equivocation about authority of voice and above prosaic equity of sign and signification" (223). But Brisman does not account for the linguistic range of voices in the multigenre poem or for the dialogized speeches of the individual narrators, who adopt different oral modes and discourses.

Within the restrictions of the lofty verse, meaning is in fact created through each struggling, feeling interpreter and through the manipulation of metre and rhythm. The communication of meaning also depends on accommodation and condescension, as well as on discursive reasoning – expression and interaction through the process of speech – which all assume a difference between signified and signifier. Moreover, the language of the speeches and narrations in the poem contains traces of extra-literary discourses from which the elevated style of epic discourse was traditionally dissociated.[7] I would suggest, finally, that Milton's formalism is in part a response to his aesthetic, social, and political concerns and that the stylistic distancing, while creating and addressing a privileged community of readers, allows him to challenge censorship practices and ensure that his voice might still be heard.

The redistribution of political power in a society that was becoming increasingly socially and historically conscious was complemented by a more modern apprehension of language. The development of language is one of the actions succeeding the loss of origin, Edward Said explains: "Human discourse, like *Paradise Lost*, lives with the memory of origins long since violently cut off from it: having begun, discourse can never recover its origins in the unity and unspoken Word of God's Being. This, we know, is the human paradigm incarnated in *Paradise Lost*" (280). The dissociation of the signifier from the signified – the *etymon* – produced only echoes or disembodied voices that returned fragments of speech. However, at the same time a new understanding of language directed attention to the transaction of words; truths emerge, then, through narratives and in the course of linear time or through the discursive "process of speech." The dependence of words on each other for meaning manifests itself not only in linear relationships of succession but also in relationships of adjacency, correlation, and complementarity, so that the truth assumes numerous shapes.

For Milton, linguistic ambiguity, the interplay of voices, and the multigenre nature of the text encourage active critical interpretation and political engagement, and are designed to involve the reader in the process of poetic composition as well as of the rebuilding of the commonwealth. Through the interaction of various discourses and the transaction among the voices inside and outside the poem, the gradual re-membering of truth is facilitated. Bakhtin's model of the novel, which he regards as a Renaissance invention, illuminates this phenomenon of a diversity that tends towards a dynamic but ultimately unachievable unity. Though categorized as monologic by Bakhtin, the epic, through exchanges with its contemporary setting as well as through its accommodation of multiple voices and problems of signification, becomes novelistic, "a dialogized representation of an ideologically freighted discourse (in most cases actual and really present)." The novel is of all the genres "the one least susceptible to aestheticism as such, to a purely formalistic playing about with words," Bakhtin adds (*Imagination* 333). Through its fluid syntax, figures of repetition, patterns of imagery and allusion, and its complex use of echoes in reiterated sounds, words, and phrases, *Paradise Lost* recuperates word-play while consciously exhibiting the tension between signified and signifier.

In an examination of the development of the Renaissance text, Gunther Kress and Terry Threadgold explain that the conflicting cultural voices of the period and social discord are represented not only by the text's linguistic ambiguities but also by its accommodation of multiple genres:

In a classical text, adherence to the rules of genre was highly regarded precisely because purity of genre ensured both fixity of meaning and social stability. Renaissance textual practices were equally "generic" but here there was no particular value associated with fixity or purity of genre. Indeed much Renaissance textual practice deliberately mixed genres, producing texts which foregrounded social instability and focused on heteroglossia, the many conflicting voices of culture. Such texts seem often only to be readable in so far as readers recognize a superordinate or "master" genre, within which the mixing of genres is embedded. Milton's *Paradise Lost* is a text whose multigeneric nature seems, for example, comprehensible even coherent to most readers in the light of its self-professed "Biblical epic" status. (220)

While Milton seemed to imply an underlying sense of social order by foregrounding the epic in *Paradise Lost*, the dominant genre remains in dialogue with the poem's other literary modes and genres, which, traditionally characterized as univocal, are transformed by their inclusion in the multigenre, politically charged text.[8] The lyric and the prophetic mode, which I discuss in chapters 3 and 6 respectively, are conventionally recognized as monologic, ahistorical, and apolitical; but in Milton's text they are dialogized and brought into a constructive engagement with political and historical issues.

In imitation of the book of Revelation, which resists closure despite its teleological imperative, *Paradise Lost* concludes with apocalyptic visions and accounts. The epic's prophetic books include various interpreters and examples of historical actors who disrupt the tragic narrative of history. The historical and political circumstances surrounding the creation of the final prophetic and symbolic text of the Bible greatly resemble the circumstances of Milton's composition of his Restoration poems, not to mention those surrounding David Pareus's publication of *A Commentary Upon the Divine Revelation*, banned earlier in the century.[9] John, the visionary author of Revelation, used a coded and veiled language to address the members of the early Christian community, who opposed Roman occupation. Identified as the warning voice in *Paradise Lost* (4.1) and *Paradise Regained* (1.18), John created what Milton describes as a multivocal, multigenre text; Milton elaborates on Origen's description of Revelation, which is explicated by Pareus in his account of the biblical text as a "Propheticall Drama" (20) and a "truely Tragicall" "Dramaticall Prophesie" (26): "the Apocalyps of Saint *John* is the majestick image of a high and stately Tragedy, shutting up and intermingling her solemn Scenes and Acts with a sevenfold *Chorus* of halleluja's and harping symphonies" (*Prose* 1:815).

The development of deliberately or strategically ambiguous discourses, including those of multivocality and prophecy, is a political strategy for challenging censorship, by which Milton was inhibited. In *Sade/Fourier/Loyola* Roland Barthes provides the following definition of censorship, which he thereafter contrasts to the invention of an alternative symbolic language: "true censorship, the ultimate censorship, does not consist in banning (in abridgment, in suppression, in deprivation), but in unduly fostering, in maintaining, retaining, stifling, getting bogged down in (intellectual, novelistic, erotic) stereotypes, in taking for nourishment only the received word of others, the repetitious matter of common opinion. The real instrument of censorship is not the police, it is the *endoxa* ... social censorship is not found where speech is hindered, but where it is constrained" (126). In his treatise against censorship, in which he denounces conformity of opinion in a similar fashion, Milton resists the foregrounding of a dominant view or single truth, an act more oppressive than the suppression of all truths:

Well knows he who uses to consider, that our faith and knowledge thrives by exercise, as well as our limbs and complexion. Truth is compar'd in

Scripture to a streaming fountain; if her waters flow not in a perpetuall progression, they sick'n into a muddy pool of conformity and tradition. A man may be a heretick in the truth; and if he beleeve things only because his Pastor sayes so, or the Assembly so determins, without knowing other reason, though his belief be true, yet the very truth he holds, becomes his heresie. There is not any burden that som would gladlier post off to another, then the charge and care of their Religion. There be, who knows not that there be of Protestants and professors who live and dye in as arrant an implicit faith, as any lay Papist of Loretto. (*Prose* 2:543–4)

The defence of critical reading applies to any kind of interpretive or imaginative activity. In this case, the authorities, the church prelates and the assembly, who conform to tradition, enforce censorship practices by discouraging the active interpretation of the different texts. The passive reader of the texts likewise promotes censorship and idolatry.

Barthes defines contra-censorship, the opposition to the establishment of stereotypes, as follows: "The ultimate subversion (contra-censorship) does not necessarily consist in saying what shocks public opinion, morality, the law, the police, but in inventing a paradoxical (pure of any *doxa*) discourse: *invention* (and not provocation) is a revolutionary act: it cannot be accomplished other than in setting up a new language ... it is in having invented a vast discourse founded in its own repetitions (and not those of others), paid out in details, surprises, voyages, menus, portraits, configurations, proper nouns, etc.: in short, contra-censorship, from the forbidden, becomes the novelistic" (126). Censorship and the monopolization of truth are challenged through the development of a new language and a discontinuous "effective" history that appropriates the dominant discourse, turning it "against those who had once used it" (Foucault 154). The language used by the iconoclast to present the counter-arguments is necessarily metaphoric, paradoxical, and elusive. According to Anthony Wood, Blackburne explains, Milton absconded "'for fear of being brought to a legal trial; and so consequently, of receiving condign punishment'" (1:136–7). Christopher Hill, acknowledging his indebtedness to Don Wolfe's *Milton in the Puritan Revolution*, reminds us that Milton was a "marked man" and censors would certainly have been alert to anything written by him. On that basis, he could not put heresies or public opinions into his last poems, "except perhaps by an 'intentional ambiguity,' warnings, innuendos, and a subterfuge wherein radically new interpretations are forged out of subtle reformulations of traditional materials" (*Collected Essays* 1.61).

Like Hill, David Quint (130–1), and Gary Hamilton, who examines Milton's "art of indirection,"[10] Annabel Patterson, in her earlier study of censorship practices, identifies the creation of a symbolic and ambiguous language as an act of contra-censorship. Announcing that her argument is hospitable to, and indeed dependent upon a belief in authorial intention – which can nevertheless not be reduced to a positivist belief in meanings that authors fix – Patterson maintains that authors build a *"functional* ambiguity" into their texts, though they ultimately have no control over what happens to the texts thereafter (*Censorship* 18). Ambiguity becomes thereby for Patterson one message that the author has managed successfully to convey. While Patterson decides not to apply her theory of functional ambiguity to her brief analysis of Milton, she does suggest that such an application would have to address the ambivalent political content that she identifies in Milton's epics and *Samson Agonistes*. Patterson reminds us that we do not know whether Milton turned to biblical reinterpretation in order to transcend his political experience or whether he was still operating in the tradition articulated by James 1 before he became king, that matters of the commonwealth "are to grave materis for a Poet to mell in" (20).[11] Milton's response to the latter would necessarily be the development of a deliberately and strategically ambiguous discourse. He invents and employs such a discourse, I have observed, when he constructs imagined political communities or provides alternative readings of history in his poems and political treatises. Nevertheless, the complex metaphorical rendering of a political or historical subject is not always a contra-censorship strategy, as Patterson explains in *Reading between the Lines*. Patterson's more recent book includes a critique of Hill in which the author notes Hill's conflicting theories about Milton's Christian resignation and his encoded political defiance (247).[12] While finding myself very attracted to the theory that political censorship is a factor in explaining the elusive representation of issues in the poems, I cannot dismiss the possibility that Milton's ambiguous statements were also very much informed both by the poet's Christian transcendence and by linguistic and referential insecurities that register in the texts.[13]

The extent to which *Paradise Lost* is a product of its social and political settings is difficult to judge. At best we can say that the one "determines" the other, not in the sense of causing it but rather in the sense of providing the limiting context to which the text must be seen as necessarily responding (Kendrick 7). If we choose to read the text in this light, then Milton's need to reassert in the face of defeat the possibility of a dialogue with or imaginative transcendence of reality must also take into account the inevitable inscription of those "traces of reality" in the language of the poem. In the exchanges between the speakers created by the "perfect, unimitable *Master of Language*" (Gildon 198), and in the conversations of the poem with socio-historical voices, language is dialogized. The dissociation of the poem from the dissonance that threatens its harmony produces more dissonance. Language bears the imprint of its confrontation with historical becoming and social struggle; it remains "still warm from that struggle and hostility, as yet unresolved and still fraught with hostile intentions and accents." The novel – a term that applies in various ways to the multigenre, multilanguage conscious text of *Paradise Lost* – subjects this discourse to "the dynamic unity of its own style" (Bakhtin, *Imagination* 331).

Milton offers numerous examples of the construction of meaning through speeches and narratives in the multivocal poem, which simultaneously accommodates various accounts of the monopolization and fragmentation of truth; in fact, not only Satan, Nimrod, and Satan-Nebuchadnezzar in *Paradise Regained*, but every narrator, including the poet-narrator, is involved in the manipulation of truth. In the following chapters I examine the development of the individual creation stories by the different interpreters of both epics whose accounts are situated in the poems' master narratives. Harold Toliver argues that Milton intends in *Paradise Lost* "to discover a style that can recite in all the tongues the glory of a single word" (154). If that is so, then some of Milton's discoveries in composing the poem are the agonistics of language and the dialogic nature of "the single word" and of the tongues that recite it. When we consider how the voices emerge and interact in the poem, we become aware that in both their socio-political milieu and in the text, words, discourse, language, and voices become dialogized – that is, they become de-privileged, and derive significance from their association with competing definitions, voices, and discourses (Bakhtin, *Imagination* 427). The resolution of the resonating or oscillating meanings is, furthermore, continually deferred.

Though the lofty epic language and the epic narrator appear to be omnipresent, *Paradise Lost* does not consist of just one mode of expression or one speaking voice – the common gloss of historicists. The poem includes rather, as Charles Gildon announces in the 1694 "*To Mr. T.S. in Vindication of Mr. Milton's Paradise lost,*" a range of mean to lofty descriptions, expressions, styles, languages, voices, and characters (198–9). These characters tell their own stories and thereby shape the complex narrative of providential and contemporary history recounted by the primary speaker. While establishing a chorus of voices and discourses and a community of fit readers, the poem simultaneously and deliberately emphasizes differences among the interpreters. By recasting the official Genesis account and fragmenting the unified teleology of both the classical epics and the monarchy's own model of history, Milton develops a counter-narrative composed of multiple creation stories. In inventing the various histories recounted by the poem's narrators, he does not attempt to uncover the original creation account or restore the primal voice; nor does he attempt to reverse the Nimrodizing or return to an Adamic language – the only one that in Bakhtinian terms had escaped the dialogic inter-orientation with the alien word, the demonic discourse. Instead, he creates a contrapuntal song, which anxiously and self-consciously celebrates its multivocality, celebrates it in what Milton, in a prose soliloquy in *The Reason of Church-Government*, identified as his own native tongue (*Prose* 1:811).

## 2 THE NARRATIVES OF HISTORY

By describing the dissociation between "name" and "fame" (12.45–7) in the story of Babel, Michael satirizes the tower builders' attempts not only at controlling linguistic meaning but also at fixing their historical identities. The rift between words and things in the account creates an ironic perspective that exposes the assumptions and critical apparatus underlying the construction of historical accounts and narratives. The agonistics of language contribute to the internal contestations of the poem and unsettle its dominant narrative. When Michael portrays God's interventions in the biblical historical narrative, particularly his act of "sow[ing] a jangling noise of words unknown" (12.55) and the later miracle of Pentecost – events that frame book 12 – the prophetic narrator highlights the possibilities of developing counter-narratives of history. Through his reemplotment of historical events and his experimentation with chronology, interpretive voices, and a range of perspectives, Milton recuperates ambiguity and offers various models of critical intervention in the official narrative.

Milton's complex construction of worldly and providential history in the poem is effectively illuminated by contemporary theoretical paradigms of narrative and historical interventions. In this section I first identify several modern and contemporary philosophical and literary models of history, and then consider how critics propose to liberate the reader's perception of the past from a narrative of continuity by encouraging interventions – critical interpretations and revolutionary actions. Historical readings that recognize the multiple voices and the discontinuous and heterogeneous processes that constitute history challenge reigning narratives and ideological formulations that censor or suppress differences. Interventions, whether literary, historical, or philosophical, do not occur in vacuums, and this is one of the lessons Milton learns in defending the revolutionary cause – unsuccessfully. In section ii of this chapter I address Milton's various discourses of historical engagement and the reemplotment in the epic of the events of providential and human history.

Friedrich Nietzsche, in *On the Advantage and Disadvantage of History for Life*, a seminal text for deconstructionists, criticizes a blind and fanatical worship of the past that neutralizes differences in order to impose order and continuity. An idolatrous "disguised theology" (45) or the "historical malady" (62) enslaves the individual: "there are no more ruling mythologies? What, religions are about to become extinct? Just look at the religion of the historical power, take note of the priests of the idea-mythology and their abused knees!" (47) The historical continuum was for Nietzsche more oppressive than institutionalized religion. By representing the individual as a latecomer to a world in which all acts of heroism have already been performed, the continuum promotes voyeurism and passivity. However, history – and Nietzsche deliberately employs the term *Historie* rather than *Geschichte* in his title, "Vom Nützen und Nachteil der Historie für das Leben" – does not have to remain a closed system but may be used advantageously, as the title suggests.[14] In fact, the youth of the nation must be made historically conscious if they are to participate in the life and advancement of a true culture, he explains (63). Nietzsche's treatment of the past should, then, be considered in terms of exercise, not exorcism: we do need history, he maintains: "I turn in conclusion to that company of hopeful ones to tell them in parable the course and progress of their cure, their rescue from the historical malady, and so their own history to the point in time at which they will again be well enough to engage in studying history anew and to use history under the dominion of life in that threefold sense, namely monumental or antiquarian or critical" (63). Nietzsche's philosophy includes two concepts of history that T.S. Eliot would later also recognize: "History may be servitude, / History may be freedom" ("Little Gidding" 3.13–14). The proliferation of a diseased, engulfing history is caused by science, which generalizes and regards things as "finished and historical, not as continuing and eternal" (70). The antidote to this "poison" is a dose of the "unhistorical" or forgetfulness, and of the "superhistorical." Nietzsche's antidotes prevent a surrender of the individual consciousness to a homogenizing world-process by engaging the other "spiritual powers" (52); art and religion challenge the sovereign historical power by redefining common historical actions as revolutionary events.

In "Nietzsche, Genealogy, History" Foucault contrasts the Nietzschean "wirkliche Historie" or "effective history" to a traditional history – the malady of history – which is based on a pretended continuity and a system that resists differences and prevents choice. Effective history is not teleological but is characterized by rupture, thus transposing the relationship ordinarily established between an event and an unviolated continuity. Foucault describes an event as a random, subversive, and unique occurrence, one that nevertheless develops in relation to monolithic systems – including the system of language – which it disrupts; an event occurs "not as a decision, a treaty, a reign, or a battle, but as the reversal of a relationship of forces, the usurpation of power, the appropriation of a vocabulary turned against those who had once used it, a feeble domination that poisons itself as it grows lax, the entry of a masked 'other'" (154). Foucault's dismantling of the comprehensive view of history is anticipated by Walter Benjamin, who describes the historical materialist taking cognizance of a historical subject in order to blast a specific era out of the homogeneous course of history and a specific life out of the era. The past for Benjamin is more than a theoretical construct: it is a political one as well. Rather than being a mimetic act, the writing of history involves seizing hold of a memory "as it flashes up at a moment of danger," thus disrupting the established historical continuum and the teleological vision called historicism. Both Terry Eagleton and Benjamin identify the inviolable force as ruling-class history and as the capitalist system, which resists intervention. Both define interventions, ruptures, recyclings, and reinsertions as necessary political actions. The revolutionary acts bring historical contestations, social differences, and class struggles to the surface again, where they might challenge the dominant discourses. Dialectical thought, which Hobbes had sought to suppress in seventeenth-century England, is, according to Benjamin, the organ of historical awakening (*Baudelaire* 176), and critical thinking is an act of revolution.

Benjamin's argument that the truth of the past and present emerges only in their collision is developed into a metaphor of history as conversation by Kenneth Burke in *The Philosophy of Literary Form*. Burke situates the writer, historian, and rhetorician – the not-always-conscious bearers of historical and ideological forces – in a socio-political context. The intervener or critical reader becomes both the reader and listener, the subject and object of the conversation, and acquires materials from the historical discussion while becoming an agent of change within it. The recalcitrant continuum of history, in which intervention makes no difference and to which single revolutionary events bear no necessary connection, is reconstructed as a forum of exchange that registers individual expressions:

Imagine that you enter a parlor. You come late. When you arrive, others have long preceded you, and they are engaged in a heated discussion, a discussion too heated for them to pause and tell you exactly what it is about. In fact the discussion had already begun long before any of them got there, so that no one present is qualified to retrace for you all the steps that had gone before. You listen for a while, until you decide that you have caught the tenor of the argument; then you put in your oar [/or]. Someone answers; you answer him; another comes to your defense; another aligns himself against you, to either the embarrassment or gratification of your opponent, depending upon the quality of your ally's assistance. However, the discussion is interminable. The hour grows late, you must depart. And you do depart, with the discussion still vigorously in progress. (Burke 110–11, my intervention)

We enter a familiar setting *in medias res*, and history begins to "make" us; the expressive act is produced by a network of discourses. At the same time, participation in the discussion allows us to leave an impression that provides the conversation with the necessary energy to continue. Individual contributions help to shape the experiences of future speakers, who are also invited to review the conversations of the past from the recently altered vantage point.[15] The conversation of history cannot come to a conclusion because all future speakers or actors will similarly enter the parlour historically burdened and will leave the conversation vigorously in progress.

Dominick LaCapra develops an even more complex model of interaction between historical and contemporary discourses. The engagement of interpreters "in a particularly compelling conversation with the past" ("Rethinking" 28) assumes that history is not transparent or monolithic and that it can only be recognized in its entanglement with contemporary voices. Historical documentation is complicated by the fact that the act of interpretation is neither purely objective nor subjective, and by the impossibility of fictionalizing or willfully projecting present concerns upon the past. Interpretation takes the form of political intervention, which involves the historian in "a critical process that relates past, present and the future through complex modes of interaction involving both continuities and discontinuities" (63).

To suggest that there are historical continuities is not to say that the past orchestrates a cacophony of historical voices into momentary cohesion, repressing and concealing disjunctures. Rather, by containing continuous forces and tendencies, history becomes a palimpsest of numerous traces and voices. For LaCapra the act of reading involves, then, a dialogical relation with the layers and voices of history: "Even if one accepts the metaphor that presents interpretation as the 'voice' of the historical reader in the 'dialogue' with the past, it must be actively recognized that the past has its own 'voices' that must be respected, especially when they resist or qualify the interpretations we would like to place on them" (64). The examination of interpretive voices and viewpoints represents a major intervention in historiography. At the same time that he addresses the conversation between past and present, LaCapra nevertheless reifies the voices of the past in this passage by isolating history's "own 'voices.'" The very engagement of the past with the present ensures that the "voices of history" continue to be heard, but not in isolation from contemporary discourses. The voices of the past that register in the text create in turn the required context for the writer's own voice, outside of which individual artistic nuances cannot be detected.

The conversation of history includes a conversation about history, one that has been transformed by literary critical discussions of narrative, point of view, and focalization. Historians who have brought literary critical discourses to bear on historical interpretation are inclined to read history as historiography or literary artifact. The poetics of historiography constitute metahistory, which identifies historical narratives as verbal fictions and exposes their structural poetic content. In *Metahistory* Hayden White characterizes the historiographical style as one that offers a particular combination of modes of emplotment – the organization of events – argument, and ideological implication. The attempt to wed a mode of emplotment with a form of argument or ideological implication that is inconsonant with it creates a dialectical tension (60, 61) and is a source of "dissonant consonance" (Ricoeur, *Time and Narrative* 1:168).

Emplotment is one of the operations that shapes our interpretation of historical narratives. Emphasizing the constructed quality of history, White defines emplotment as a mode of explanation: the act of "providing the 'meaning' of a story by identifying the *kind of story* that has been told" (*Metahistory* 7). The critic or historian is compelled "to emplot the whole set of stories making up his narrative in one comprehensive or *archetypal* story form" (8). The archetypal forms consist of romance, tragedy, comedy, and satire.[16] Culture makes sense of personal and public histories by encoding events in plot structures and by presenting the events from different perspectives. In so far as the acts of narration and the emplotment of events change the meaning of the events and of the narrative, they are revisionist and reconstitute the world and the interpreter of it.

Psychoanalysis adds another critical dimension to historiography. The analyst encourages a re-engagement and revision of the personal history to make the patient aware of his "overemplotment" of particular events. In the process of narrating his history the patient works through events and restructures them in order to cast himself in another role and construct an alternative life. The therapy involves working through experiences by remembering and recounting them, thus creating a dialogue with the past, one that imitates the historian's own confrontation with artifacts and documents. The exchanges with personal or political history involve a transferential relation; LaCapra uses the term in the modified psychoanalytic sense of "a repetition-displacement of the past into the present as it necessarily bears on the future" (*History and Criticism* 72). Transference is an act of repetition with variation, which resists at once a total identification with and a complete dissociation from one's self, culture, or history.

*Providential history*

In book 20 of the *Iliad* Aeneas confronts Achilles and admits: "The tongue of man is a twisty thing, there are plenty of words there / of every kind, the range of words is wide, and their variance / The sort of thing you say is the thing that will be said to you" (248–50). The characters' exchange is deemed futile by Aeneas, who returns to military combat. Rehabilitating Homer's twisty words, Milton replaced military battles with debate and verbal contest, in which the poet-revolutionary was most actively engaged during the Civil War and to which he returned when writing *Paradise Regained*. Milton announces that his own contribution to the cause did not take the form of military involvement but of alternative personal and political engagement through writing. Anticipating Abdiel's defence in *Paradise Lost* 6.121–6, Milton justifies his fight for the truth through argumentation in *A Second Defence*:

For I did not avoid the toils and dangers of military service without rendering to my fellow citizens another kind of service that was much more useful and no less perilous ... I exchanged the toils of war, in which any stout trooper might outdo me, for those labors which I better understood, that with such wisdom as I owned I might add as much weight as possible to the counsels of my country and to this excellent cause, using not my lower but my higher and stronger powers. And so I concluded that if God wished those men to achieve such noble deeds, He also wished that there be other men by whom these deeds, once done, might be worthily praised and extolled, and that truth defended by arms be also defended by reason – the only defence truly appropriate to man.   (*Prose* 4:552–3)

The terms used to describe physical labour are employed to characterize intellectual activity and the recording of heroic deeds. The personal testimony offered in the political treatise by the revolutionary, who identified himself as a country of one,[17] suspends the account of national history. At the same time, the text becomes the site for the redefinition of critical intervention and for the representation of alternative political actions.

Milton's original design of historical progress was informed by classical models of history adapted by Renaissance humanists. In accordance with classical tradition, the histories emphasized the role of fortune and the cyclical patterns of events. Historians like Machiavelli and Bodin argued that the political obligations of the man of letters entailed a return to a pragmatic and moral interpretation of the past, which taught the art of survival by rewarding people with fame or punishing them with anonymity. The Christian view of history and the revival of millenarianism inspired by the Reformation challenged the humanists' reading of the ancients and presented instead a providential pattern of events, tracing a linear progression from the creation to the Last Judgment. Milton negotiates between the ancient and Christian models in developing a providential account of history that is influenced by moral causation and human action predicated upon right reason.

The story of God's interventions constitutes providential history, which is brought to fulfilment by human actions. At the beginning of the Civil War many of the revolutionaries were strongly attracted to millenarianism – the belief in the thousand-year reign of Christ and the saints on earth after the destruction of Babylon and the binding of Satan – and were convinced that the Long Parliament would precipitate the national cause and the Second Coming. The Puritan integration of necessity and freedom cast the individual as a player in and reader of providential history. "Indeed there are [hi]stories that do ... give you narratives of matters of fact," Cromwell maintained, at the same time acknowledging that the course of human history remained a mystery (Hill, *Englishman* 241). The intercession of individuals, who interpret Providence and persuade others to participate actively in the cause, could, nevertheless, hasten the results.

In his comparison of the Calvinist and Leninist dilemma about the antithesis between voluntarism and fatalism, Fredric Jameson offers a Hegelian solution in which "the past is necessary and its chain of events as inevitable as in any Providential scheme, but where the understanding has nothing whatsoever to do with the possibilities of action in the present" (44) because those actions are taken in but not within time. One cannot know whether an action might have proved successful until it is attempted. Only in retrospect, then, do interventions register and become meaningful. Providential history is itself subject to reinterpretation when the individual actor or speaker affects conversations about the present and future by rereading the past.[18]

The Puritans' disillusion with Cromwell's reign and the results of the Revolution unsettled this providential and millenarian reading, compelling them to acknowledge the inscrutability of God's ways. Inscrutable, but necessarily so, Milton admits. Guilty of having imposed an artificial linearity on the course of providential history, which charted a direct course from tyranny to the establishment of God's kingdom on earth, Milton develops a more open-ended interpretation of history. In book 3 of *Paradise Lost* he works through the dialectical relationship between providential and worldly history by putting harsh words – which have no biblical frame of reference – into the mouth of God, who declares the freedom of a yet uncreated humanity to author its own destiny. The Father's speech anticipates Adam's lament in the final books as he watches helplessly while the tragedy of human history unfolds (11.770–6). God insists vehemently, though somewhat defensively,

> if I foreknew,
> Foreknowledge had no influence on their fault,
> Which had no less prov'd certain unforeknown.
> So without least impulse or shadow of Fate,
> Or aught by me immutably foreseen,
> They trespass, Authors to themselves in all
> Both what they judge and what they choose; for so
> I form'd them free, and free they must remain,
> Till they enthrall themselves: I else must change
> Thir nature, and revoke the high Decree
> Unchangeable, Eternal, which ordain'd

> Thir freedom: they themselves ordain'd thir fall.
> The first sort by thir own suggestion fell,
> Self-tempted, self-deprav'd: Man falls deceiv'd
> By th' other first: Man therefore shall find grace,
> The other none: in Mercy and Justice both,
> Through Heav'n and Earth, so shall my glory excel,
> But Mercy first and last shall brightest shine. (3.117–34)

By dissociating divine will from foreknowledge, the Creator relinquishes control of humanity's destiny. At the conclusion of this speech, however, God adopts the voice more of Mercy than Justice, anticipating his reemplotment of human history. God will not repeal the death sentence conferred upon a disobedient humanity; however, divine intervention after the Fall does extend the narrative of history so that the actors and readers might interpret their transgression, like the defeat of the Revolution, as a single event in a larger process.

When the monarchy again seized control over the nation's history Milton had already abandoned his plans to write a tragedy, "Adam unparadiz'd," and in the Restoration years composed instead the ten-book poem. In his account of biblical history, Milton acknowledges the impossibility of the individual's intervention in the course of English history, deciding that narrative rather than drama is the appropriate genre for portraying the Fall and the story of human experience after the Fall – by extension, the failed Revolution. Thus the dramatic and lyric moments of *Paradise Lost* become ruled over by the "narrative imperium."[19] In the development of the poem's second edition, the twelve-book epic, Milton, who works through the experience of defeat, reconfigures the events of the plot so that the emphasis in the concluding scenes falls less on the original transgression than on the recovery, which involves a reemplotment of humanity's tragic history.[20]

Through his reorganization of the tragic events Milton disrupts the historical continuum, which would have ensured a satanic victory, a triumph for a tyrant. In opposition to interpretations of Satan's heroic revolutionary impulses, I argue in chapter 3 that Milton's antagonist in *Paradise Lost* is less a rebel than a defender of the status quo, intent on maintaining the closure of the existing historical and political systems. He is, for example, overly protective of his place in the divinely established hierarchy, and resents the intrusion of others who might usurp his position (2.467). Satan is particularly threatened by the elevation of the Son: "By Decree / Another now hath to himself ingross't / All Power, and us eclipst under the name / Of King anointed" (5.774–8). As the protector of the established order, the devil is the tyrannical force behind the creation of a reigning narrative. In *On the Advantage and Disadvantage of History for Life* Nietzsche denounces the "historical power" by associating its perpetuation with egotism, embodied ultimately in the prince of the world himself:

> The purest and most truthful adherents of Christianity have always questioned and impeded rather than promoted its worldly success, its so-called "historical power"; for they used to take a stand outside the "world," and did not concern themselves with the "process of the Christian idea," which is why they have mostly remained quite unknown and unnamed by history. Expressed in a Christian way: the devil is the regent of the world and the master of successes and progress; he is the real power in all historical power, and so it will essentially remain – even though this may ring quite painfully in the ears of an age which is used to the deification of success and historical power. (56)

The construction of a world process that absorbs all dissension must, therefore, be interrogated by those who challenge the "mass-produced" system of history by exposing its narrative quality and the many episodes and multiple voices of which it is composed.

In the final book of the epic Milton invites a critical reading of the double-voiced, prophetic account of human history that includes the stories of such unnamed or minor characters as Cain and Abel, Seth, Enoch, Noah, Nimrod, Ham, Abraham, Isaac, Jacob, Joseph, Pharaoh, Moses, Aaron, Joshua, David, and Solomon. The story of Nimrod reminds us that the course of history can be frustrated and that it includes tragedies and setbacks. At the same time the account portrays history as a composite construction, one open to penetration. While confirming the inevitability of humanity's tragic destiny, the falls of Satan, Adam and Eve, and other biblical figures like Cain and Pharaoh also testify to the free will of the individual actors. Curiously, Milton suggests that the effects of tyranny or tragedy could or even should be erased. The Son roots out but does not destroy the fallen angels at the conclusion of the war in heaven. Moreover, in book 12, as we have seen, God intervenes, but rather than destroying the tower and restoring the originally pastoral society, adds to the confusion by causing the dispersion that Nimrod's followers initially sought to prevent. "Tyranny must be, / Though to the Tyrant thereby no excuse," Michael declares in response to the story of Nimrod (12.95–6) and in contradiction to "necessity / The Tyrant's plea," used by Satan to excuse his "devilish deeds" (4.393–4).

In this chapter I have demonstrated that the concept of an isolated historical event or critical intervention is a fallacy. While it is difficult to determine how specific events, interventions, identities, and voices develop in relation to the larger narratives – socio-political or literary – we can say that they condition each other by creating contexts in which exchanges occur. Christopher Kendrick observes that there is a strong sense in which political revolutions are made by the cultural revolutions that precede them (7). Andrew Milner explains in *John Milton and the English Revolution* that social and political crises rarely, if ever, emerge from nothingness (182). Using a historical example, he asserts that it is surely inconceivable that the ideological preconditions for the Exclusion Crisis – informed in part by Milton's own Restoration writings – had not already been established prior to 1678. Applying a more radical perspective, Eagleton notes that the soldiers of the first Russian Revolution, of 1905, carried copies of *Paradise Lost* with them and read the poem enthusiastically as a libertarian text (*Introduction* 8 n 22). The text thereby not only reflects certain discursive practices and ideologies but creates them. The attempt to furnish evidence for such assertions often ends, however, in the foregrounding of historical over literary texts and in the suppression of the tensions and multiple voices of literature. By examining the complexities and conflicts in the literary text, we do not relegate "reality" or politics to a place outside the text. Instead we analyse its historically freighted language and multivocal nature, thus establishing a continuing exchange between literary and historical voices and between the networks of passages and episodes that constitute the textuality of the poem.

# 3 "I now must change Those notes to Tragic" The Sad Task of Raphael, Satan, and the Poet-narrator

The act of narrating the Genesis story is constantly frustrated; even the angelic historian finds the task daunting: "Immediate are the Acts of God, more swift / Than time or motion, but to human ears / Cannot without procéss of speech be told" (7.176–8). As the subject of a critical and self-conscious text, the original account of earth's creation is fragmented;[1] and because the account competes with creation stories presented by the different characters in the poem, it is also decentred. The official historical and epic narratives are constantly intercepted by the multiple narrators in *Paradise Lost*, who all create their own histories and imaginary worlds. In each case the narrative act comes unsolicited and is characterized as morally ambiguous or dangerous. The presentation of the individual autobiographical accounts is likewise complicated, and in their attempts at remembering their personal histories the speakers of *Paradise Lost* continually draw attention to the limitations of language that impede self-representation. In fact few characters in non-dramatic texts written prior to *Paradise Lost* have as much opportunity to tell their own stories and are, at the same time, plagued by as many difficulties with narration as Milton's characters. In this chapter I will examine the "Sad task" of narration and of historical interpretation in which Raphael, Satan, and the poet-narrator participate. This "Sad task" refers not only, like Aeneas's "sad remembrance" (2.3–6), to the recollection of tragic historical events, but also to the problems of verbal and self-representation. Referential insecurity, subjective expression, and heightened self-awareness in the accounts of Satan and the poet-narrator are concentrated in the soliloquy – a primary site of internalized agonistic strife in the tragic epic.

## 1 "LIK'NING SPIRITUAL TO CORPORAL FORMS"

In the drafts of the Trinity Manuscript, Milton designed the histories of the war in heaven and the creation of the earth in books 5 and 6 and book 7 respectively as choric songs recited by an omniscient narrator. However, in *Paradise Lost* Milton directs attention to the act of interpretation and mediation by turning the narration over to a particular speaker, Raphael, who offers a partisan though authoritative and, in various ways, authorial, reading of history. Later making a disclaimer to knowledge, Raphael establishes a forum for and welcomes the presentation of another episode of the Genesis story: the creation account of Adam, who in book 8 entertains and educates the angel with his story. Raphael is technically a secondary narrator, but one of higher status in the hierarchy of creation and discourse than Adam and certainly than the blind and fallen poet-narrator, whose vision is impaired by the Fall – that is, by his participation in the postlapsarian account he describes. At the same time, Raphael's narrative supplies information to which the angel could not possibly have had access, including knowledge of Satan's speeches to his cohorts and of the invention of "devilish Enginry" (6.553) (Gilbert 63–4). As a historian Raphael speaks in the first person (6.373), though having cast "Raphaël" as an actor in the drama (6.363) and on occasion also employing the first person plural, as in 5.628 or 6.91, 200, and 571ff. Ultimately, then, the narrative is double-voiced, combining the perspectives of Raphael and of an omniscient narrator.

Donald Bouchard argues for the angel's partisanship, claiming that Raphael fails to realize that his own side in the war is as much at fault as his opponents are (130). Raphael, however, does recognize that the "perverseness" that resides in the "hapless Foes" (6.788, 785) is also apparent in the theatrical antics of the loyal angels (6.594, 662–70), who do little to further the Good Old Cause. Potentially more dangerous than military engagement is the act of recounting the physical and internal conflicts of the combatants. Raphael's involvement in the war actually contributes less to his partisanship than do the difficulties he experiences as a historical narrator. The questions Raphael asks prior to narrating the account are rhetorical, and yet they address a range of epistemological, ontological, and even legal issues, thus problematizing the acts of mimesis and historical interpretation. A skilled orator who is attempting to clarify or "make plain" in an effort to secure confidence in his pupil (Swaim 176), Raphael is at times an unreliable narrator (Bouchard 130) and a prevaricator and fumbler (Rajan, "Osiris" 222). Yet his unreliability is in part a function of his employment of a flawed medium and of his participation in the narrative act, which "always entails a measure of opacity" (Kermode 25). The "Divine Interpreter" becomes, then, responsible for creating a metaphorical and highly complex, potentially illegal argument – which Johnson would describe as "confused" – on the relationship between the tragedies of heavenly and worldly history.

Prior to his account of the episode on the war in heaven, Raphael self-consciously delineates the difficulties involved in re-presenting pre-human history. The preface to the war illustrates the convergence of conflicting images, viewpoints, and modes of expression:

> High matter thou enjoin'st me, O prime of men,
> Sad task and hard, for how shall I relate
> To human sense th' invisible exploits
> Of warring Spirits; how without remorse
> The ruin of so many glorious once
> And perfet while they stood; how last unfold
> The secrets of another World, perhaps
> Not lawful to reveal? yet for thy good
> This is dispens't, and what surmounts the reach
> Of human sense, I shall delineate so,
> By lik'ning spiritual to corporal forms,
> As may express them best, though what if Earth
> Be but the shadow of Heav'n, and things therein
> Each to other like, more than on Earth is thought? (5.563–76)

Henry John Todd, Merritt Hughes, and John Carey and Alastair Fowler, in their respective editions of Milton's poems, interpret the verses in a Platonic context by citing the poet's indebtedness to Plato's *Timaeus* and Cicero's *Timaeus ex Platone*, which describe the earth as an image, reflection, or shadow of heaven. If Raphael were a Platonist, however, would not the effort of unfolding the secrets of another world by imitation and accommodation – that is, by employing the flawed language of "corporal forms" – be a futile or impossible endeavour rather than an illegal act? A Platonic reading of the passage could not account, moreover, for Raphael's suggestion that the earth as an image of heaven may in fact resemble the invisible world to a greater extent than humankind realizes.

The relationship between the two is in fact synecdochic as well as analogous, and limited human perception has failed to recognize it as such.

William Madsen rejects the Platonic interpretations of the passage, and like Jon S. Lawry equates "shadow" with the Christian sense of foreshadowing and adumbration, thus privileging a typological reading of *Paradise Lost* (519). He argues that when Michael later explains the development from the Mosaic law to Christian works of faith in terms of the progression from "shadowy Types to Truth" (12.303), he is presenting a view of history of which the Platonist has no conception. For Michael, we could say, the difference between the stages of historical progress is one of degree rather than kind. The relationship between matter and spirit and between earth and heaven in Raphael's prefatory passage may be construed in like terms. Madsen's typological reading foreshadows that of Jackie DiSalvo, who inverts the Platonic doctrine that regards earth as a simulation of an ideal model. She suggests that the account of the war in heaven is informed by Milton's experience of England's tragic Revolution (192), an observation anticipated by Blackburne's comment, "How plain are the civil wars imagined in the sixth book?" (2:623)[2] The multiple critical readings of the passage contribute to its existent ambiguity; DiSalvo's interpretation, which politicizes and contemporizes the account, exposes, specifically, its functional ambiguities. While the question with which Raphael's speech concludes provides the listener and reader with an alternative, prophetic glimpse of the earth, its tragic future, and perhaps of England's own political history, it does not completely deny the earth's status as a shadow; nor does it cancel Raphael's confession about the difficulties of translation.

The preface in which the angel outlines his intent to translate spiritual matters, that is, to bring heaven down to earth, invites comparison with his account of the scale of nature (5.469–503). The interpreter conflates matter and spirit in the passage and, using the Platonic symbol of the tree, describes humanity's potential metamorphosis into pure spirit. However, in order to teach Adam the nature of obedience and the steps by which to ascend to God, Raphael, who is literally converted to proper substance, metaphorically inverts the scale of nature by "lik'ning spiritual to corporal forms" (5.573). In converting spirit to substance and recounting history, Raphael recognizes that words betray him, but verse makes the sad task possible. The problems of comparing worlds with different languages and diverse means of measuring time are at once overcome and made all the more apparent by the reachings of the verse. The passage oscillates between descriptions of heavenly and secular images, past and present events, and suspended moments and linear time, thereby challenging and simultaneously reaffirming the distinctions. Examining the passage more closely, we discover how Milton uses verse to juxtapose otherwise opposing concepts of time and states of being. In the preceding Platonic description of the scale of nature, Raphael associated intuition primarily with angels, and discursive reasoning – which differs in degree, not kind, from intuition – with human reason. However, the angel himself must resort to discourse, that is, to "running to and fro" in his attempt to compare the two worlds.

The discursive language is, at the same time, self-conscious. In the prefatory passage to the war in heaven describing Raphael's attempts at accommodation, the verses – *versus* in Latin – imitate the action of regular return:³ sentences are broken up into poetic lines that reveal a fluid syntax and possible connections between contrasting terms. Beginning in line 563, "High matter" is accommodated to "men," that is to human understanding, and the act of "relating" is consequently a "Sad task and hard." "Human sense" is juxtaposed in line 565 with "invisible exploits," and the modifying phrase "of warring Spirits" is suspended until the following verse, where it is appropriately placed next to "without remorse" (567). In the subsequent line "ruin" and "glorious" are contrasted, and in line 568 the description of the once "perfet" reign of the devils is cut short in the verse when Raphael reveals his plan to unearth the mysteries of heaven, "The secrets of another World, perhaps" (569). The word "perhaps" refers us back by its sound and sense to "secrets." But it also has an anticipatory function: it directs attention to the suggestion that the narration of high matter is "Not lawful." Moreover, the word anticipates Raphael's use of the ambiguous phrase "perhaps / Herafter," which offers a vision of an imagined world or alternative political future.

The suggestion of the illegality of the narrative act is undercut by Raphael's following announcement that the relationship between model and image, between heavenly and secular history, is perhaps closer than on earth is thought. The verse, however, again redefines the terms of the relationship by balancing "perhaps" with the equally conjectural "What if." The juxtaposition of "not lawful" with "for thy good" in line 570 emphasizes the paradoxical and precarious nature of the upcoming narrative account for both the speaker and his audience. While Raphael teaches obedience, his own obedience is being tested. The succeeding verse reassures us that the revelation of the secrets is legally and divinely sanctioned.

Yet the announcement does not ease the tension: in the same line Raphael reminds us that he is conveying high matter to humans with limited understanding by ending the verse with the word "reach" and leaving the modifying phrase "Of human sense" for the next line. Though Raphael may have satisfied the legal requirements for the narrative act, his subject-matter remains out of bounds.

The juxtaposition of spiritual and corporal forms in line 573 again draws attention to their oppositional relationship, while simultaneously recalling the fusion of divine spirit and earthly matter in God's creation of humanity described in *The Christian Doctrine* (*Prose* 6:316–17). In narrating the war in heaven, Raphael develops a dialectical relationship between spirit and substance through the act of delineation. If the spiritual and the substantial are more similar than was previously thought, and if the narrative act is potentially unlawful, then Raphael's delineated account must be more than simply an outline or a shadowy impression of the actual event. Line 574, "As may express them best, though what if Earth," articulates more explicitly what the structure and syntax of the verses have already suggested: if properly perceived, contraries will reveal their similarities. Through his poetic speech, then, Raphael compels us to reconsider the effects of accommodation. The likening of spiritual to material forms "As may express them best" is, in Milton's terms, condescending; however, the word "though," which introduces the subsequent proposition that earth may be more like heaven than humankind recognizes, raises the possibility that the shadowy world and its history may not be mere reflections of what lies above or behind after all. Raphael invites us to consider the distinction between earth and heaven in terms of the difference between night and day in heaven, where the change to twilight is welcomed:

> ambrosial Night with Clouds exhal'd
> From that high mount of God, whence light and shade
> Spring both, the face of brightest Heav'n had chang'd
> To grateful Twilight (for Night comes not there
> In darker veil). (5.642–6)

Raphael's parenthetical alignment in this passage is one of several throughout his narrative. In each case, the alignment marks a distinction between heavenly and worldly experience. But the preface to the narration of the war has already provoked a reexamination of the interconnection of the diverse experiences. The image of heaven, rather than being a copy of an ideal, or even a silhouette or outline of a painting (Madsen 522), can legitimately be perceived as a "lively shadow" (*PL* 8.311). In the final line of Raphael's introductory passage, the angel's suspicion that the image is in fact very like the ideal model is juxtaposed with the limited understanding of earth's inhabitants, particularly the Platonists, who see otherwise. This one brief concluding remark in Raphael's prologue adds a new dimension to our reading of the relationship between the ontological status and the histories of the two worlds that he compares.

The monovocality of the preface is challenged not only by its discussion of comparative strategies but also through its intertextuality and inclusion of different voices. Raphael's words "Sad task and hard" allude to those of another "secondary narrator" – Aeneas, who began the account of his tragic history in the same way. Despite Raphael's angelic status, his inferior position in relation to the official narrator is suggested by this connection to Aeneas. The prefatory passage to the war in *Paradise Lost* also echoes the "doleful tale" of the Duke of Buckingham in *A Mirror for Magistrates*, which I examine in the first section of part 2, and it anticipates the anxiety of Milton's poet-narrator as he changes his notes to tragic. While the divinely sanctioned authority of the angel should prevent him from having any misgivings at all about the narrative act, Raphael's reliance on human discourse connects him with the other narrators in the poem. Moreover, even if his reference to the precarious nature of narration is merely a disclaimer, Raphael, like the poet-narrator, still betrays self-consciousness in the monologue. By directing attention to the methods of accommodation, the speakers make us all the more acutely aware of the presence of a mediating, partisan voice in the historical narratives. In turn, the metafictional and lyrical moments, the interjections, as well as the authorial intrusions and proems of the poet-narrator, though seemingly monovocal, reveal the speakers' concern about their performances and their awareness of an audience.

The act of translation that Raphael identifies is, on one hand, an act of condescension, one that depends on power differentials or hierarchically constructed relationships. Yet the announcement of difference implicit in the process of accommodation paradoxically calls for its opposite. Raphael, in his prologue to the impending tragedy, proposes the possibility of a correspondence between the shadowy image and the model. Through the imagination, then, the act of comparison reveals a similarity of form and the balance of its parts. Raphael's question, "what if Earth / Be but the shadow of Heav'n," at once alerts us to the limited nature of human understanding, which is perhaps guilty of having established an artificial hierarchical relationship between otherwise like things, and reveals the possibility of expanding human capacity to receive and transcend the limits of the information imparted. The act of accommodation, then, brings matter and spirit, discursive and intuitive processes, linearity and simultaneity, and lyric and dramatic voices together in a constructive tension.

## 2 THE ANXIETY OF INFLUENCE

The reason Milton wrote in fetters when he wrote of Angels & God, and at liberty when of Devils & Hell, is because he was a true Poet and of the Devils party without knowing it
William Blake, *The Marriage of Heaven and Hell*

> Others more mild,
> Retreated in a silent valley, sing
> With notes Angelical to many a Harp
> Thir own Heroic deeds and hapless fall
> By doom of Battle; and complain that Fate
> Free Virtue should enthrall to Force or Chance.
> Thir Song was partial, but the harmony
> (What could it less when Spirits immortal sing?)
> Suspended Hell, and took with ravishment
> The thronging audience.   (*Paradise Lost* book 2)

The speeches of the two other narrators in *Paradise Lost* who undertake the sad task of recounting tragic events exhibit, like Raphael's preface, an ambiguous, intertextual, and multivocal quality. Because the narrative act for Satan and the poet-narrator involves the relation of personal tragedy more than it did for Raphael, I have foregrounded the issues of self-representation and subjective expression in my examination of their accounts.[4] Part 2 focuses on the strife between the two authoritative voices that is dramatized in the narrators' monologues – the discourse of the divided self, of which the multivocal poem is intensely distrustful.[5] Despite the apparent opposition between Satan and the inspired narrator, the poem develops out of the ambivalent relationship between these two voices and, in particular, between the poet's language and both the monological discourse and the wandering signification of the devil's speeches.[6] "Opposition is not necessarily enmity; it is merely misused and made an *occasion* for enmity," Freud contends in *Civilization and Its Discontents* (49). The allusions to Bacchus and Nimrod in the accounts both of Satan and the dominant narrator complicate our understanding of the interrelated identities of the two epic poets. In the invocation of book 7 the narrator announces that he is threatened by the surrounding dissonance and also compares his poetic enterprise to the daring ascent to the heavens made by Bellerophon – who ended up blind (Hollander 116). The poetic flight recalls, moreover, the vain attempt by Nimrod to reach the heavens through the construction of a tower. Like Satan immediately after his fall, the world's first tyrant remains unnamed in Milton's poem, and the rebel's unfinished work is left "Ridiculous" and in confusion (12.62). The Christian Orphic poet, who boldly proposes to "soar / Above th' *Aonian* Mount" (1.14–15), in turn fears at once the fragmentation of his artistic creation and his own tragic fall.

A psychoanalytic approach to the relationship between the epic poets in *Paradise Lost* challenges our assumptions about the poet-narrator's dominance and the politics of voice in the text. In a Freudian context, aggression is antithetical to civilization, and at the same time strife and competition are the bases for human activity (49) as well as human creativity. Freud applies his account of the evolution of civilization to personal development in locating the origin both of the "super-ego of an epoch of civilization" and of an individual (78) in guilt, aggression, and fear of and resistance to authority. Hailing Freud as the prophet of the agon and of its ambivalences (*Agon* viii), Harold Bloom adopts the model developed by his precursor for his theories about poetic interpretation and criticism. *Kairos*, the "fusion/defusion of the fundamental drives, love and death" (*Agon* 36), is the heart of poetry, even the figuration for poetry itself. Bloom defines *kairos* as "image of voice," "crossing," "poetic stance," or primal ambivalence in the Freudian sense (38). The example in *Paradise Lost* of Satan's rebellion against divine authority, cited throughout *The Anxiety of Influence* and *Agon: Towards a Theory of Revisionism*, supports Bloom's contention that the mind cannot conceive of interpretive power without the demigod or king whose power must be usurped.

In *Paradise Lost* the contest between Satan and the poet-narrator, which is represented in the soliloquies and dramatic speeches of both characters, becomes one of the primary sites of strife. In section i I examine the narrative and oratorical strategies of Satan in the monological speeches of the tragic epic and then focus in section ii on the poet-narrator's dialogized voice and his negotiation between "barbarous dissonance" and multivocality in the official narrative. Bloom's implicitly hierarchical model of interpretation (*Agon* 43) effectively illuminates Milton's account of Satan's agonistic struggle with God. This contest leads eventually to Satan's misreading of history and to the devil's retreat into both wilful narcissism and incessant autobiography. In my discussion of the poet-narrator's role in *Paradise Lost*, the Bloomian theory of the agon is placed in a constructive tension with the Bakhtinian definition of authority, in which power is dispersed among multiple voices to create a plurality of centres of consciousness, displacing the "single and unified authorial consciousness" (*Problems* 6). Implicit in the tenuous signified-signifier association in the tragic accounts of both poets – and also represented by the hierarchical and heretical relationship between the Father and the Son – is both a sense of anxiety and loss as well as the possibility for greater interaction among the other *characters*. The accommodation in the poem of concepts, such as contending interpretive voices and narrations, mixed genres, and – particularly in the scenes involving Satan – comedy, parody, and irony, tells us something about the poem's agonistic composition and the conditions that informed its creation.

*Satan's partial song*

The epic begins not with the Genesis creation story but with Satan's own tragic history, from which Milton struggles to dissociate his own poetic origin and creativity.[7] At the beginning of the poem, the vision of the Muse from whose view "Heav'n hides nothing" (1.27) is displaced by the perspective of Satan, who comments on the change he sees in Beelzebub: "If thou beest hee; But O how fall'n! how chang'd / From him, who in the happy Realms of Light / Cloth'd with transcendent brightness didst outshine / Myriads though bright" (1.84–7). Here Milton recalls Aeneas's encounter with Hector's ghost (*Aeneid* 2.358–9), who in the classical epic represents the defeated warrior Hector, but who also acts as a prophet of Aeneas's triumph (2.381–2). Satan is interested in his companion's countenance and words, both because Beelzebub reminds him of his own tragic past and fallen condition and because Beelzebub, as type of prophet (1.143–55), inspires Satan to author the devils' destiny (1.157–91). Satan, then, is the modern poet who misreads and rewrites the past (Bloom, *Anxiety* 20–1). The resulting anxiety produces a satanic counter-epic, one imitated by the devils, and one that recounts the demonic poets' "Heroic deeds and hapless fall" (2.549). Satan's own darkened vision is thereby inscribed as a comedy and as comic revelry in the official tragedy.[8]

Throughout the poem Satan denies the dialectical nature of expression and narration by composing his autobiographical history in formalist and absolutist terms. Raphael, Michael, and Adam and Eve are confronted by situations that they interpret in the context of providential history, while Satan, by contrast, generates his story. Having suppressed his past and all contending voices from the start, Satan, the dictator of Pandemonium, "dwells within his abstract potential and cannot confront situations at all" (Grossman 37). The narrative that the mock-author develops expresses the forms by which consciousness "both constitutes and colonizes the world it seeks to inhabit comfortably" (White, *Tropics* 99) and also exposes the Sin-ful consequences of the imaginative act of colonization. Satan's misreading of his story produces the anxiety from which the satanic epic and the devils' destiny are made. The fall of Satan and the devils is continually rehearsed in their literal re-enactment of the original temptation to which they themselves fall prey in book 10. The script they write later in the poem is a chapter of the "partial" – partisan and fragmented – song identified in book 2. The satanic literary creation is the heathen, mythological, and comic counterpart to the tragic Genesis story of original sin. Again the fruit proves bitter, for the myth of the Titans Ophion and Eurynome ends with the expulsion of these first Olympian rulers by Saturn and Rhea (10.578–84).

The authoritative position that Satan assumes in revising the past is one he adopts in the first public address to his cohorts after their fall. The poet-narrator represents Satan as a tragic classical hero who succeeds in enchanting his followers by his splendour, though he is darkened like the eclipsed sun. The sun in eclipse perplexes monarchs (and royalist censors)[9] with fear of change, according to the narrator (1.594–8). In book 4 Satan will find himself similarly overshadowed by the sun, "the God / Of this new World" (4.33–4). A fallen monarch who conceals his defeat, Satan holds his audience mute in anticipation of his oration: "Thrice he assay'd and thrice in spite of scorn / Tears such as Angels weep, burst forth: at last / Words interwove with sighs found out thir way" (1.619–21). Satan uses rhetoric and gestures to smooth over any signs of conflict or self-contradiction, as the narrator reveals in his critique of Satan's stage-work. Still the relationship between the poet and the devil he portrays is not simply oppositional but is built as well as on identification and a shared interest in contest and performance, including verbal performance. The poet-narrator also betrays his attraction to classical heroism, despite his proposal in the fourth proem to replace the descriptions of epic wars and battles – the kind that fill the classics and, ironically, book 6 of *Paradise Lost* – with illustrations of "the better fortitude / Of Patience and Heroic Martyrdom

/ Unsung" (9.31–3). The poem in fact develops out of the struggle inspired by the equal pressures of the poet's fascination with the ancients, his allegiance to the scriptural tradition, and his desire to assert his own voice. The description of Satan as a hero who, though fallen, possesses a form that has "yet not lost / All her Original brightness" (1.591–2) testifies to his grandeur as well as to the poet's muted admiration for the classical antihero. The characterization of Satan as an actor, deceiver, and simultaneously a champion – the meanings of the epithet *agonistes*[10] – heightens the tension between the carnivalesque[11] and the tragic in this portrait, which anticipates the same in the dramatic representation of Samson's agonistes.

Drawing on classical and Renaissance texts for the above description (1.619–21), Milton appropriates an epic formula – conventionally used in accounts of military combat and ceremonial action – to represent the Periclean orator at the point of addressing his audience in a mode that is at once formal and confessional.[12] For his portrait of Satan as a statesman, orator, and tragedian in book 1 Milton is indebted to Virgil's descriptions of Aeneas (2.1–6; 6.949–52) and, more immediately, to Thomas Sackville's portrait of Henry, Duke of Buckingham, in *The Mirror for Magistrates*:

> Thryse he began to tell his doleful tale,
> And thrise the sighes did swalowe up his voyce,
> At eche of which he shryked so wythal
> As though the heavens rived with the noyse:
> Tyll at the last recovering his voyce,
> Supping the teares that all his brest beraynde
> On cruel Fortune weping thus he playnde.   (547–53)

The account of the fallen monarch in *Paradise Lost* fragments and parodies the instructive histories that make up *A Mirror for Magistrates*. The agonistic interplay of the two tragic scenes heightens the parodic character of the satanic performance. Buckingham's and Satan's sad task of recounting the narratives complements the tragic subject-matter of the histories. However, while Buckingham confronts his experience, offering it as an example by which readers might learn to check their own actions and political ambitions, Satan deliberately misreads the tragedy of his rebellion to deny its relevance. *Paradise Lost* and "The Induction" of Sackville's tragedy both conclude with a panoramic account of a world demonized by human perversity. However, *Paradise Lost* – particularly the twelve-book version – extends the process of working through the tragedy it inscribes by offering an alternative though darkened vision and narration of humankind's destiny. Milton's poem, then, mediates between the imperial triumphs prophesied by Virgil, the purgation and redemption of souls in Dante, and the tragic history dramatized by Sackville.

In *Paradise Lost* the devil's first public speech, to which he refers in book 4 as one of his "vain boasts," presents a resolved argument. His deliberative rhetoric – rhetoric addressed to a political assembly or ruler to persuade the listener to some course of action on a public issue – is directed at an audience of one; it renders its listeners mute prior to its presentation and makes no mention of them afterwards. The dialogues between Satan and the fallen angels are equally ineffective and take on the character of manipulative rhetoric because Satan prevents all exchanges and critical readings of authority (Lewalski, *Rhetoric* 80–4). Satan's control of the outcome of the infernal council in book 2 is a primary example of his attempts at censoring dissenting voices and the devils' own epic history.

Inverting the colloquy between Father and Son in book 3, which culminates in the book 7 Genesis creation account, Satan, the voice of tyranny, develops an absolutist language and speaks in isolation in book 4, effectively silencing the poem's other voices. In his mock invocation on Mount Niphates, Satan initially acknowledges the presence of an addressee, thereby echoing the words of the poet-narrator, who invokes Urania. Failing to recognize the complex identity of his addressee, however, Satan calls on the Sun directly in a scene of personal confession and of critical judgment (Carey and Fowler, eds., bk 4, n 30):

> O thou that with surpassing Glory crown'd,
> Look'st from thy sole Dominion like the God
> Of this new World; at whose sight all the Stars
> Hide thir diminisht heads; to thee I call,
> But with no friendly voice, and add thy name
> O Sun, to tell thee how I hate thy beams.   (4.32–7)

The word "sole," suggestive of "sol," is juxtaposed with "Dominion" and located at the centre of verse 33. However, by the end of the soliloquy, Satan – the self-proclaimed king who is threatened by the Sun, just as he is "eclipst" by the Son (5.776–7) – displaces the "Sun," proposing to dominate and colonize the "new World" of humanity. The development of a relationship between the self and the other in this speech is an act of solipsism. In the epic both the poet-narrator and Adam call out at different times to the Son and the Sun respectively and likewise project a name and identity on the addressees. However, unlike Satan's soliloquies, these invocations develop into exchanges between the speaker and the addressee.

The orientation of the soliloquy and apostrophe towards an object world that cannot respond marks the change in emphasis from auditory to visual perception that suspends dialogue altogether. The vocative is thereby reduced to the descriptive, "eliminating that which attempts to be an event"; what is at stake is "the power of poetry to make something happen" (Culler 140). Satan develops a language of absolutes that fixes the relationship between signifer and signified, and he adopts reductive rhetorical strategies in part indebted to Ramism: "The Ramist arts of discourse are monologues ... the orientation of Ramism [is] toward an object world (associated with visual perception) rather than toward a person world (associated with voice and auditory perception). In rhetoric, obviously someone had to speak, but in the characteristic outlook fostered by the Ramist rhetoric, the speaking is directed to a world where people respond only as objects – that is, say nothing back" (Ong 287). This rhetoric renounces any possibility for invention within a speaker-auditor framework because verbal communication and understanding are denied.

In the soliloquy Satan's memory is awoken first by conscience, then by the Sun's beams, which brought "to [his] remembrance from what state / [He] fell" (4.38–9), and finally by his recognition of his difference from the creator. The acknowledgment of a higher authority is potentially liberating, thus revealing a dialectical relationship between obedience and freedom. "A grateful mind / By owing owes not, but still pays, at once / Indebted and discharg'd; what burden then?" (4.55–7), Satan admits, recognizing that unmerited advancement leads only to further decline (89–92). Plunging ever deeper into his *self*-made hell, however, he eventually shuts out all memories and creates for himself an identity that resists interrogation and is allegedly immune to difference and alteration – the projection of "A mind not to be chang'd by Place or Time" (1.253). By repressing the history of the Fall, Satan evades all responsibility; his rhetoric is filled with passive constructions and suppositional statements. The fragmentation of the past is represented by the truncated lament and parodic consolation that bring the soliloquy to its abrupt conclusion (Lewalski, *Rhetoric* 99). The devil ends his self-confrontation, silences the voices that speak of his relationship to God and history, and announces unambiguously in a statement of anti-creation: "So farewell Hope, and with Hope farewell Fear, / Farewell Remorse: all Good to me is lost; / Evil be thou my Good" (4.108–10).

The reign and relation of Satan's own narrative is intercepted in the larger context of the poem both by the retrospective and anticipatory stories of the other characters and by Satan's own contradictory voice. The soliloquies jar with the linear narrative and the public speeches that he orates. Temporarily suspending the related events, the soliloquies offer a particular point of view on the action, one that replaces the choric commentary in the early plans for the tragedy. Satan here is a choral character who distances himself from the action while providing the spectator-reader with an alternative, though largely distorted or ironic, reading of events. Interrupting the narrative, the soliloquies project a will-to-sameness and allow for only a singular perspective. Their meditational mode and psychological content make them resistant to other viewpoints. Yet the language of the soliloquies inevitably resists absolutes and splinters, thus taking revenge on those who would use it to suggest that there are no alternatives to a given thought or action.

The complex attempts at self-representation in the soliloquies challenge the hegemony of cultural and literary expression established in the traditional epic and tragedy and, more specifically, destroy "that naïve wholeness of one's notions about the self that lies at the heart of the lyric, epic, and tragic image of man" (Bakhtin, *Problems* 120). Milton's lofty poem registers its anxiety with the soliloquies, monologues, and apostrophes that it nevertheless accommodates. As the forms of the discourse of the divided self, the monologic speeches, which are very much dialogized throughout the poem, expose the composite, contradictory nature of identity.

Despite their personal and psychological nature, Satan's soliloquies retain a public, rhetorical, and oratorical quality that reveals the devil's manipulation of his audience, while also indicating that genuine self-expression eludes the artificer of fraud. If we compare the public speech made after the rebel angels' fall with Satan's first soliloquy, we find a similarity in style and argument. Lewalski explains that Satan's soliloquy can in fact be divided into the parts of the judicial oration (97ff). The language of this eloquent orator is crafted and contrived, even when his subject is seemingly most personal. In the subsequent book Milton invites a comparison of Satan's mock invocation with the unmeditated orisons of Adam and Eve.

When Satan does not soliloquize, he often serves as a focalizer whose perspective is presented by the official narrator. The gaze of Satan contributes to the "reign" of a linear and totalizing narrative. In book 2 Satan's narcissistic and destructive gaze leads to the rape of the "double-form'd" Sin, who merely echoes her lover's/father's tautological language. We experience Eden in book 4 through the eyes of Satan, who, in the likeness of a cormorant, is perched on the tree of life (194–201). The poet-narrator superimposes his vision of Eden on Satan's, but the account of the garden is nevertheless characterized by negative comparisons and anachronisms – the product of a distorted and distant perspective. In the garden, which the poet-narrator regards as "A happy rural seat of various view" (4.247), the Fiend "undelights all delight" through his censoring vision. Satan, "still in gaze" (356) and in "couchant watch" (406), alternates between voyeur and exhibitionist, providing an audience for Eve, who recounts the story of her enchantment with the reflection she sees. Through his tyrannical gaze, the voyeur attempts to define and master the object of inquiry. Voyeur and exhibitionist both avoid the "other" role. However, by objectifying what he sees, Satan, the actor who becomes a spectator, is himself transformed into a passive object. The mechanism of reversal-aggression towards an object is turned back upon the self, thus preventing dialogue (Schwartz 55).[13]

Tormented by his exclusion from the joyful scene in Paradise, Satan curses the "Sight hateful, sight tormenting!" (505) and finalizes his plans for destruction. In this soliloquy Satan reduces the garden to a *hortus conclusus*: "first with narrow search I must walk round / This Garden, and no corner leave unspi'd" (4.528–9). The gaze that Eve identifies when recounting her dream in book 5 (47, 57) is the same totalizing gaze that provokes her book 9 fall. The Satanic eye is mentioned again in book 8, where Raphael admits to Adam that on the sixth day of creation he was absent on a mission to capture any *spies* intent on mixing "Destruction with Creation" (236).

In the first soliloquy of book 9 Satan again declares his plan for anticreation: "only in destroying I find ease / To my relentless thoughts" (129–30). Ironically, his language anticipates his perverse metamorphosis or demonic incarnation (9.166) into the serpent; the temptation scene is signalled by the alliterative "s" sound of Satan's words used to address Eve thereafter:

> Revenge, at first though sweet,
> Bitter ere long back on itself recoils;
> Let it; I reck not, so it light well aim'd,
> Since higher I fall short, on him who next
> Provokes my envy, this new Favorite
> Of Heav'n, this Man of Clay, Son of despite,
> Whom us the more to spite his Maker rais'd
> From dust: spite then with spite is best repaid.   (171–8)

The speech recounts the act of the divine creation that culminates in the fashioning of Adam and Eve, an event that proves to be the devil's greatest source of torment. Satan turns his spite on Adam, whose creation by God he reduces to an act of vengeance against himself; he thus misreads the historical event, returning Adam – "this Man of Clay, Son of despite," "rais'd / From dust" – to the clay and dust from which God originally created him. In the fifth soliloquy – Satan's most solipsistic speech addressed to his own thoughts, one that best reflects his own divided mind (9.473–93) – the devil provides an impressive portrait of Adam that contradicts his previous description. As Satan himself realizes, however, revenge, like language, "ere long back on itself recoils." Satan later is literally transformed into the serpent that consumes and becomes dust (10.566; 208). Moreover, he is reduced to uttering spite through his hissing (10.543), which recalls the dire "noise / Of conflict" produced by the warring angels (6.211–12) and the "dismal universal hiss" from the serpents' "innumerable tongues" (10.507–8). The language of the soliloquy also imitates the cannon fire: the diction – "recoils," "well aim'd," and "fall short" – characterizes the temptation speech as a militant action.

Satan is described prior to his first speech as standing above his cohorts in a shape and gesture proudly eminent "like a Tow'r" (1.591). The tower, a traditional emblem for the Son (Carey and Fowler, eds., bk 1, n 591), is here representative of Babel. The numerous creaturely disguises that the harlequin adopts throughout the narrative ridicule his once stately form and performances. Likewise, the meaning of his eloquent speech splinters; the many conflicting significances conveyed by his words flame out defiantly towards heaven (1.663–9) only to "recoil" and wound the speaker himself. Both the militant language and the past return to haunt and mock him. Satan's soliloquies, particularly the two in book 9, suppress all contesting voices and perspectives and gradually become more inwardly directed. In contrast, the monovocal speeches of Adam and Eve – who in their prelapsarian condition utter the demonic discourse in books 9 and 10 – are eventually transformed into complaints, lamentations, elegies, and prayers. At once recounting and participating in Satan's fall and humanity's original sin in book 9, the poet-narrator exposes the dialogical nature of his speaking voice that also moves between the postlapsarian soliloquy and the restorative dialogue.

*"But drive far off the barbarous dissonance"*

A solo voice sings not in harmony by silencing the rest.
Eva Figes, *The Tree of Knowledge*

The discordant harmony that, according to Tasso, characterizes the

Renaissance epic counterpoints the "barbarous dissonance" of Bacchus and his Revellers that resounds in *Paradise Lost*. The allusion in the third invocation to the dismemberment of Orpheus by the Revellers has symbolic and, as I will demonstrate, historical importance (7.32–8). The Thracian Bard's death ends the singing and leaves only images of voice or echoes out of which the Revellers compose their comic, "partial" song (2.552) – one that is disharmonious and favourable only to themselves and one that echoes the demonic poets' epic history of their own fall (2.549). The description of "*Bacchus* and his Revellers, the Race / Of that wild Rout" (7.33–4) anticipates the account in book 12 of the unfinished tower left "Ridiculous" (12.62) and of the rebellious Nimrod, to which the name of Bacchus as law-giver and corrupt monarch is linked.[14]

The demonic bacchic dissonance that his poetry attempts to evade endangers the song of Milton's Orphic poet – the dominant voice of the official narrative:

> But drive far off the barbarous dissonance
> Of *Bacchus* and his Revellers, the Race
> Of that wild Rout that tore the *Thracian* Bard
> In *Rhodope*, where Woods and Rocks had Ears
> To rapture, till the savage clamor drown'd
> Both Harp and Voice. (7.32–7)

As he does in reference to Nimrod, Milton activates the etymology of Bacchus's name in the harshly alliterative verses. Bacchus "was so call'd from a Greek Word which signifies to *revel*" (Tooke 70). Bacchus and Nimrod are different representatives of one dialectic, constituting the extremes of a continuum of voice. However, Bacchus's antithetical relationship to Nimrod and the symbolic pole of multivocality is challenged in the poem; in fact, Bacchus's name and various mythological identities are closely connected with those of Nimrod. Nimrod, like Bacchus, is responsible both for political anarchy and cacophony, as well as for monarchy and the censorship of voice, including the poet's (Orpheus-Lycidas's) own voice. The Master of Revels employed by the monarch was the primary censor, as Milton, who makes cacophony synonymous with censorship and tyranny, recognized (*Prose* 2:518).[15] Andrew Tooke, in *The Pantheon*, would offer five pieces of evidence to prove that Bacchus, the corrupt monarch, is Nimrod (81). The second reason he provides reads: "They think the Name of *Nimrod* may allude to the *Hebrew* Word, *Namur*, or the *Chaldee*, *Namer*, a *Tyger*. And accordingly the Chariot of *Bacchus* was drawn by Tigers, and himself cloath'd with the Skin of a Tiger" (81). Du Bartas likewise alludes to the relationship between Nimrod and Bacchus by describing the confusion caused by the former as "a jangling noyse not much unlike the rumors / Of *Bacchus* swaynes amid their drunken humors" (2.2.2.191–2).

The poet-narrator's resistance to the demonic bacchic revelry in composing his "great Argument," his genesis account, becomes one of the primary sources of agonistic strife in the poem at large. The problems of expression, which register even in lofty verse, are particularly evident in the lyrical moments of Milton's epic. The narrator's awareness of the distinction between name and signification in the third proem, in which he invokes the "Voice divine" (7.2), opens into this highly self-conscious scene. In the same proem, however, Milton's poet-narrator, who is confined to the "Native Element" (7.16), associates himself with Orpheus, fearing "the barbarous dissonance" that is a product both of the fallen satanic discourse that pervades and threatens the tragic epic and of the historical political conditions to which its style is answerable. Blackburne asserts confidently: "Could the character of Charles the Second, with his rabble rout of riotous courtiers, or the cavalier spirit and party just after the Restoration, be marked stronger and plainer than in the beginning of the seventh book?" (2:623). The reference in *The Readie and Easie Way* to the diabolical royal pamphleteers "[creeping] out of thir holes, thir hell" – pamphleteers whom Milton identifies as the "tigers of Bacchus ... inspir'd with nothing holier then the Venereal pox" (*Prose* 7:452–3) – provides one possible gloss for Bacchus and his Revellers. Here Milton's images recall not only the feminized royalist confusion – which "fatally stupifi'd and bewitch'd" the people (*Prose* 3:347) – but as well the "language of [the Tory scribblers'] infernal pamphlets" (*Prose* 7:452), which maligned the poet-revolutionary himself, and the "contradictions [knit by the king] as close as words can lye together" (*Prose* 3:372–3), a reference that links linguistic with sexual ambivalence.

The authority of the official narrative voice is threatened in a variety of other ways in *Paradise Lost*. The poet-narrator proposes in the fourth proem to replace the descriptions of epic wars and battles with illustrations of "the better fortitude / Of Patience and Heroic Martyrdom / Unsung" (9.31–3). The psychological rewriting of the traditionally heroic subject-matter to compose a poem that is even more heroic depends, according to the narrator, on his being inspired by the Muse. Indeed, we are led to believe that the voices of the Muse and the poet have already merged; thus the final proem becomes the only one of the four that is not an invocation. Ironically, the threat of univocality inspires thoughts of uncertainty, even meaninglessness:

> Mee of these
> Nor skill'd nor studious, higher Argument
> Remains, sufficient of itself to raise
> That name, unless an age too late, or cold
> Climate, or Years damp my intended wing
> Deprest; and much they may, if all be mine,
> Not Hers who brings it nightly to my Ear.   (9.41–7)

The poet-narrator's primary concern is not the possibility of being muted; he is more threatened by the tyrannical imposition of a single perspective and by the possibility that "all be mine / Not Hers." Presumption and failed dialogue render him potentially more vulnerable to "an age too late, or cold / Climate, or Years."[16]

The domination that the poet-narrator achieves by controlling the historical epic narrative becomes at times difficult to detect when it moves us without provoking the resistance we otherwise experience in reference to an omnipresent voice. The narrator continually moves from acute self-consciousness to anonymity. Yet anonymity paradoxically calls attention to the identity that has been displaced, and Milton's mastery is achieved by the suppression and deconstruction of his own identity. In fact, absence and silence expose his behind-the-scenes performances, according to Wayne Booth, who argues for the complete artificiality of authorial objectivity or impersonality. Direct addresses to the reader, obstructive commentary, shifts in point of view among the characters, inside views, and the presentation of reliable statements by dramatized characters are all suspect and thus testify to the author's manipulating presence. "But why stop here?" Booth asks: "the author is present in every speech given by any character who has had conferred upon him, in whatever manner, the badge of reliability" (18). But why even stop here? Every recognizably personal touch, distinctive literary allusion, metaphor, and symbol becomes for Booth a sign of evaluation. Even the choice to expunge the authorial voice completely betrays a decision and an authorial voice (20).

The complex representation of voice in the literary text has political implications. Even in reference to "multivocal" texts we must ask how the chorus of voices is actually orchestrated; an author may presume to let others tell their own stories, but there remains the issue of the legitimacy of this democratic constitution. Is there a controlling, constituting agent behind the conversation, and what is the extent of his control? We could say on one level that Milton manipulates both understanding and response to the point of actually casting his intended readers – the "fit ... though few" – as (choral) characters in the text. Though including different perspectives attributed to the speakers and characters, the author is in the end, then, composing a text that is no more multivocal than the classical epics, which, according to Bakhtin, were mediated entirely by one narrator. According to such a reading, the author himself ultimately hides behind the mask of the other, while in some way orchestrating and appropriating the voices of the poem's various interpreters – the "mouthpieces" (Cyr 309).

Both Milton's poems and his pamphlets convey the difficulties and dangers of writing *in propria persona*. Defying the Aristotelian dictum that the poet not speak *in propria persona*, Milton develops a type of authorial presence in the poem, which provoked critics like Coleridge to hail Milton as the "deity of prescience" and announce in *Table Talk* that "John Milton himself is in every line of Paradise Lost" (Wittreich, *Romantics* 270).[17] Yet Milton chooses to differentiate between the voice of the author and those of the characters he develops (*Prose* 1:880). Milton's attempt at self-justification in *An Apology against a Pamphlet* prompts a distinction between the authorial voice and that of the Confuter, Hall, whom the author impersonates in the act of ventriloquization: "he who was there *personated*, was only the *Remonstrant*; the author is ever distinguisht from the person he introduces" (*Prose*, 1:880). Jonathan Goldberg deconstructs this claim: "such a 'distinction' of person from the personated, as quotation-within-quotation suggests, with its ability to slide away from the stabilization of the referent, is a virtual impossibility" (*Voice* 213). This critical approach to the text, which recognizes the tyranny of the authorial voice, could certainly uncover the contradictions and tensions that would otherwise be glossed over in a text in which the author is seen to distribute his power or to detach himself. However, it would not account for the fact that the author's self-definition is informed by extra-literary influences that are as resistant to appropriation as they are subject to it. The formation of an authorial voice is accomplished not at the expense of but in reference to a socio-historical context, and, in the case of *Paradise Lost*, a period of dissent that the poem invokes and responds to in different ways. In the process of examining the poem's relationship to its contemporary setting, we become aware not only of the poet-narrator's own dialogized voice and of the multiple speakers in the poem but as well of the language of tyranny and of multivocality that informs his discussions of the politics of voice.

As Milton's speaker announces in the poem, the suggestion that the "mortal voice" of the poet may be speaking alone (9.41–7) affords the possibility of meaninglessness or bacchic cacophony: "if the speaker depends solely on himself, his 'evil days' will be read as the expression of 'evil tongues,' a reminder of the confusion of tongues in Babel and an expression of disorder" (Bouchard 109–10). The soliloquy, monologue, apostrophe, and even the invocation in *Paradise Lost* are postlapsarian modes of discourse that reveal the conflicted nature of the speakers. The consequences of soliloquizing are repressed by the internally divided Satan, who, as we have seen, tyrannizes over the other voices in the poem. The reformation of the soliloquy, which begins, paradoxically, in the more self-conscious moments of the poet-narrator's invocations and leads to creation of the elegies, laments, and dramatic exchanges in *Paradise Lost*, is advanced in *Paradise Regained*. The Son's dialogic soliloquy makes possible a humanizing self-confrontation that develops into his debate with Satan, the subject of chapter 6.

Bouchard remarks on the ill-fated journey of the erroneous narrator in the poem by pointing to the numerous false starts, hesitations, and interruptions balanced by presumptions, faulty identifications, accusations, and counter-accusations, beginning nowhere and leading "God knows where" (108). The whole enterprise may be jeopardized. Bouchard explains that Milton's response to this danger and confusion involves the creation of two voices – that of the narrator and of Milton's Muse – which control two different narrations in the poem. The narrator's composition is a temporal construction: "it is successive, linear, tedious, and doomed to failure" (109). The Muse, by contrast, establishes through conversation and play with God a "sort of oblique counter-point to the sequential action of the poem" (110) that "recreates the circularity and perfection of the creation."

The argument about the two distinct voices is more problematic than the structuralist approach suggests. The speeches of the voices actually intersect in the narrative, which moves easily from retrospective to atemporal lyrical moments to prophecy, accommodating multiple time-frames. Moreover, point of view in the epic is often ambiguous: the narrator, for example, speaks initially of "all our woe" (1.3) and thereafter relinquishes authority to the Muse, who assumes control over the narrative in line 34 and recounts the history of Satan's fall and classical epic journey. However, in the subsequent book, the poem returns, without warning, to the intervening words of the fallen narrator, who describes the key of Sin as the "Sad instrument of all our woe" (2.872). The shift back to the official narrator's voice is, then, signalled prior to the second invocation. Changes in voice not indicated by a move to direct speech are difficult to mark. If the poet does initially introduce us to two speakers, one telling the story and the other taking dictation, he soon thereafter unifies the speaking voices and, at the same time, attributes a range of identities to the main epic narrator.[18]

In *Paradise Lost* the poet-narrator mediates and speaks through the poem's other voices, as well as affirming his privileged position and authority in the four proems. At the same time, we hear him speak less confidently in the later invocations, and we hear less from him generally by the end of the poem. Despite the claim that he has monopolized the poem, the poet-narrator's own voice is dialogized, and he is in fact relieved of significant parts of the narration by other characters who recount their own stories in the episodes of this modern epic. Just as the proems are of much greater significance than Samuel Johnson allowed, so too are the episodes of *Paradise Lost* more than just extraneous and accidental parts of the epic. Whereas the retrospective stories of Aeneas and Odysseus are of lesser importance than the primary narrations in the respective classical epics, Raphael's, as I have shown, and Michael's narrations compete in importance with that of Milton's poet-narrator.[19] Though *Paradise Lost* is also largely retrospective, the historical prophecy presented by Michael on the hill of the Visions of God rather than in the underworld is located at the end of the poem, unlike that in the *Odyssey* or *Aeneid*. Moreover, Milton's tempered political and millennial hopes are in the end presented as the subject not only of a revelation but of an exchange between two speakers that leaves the poem open-ended.

In characterizing the poet-narrator's voice as dialogical, I am not denying its status as an authoritative and public voice. By foregrounding the poet-narrator's words while simultaneously accommodating multiple interpreters and creation accounts, the text reflects and endorses the establishment of a socio-political system based on hierarchically structured relationships in which contributory elements nevertheless interact. Privilege in fact becomes a function not primarily of the narrator's dominating presence and claims to inspiration – which the poem in fact problematizes – but of his relationship to the poem's other narrators. At the same time, the exchanges among the diverse voices are often not easily distinguishable from the poet-narrator's preoccupation with self-legitimization.

Identity and voice develop in reference to surrounding constructs and contexts, as Milton realized when his own voice was muted by the failed Revolution. Language, rhetoric, and verbal expression shape identity and determine status once the speaker is severed from established forms of identity or centres of power inside or outside of the poem. The abandonment of the drama for the epic narrative – traditionally controlled by a single omniscient voice – is one response to the experience of defeat. In the ten-book epic, the tempering of the narrative voice through the inclusion of various interpreters – whose presence is made even more apparent in the later twelve-book epic – is, in turn, indicative of the attempt to lay the pattern for a more democratic or dialectical social order and at the same time to redefine the terms of self-expression. The poet-narrator's public voice is authoritative and in various ways authorial. However, the representation of the narrator, like that of the author himself, is influenced by conflicting literary and social codes that inform self-definition and also restrain individual desire and imagination.

A literary or socio-historical consciousness as much empowers as impedes the expression of voice. If, as Joan Webber argues, the seventeenth-century cosmic personality probably gave rise to the future omniscient first-person author (256), then the presentation of this consciousness simultaneously contains within it the seeds of its own undoing. The eventual disappearance of the omniscient, controlling narrative voice, which comments on the lives of all characters and knows their secrets, coincided with the breakdown of colonialism (Mascia-Lees 30). If we decide to argue for the complete autonomy and equality of all the represented voices of the poem, the results, however, differ little. Tyranny, the insolence of a despot, and democracy, the insolence of the unbridled commonalty, both lead to anarchy, Milton, like Herodotus, reminds us. A more contemporary critical analogue is relevant here as well. The modernist and postmodern transformation of fiction is characteristically multivocal, as Bakhtin has shown, and encouraging of ambivalence and multiplicity. The contest of voices must, nevertheless, continue; the equalization of voice that denies all difference is socially and politically oppressive rather than liberating. Such readings ignore or obscure exploitation and power struggles and offer no ground for fighting domination and effecting change, or even addressing the need and possibility thereof (Mascia-Lees 29).

The controlling voice of Milton's text does ventriloquize:[20] it reconstitutes and at once disempowers the represented voices no matter how eloquently, experimentally, or sympathetically it attempts to speak for them. The act of appropriation is most dangerous and damaging when it is used to justify a power differential among the voices. An examination of the politics of the orchestration of voice requires that we invoke that hierarchy of discourse but, in doing so, discover that appropriation is also the site of resistance (London 4). In a poem like *Paradise Lost* there are a number of conversations taking place between different voices, discourses, and meanings despite and precisely because of the overt presence of a primary authorial voice and the lofty style.

Out of the conflict between dissonance and multivocality, the poem emerges. Milton includes in the poem's linguistic range not only the competing voices of Satan and the primary speaker but also a chorus of narrators – Sin, Eve, Raphael, Adam, and Michael – who all serve as interpreters and relaters of their own histories. Through the dialogue between God and Christ, in which the latter is elevated on the basis of merit, the rebellion of one-third of the angels is precipitated. In reaction to the uprising, Abdiel finds a voice and acknowledges in reference to Christ: "how far from thought / To make us less, bent rather to exalt / Our happy state under one Head more near / United" (5.828–31). The narration of the war in heaven and the creation account by Raphael, who makes a disclaimer to knowledge (8.229), inspires Adam's relation of his own creation story. Similarly, Eve, who has the last word in the poem – excluding the narrator's description of the departure from Eden – is born out of the dialogue between God and Adam, and borne out of the chaos of her own imaginary sphere, from which she is, however, never wholly dissociated. These conversations between the speakers in the poem connect the oral histories of the individual speakers to each other and to the poem's official narrative.

In composing *Paradise Lost*, Milton created a self-conscious text that reflects the motivations for and methods of the poet's complex orchestration of voices. Yet if Milton deconstructs one hierarchy of discourse in his writings and establishes others in its place, can we maintain that he is really interested in change or exchange, poetic or extra-poetic? Yes, if we first recognize the distinctions Milton draws between different types of authority and between the hierarchies he constructs. If the poem on the one hand is concerned with contesting various kinds of authority, including the privileged status affixed to the single voice as the guarantor of truth, it is, on the other, deeply involved in the representation and justification of an alternative means of orchestrating voices and discourses, and perhaps of creating new worlds. As I will discuss in the subsequent chapter, the poet is, however, least inclined to resist hierarchical modes of thinking when discussing gender relations and the politics of conversation.[21]

# 4 The Gendered Hierarchy of Discourse

> Thou art my Father, thou my Author, thou
> My being gav'st me; whom should I obey
> But thee, whom follow?       *Paradise Lost* book 2

The complex interconnection of discursively linked debates about seventeenth-century politics and strained gender relations that lay at the heart of the "crisis of order" in the period (Underdown 36) informs this chapter on the gendered hierarchy of discourse in *Paradise Lost*.[1] Social disorder results from the violation of the natural and divine laws that decreed that women – who were made in the image of the fatally beguiling Eve herself – must never attempt to usurp the dominant male position. Milton insists in *Tetrachordon*:

seeing woman was purposely made for man, and he her head, it cannot stand before the breath of this divine utterance, that man the portraiture of God, joyning to himself for his intended good and solace an inferiour sexe, should so becom her thrall, whose wilfulnes or inability to be a wife frustrates the occasionall end of her creation, but that he may acquitt himself to freedom by his naturall birthright, and that indeleble character of priority which God crown'd him with. If it be urg'd that sin hath lost him this, the answer is not far to seek, that from her the sin first proceeded, which keeps her justly in the same proportion still beneath. (*Prose* 2:589–90)

The woman falls a second time by failing to fulfil the "end of her creation" – that is, by not satisfying the requirements of marriage, which Milton characterizes as "a meet and happy conversation" (*Prose*, DDD 2:246). Emphasizing the close relationship between sexual and social intercourse in the word "conversation," he identifies the two ends of marital conversation in *Colasterion* as procreation and dialogue.[2] In *Paradise Lost* the word recurs when Adam is expressing to God his unsatisfying communication with the animals and his consequent desire for "Collateral love" (8.426). The conversations between Adam and Eve and between men and women of seventeenth-century England were, nevertheless, not to proceed as exchanges between equals. The disruption by women of hierarchical relationships – marital, social, or political – was judged unnatural, even monstrous.

In this chapter I examine the autobiographical stories of Sin, Eve, and Adam, which are shaped by the gendered hierarchy of discourse established by Milton in the poem. In satirizing civil disorder and political tyranny in the early Restoration years, Milton employed the tradition of the Renaissance literature on prodigy, which taught the natural by exposing the unnatural as inversion, contrariety, and feminized confusion. The rhetoric of feminized unruliness is used most strikingly in Sin's narrative of her prodigious creation and her encounter with the epic's classical antihero – Satan. The various sources – classical myths, Renaissance allegory, and seventeenth-century popular and political culture – that inform this intertextual episode connect the corruption of the natural and political orders with the violation of traditional roles. In portraying Satan's journey of anti-creation, Milton takes a detour through the woman's body, which is represented as monstrous. Monstrosity is the product of Satan's brain and of Sin's womb; the move towards destruction undertaken by Satan is mapped out on the "double-form'd" female Sin (2.741), whose body and story become the sites of the confusion of tongues, identities, and gender roles. Milton's later portrayal of the primary female character in the poem does not redeem the portrait of Sin or repair the effects of sinfulness. In fact, the male author assigns Eve at best a secondary hero status and appropriates both her voice and creative potential, represented in *Paradise Lost* by Adam's possession of the lyrical female space that Eve constructs in narrating her earlier creation account. Adam's re-membering of Eve's story in book 8 indicates that female expression and creativity must be channelled into male agency to be authorized. Finally, Milton assigns Adam rather than Eve a major role in the unfolding of Michael's prophetic revelation and narration, which I examine in chapter 5.

## 1 SIN'S NARRATIVE

In this first section I analyse the interrelated discourses of political anarchy, gender inversion, and monstrous births in the book 2 encounter of Satan, Sin, and Death. The intertextual account of Sin's history is at once strategically distanced from and at the same time heavily freighted with topical concerns. This allegorical scene has traditionally been interpreted in the context of its Ovidian and Spenserian sources, but its dialogue with contemporary discourses of culture and politics also merits consideration.[3] In this section I interpret the meeting of the demonic trinity as a site of political turmoil, the confusion of identities, and incest, mapped out on the female body of Sin. In his confrontation with his progeny, Sin, Satan exposes his own "double-form'd" nature: Satan, I argue, is the political and intellectual component of the Satan-Sin hybrid, while Sin is made in the image of the monstrous woman who violates her non-public, apolitical role. Milton, then, does more than merely reproduce classical, Renaissance, and popular discourses in his account: he offers a subversive reading of contemporary issues, which he translates into the conventions of allegory and satire, creating a complex dialogue between literary and extra-literary texts and the conflicting voices, contested identities, and political allusions in the poetic account.

The narrative begins when Sin initiates an exchange with Satan just as Eve begins the conversation with Adam in book 9 prior to the Fall. Sin's unsolicited story provokes Satan's recollection of his repressed attraction to Sin and of his crimes of pride, lust, and sinfulness. Having recognized her father immediately (2.727), Sin reveals surprise about her alteration and about Satan's failure to know her: "Hast thou forgot me then, and do I seem / Now in thine eye so foul, once deem'd so fair / In Heav'n?" (2.747–9). Glossing over the difference between herself and Satan in an attempt to convince her father and lover of their union, Sin appeals to her "Author" Satan in a mock prayer: "Thou art my Father, thou my Author, thou / My being gav'st me; whom should I obey / But thee, whom follow?" (2.864–6). This demonic declaration will be translated in book 4 into an acknowledgment of female submission and obedience made by the newly created Eve; having been redirected into the paternally constructed symbolic order – in Lacanian terms – she reflects on how God warned her away from the image of herself on which she had been fixed.

Sin's history of her creation recalls the story of Narcissus in the *Metamorphoses*: "full oft / Thyself in me thy perfect image viewing / Becam'st enamor'd" (763–5). The Ovidian myth is prefaced by an account of Cephisus's rape of Liriope, who gives birth to Narcissus, and includes an exchange in which Liriope asks Tiresias whether her son Narcissus will live to a ripe age. "Except himselfe he knowe," is the response (Sandys 3.345); George Sandys translates the answer as "If he know not himselfe" (156). Though in various ways he represents Milton's version of Narcissus, Satan, who literally fathers and perpetuates narcissism, here imitates Cephisus. Having denied the changes he has undergone, Satan, upon meeting Sin, fails to recognize this image of himself. Nevertheless, Satan's inquiry about the words of the stranger, Sin, betrays his identification with Sin; he remarks in an appropriately epanaleptic, tautological statement: "So strange thy outcry, and thy words so strange" (2.737). In Milton's demonic recasting of the Ovidian myth, Sin becomes the voice that draws Satan into an encounter with his duplicitous self. Her story of Satan's former attraction to Sin also forces him to acknowledge the "dire change / Befall'n" (820–1) them both. The confrontation with the once desirous image of himself ends for Satan, as for Narcissus, in the confrontation with Death.

Sin's account of her membership in the demonic trinity and of her horrific metamorphosis rewrites the Ovidian myth of Scylla and Glaucus in book 14 of his *Metamorphoses*. The myth describes Scylla's transformation into a monstrous, double-formed creature by Circe, who, in her uncontrollable jealousy of Glaucus's attraction to her rival, takes this revenge on Scylla. When Scylla descends into a pool of water up to her waist, she witnesses the disfigurement of her loins by barking monsters that surround her. Not believing them to be part of her own person, she futilely attempts to drive them off. This virgin at once resists her transformation and resents the burden that maternity places on her. However, her desire to evade the process of metamorphosis results in a more terrible metamorphosis. The barking monsters become the support for her truncated thighs and for the womb that emerges from her dissolved lower parts (14.62–72). When, in her hatred for Circe, Scylla deprives Odysseus of his companions, Scylla, like Sin, becomes responsible for bringing confusion and death into the world.

In his portrait of Sin, Milton draws on the classical rhetoric of feminized unruliness, irrationality, and moral ambiguity as appropriated by Renaissance authors. In *The Faerie Queene*, the canto 1 account of the dragon Errour includes a heavily allegorized description of the hybrid, half-serpent, half-woman, breeding, vomiting dragon whose body is "full of filthie sin." Spenser's wood, in which Errour's den is located, has a labyrinthine interior and is characterized by "diverse doubt" and "turnings" that pose a moral threat: "God helpe the man so wrapt in *Errours* endlesse traine" (1.1.18). The dragon later reappears as the Blatant Beast – the offspring of incest, that of Echidna and Typhaon and of Cerberus and Chimaera, who threaten the whole moral, allegorical, and poetic enterprise. Upon being attacked by Red Cross Knight (1.1.20), Errour pours out her black, inky blood. The linguistic confusion is inscribed on the body of the false apocalyptic prophet, who vomits "poyson horrible and blacke" that contains books and papers and "loathly frogs and toades."[4] The production of the speculative and misleading philosophy that fills the books that Errour vomits would be associated by Francis Bacon and Milton with error, pride, and narcissism (*Prose* 1:250).

Spenser's moral, allegorical account of the confrontation with the monster Errour anticipates George Sandys' reading of the Ovidian account of Scylla's metamorphosis, which became available in print during Milton's undergraduate days at Cambridge:

*Scylla* represents a Virgin; who as long as chast in thought, and in body unspotted, appears of excellent beauty, attracting all eyes upon her, and wounding the Gods themselves with affection. But once polluted with the sorceries of *Circe*; that is, having rendred her maiden honour to be deflowred by bewitching pleasure, she is transformed to an horrid monster. And not so only, but endeavours to shipwracke others (such is the envy of infamous women) upon those ruining rocks, and make them share in the same calamities. That the upper part of her body, is feigned to retaine a human figure, and the lower to be bestiall; intimates how man, a divine creature, endued with wisdome and intelligence, in whose superiour parts, as in a high tower, that immortall spirit resideth, who only of all that hath life erects his lookes unto heaven, can never so degenerate into a beast, as when he giveth himself over to the lowe delights of those baser parts of the body, Dogs and Wolves, the blind & salvage fury of concupiscence. (Sandys 645)

The classical episode is recast as a Christian lesson that recalls the words of St James: "When lust hath conceived, it bringeth forth sin: and sin, when it is finished, bringeth forth death" (1:15), and which in turn is couched in the language of female physicality and immorality. The hellish hounds bred by Scylla in the *Metamorphoses* are manifestations of their mother's lust and yielding to base desires. Moreover, in attempting to become an object of desire, the woman resists her essentially passive role and is consequently transformed into a monster. In Milton's epic the punishment for sinfulness is allegorized in a similar scene in which Sin's hell hounds torment their mother unceasingly. They are the after-effects of an incestuous act whereby Satan penetrated the closed gates through which none could pass "Without [her] op'ning" (777). The ravaging of hell is thereby associated with the violation of Sin's body.

In the Preface to *The Great Instauration,* Bacon appropriated the myth of Scylla's transformation differently from Sandys to illustrate the abuses of scholastic philosophy: "the state of learning as it now is appears to be represented to the life in the old fable of Scylla, who had the head and face of a virgin, but her womb was hung round with barking monsters, from which she could not be delivered" (4:14). In book 1 of his earlier *Advancement of Learning* Bacon explained:

such is their method, that rests not so much upon evidence of truth provided by arguments, authorities, similitudes, examples, as upon particular confutations and solutions of every scruple, cavillation, and objection; breeding for the most part one question as fast it solveth another ... the fable and fiction of Scylla seemeth to be a lively image of this kind of philosophy or knowledge; which was transformed into a comely virgin for the upper parts; but then *Candida succinctam latrantibus inguina monstris,* [there were barking monsters all about her loins:] so the generalities of the schoolmen are for a while good and proportionable; but then when you descend into their distinctions and decisions, instead of a fruitful womb for the use and benefit of man's life, they end in monstrous altercations and barking questions. (3:286–7)

Bacon's imaging of the scholastics as Scylla-like monsters articulates the force of Milton's allusive connection between Sin as sprung from Satan and the sin of the philosophizing devils in book 2 of *Paradise Lost* (555–69).[5] The connection is joined, significantly, by the sign of a beauty horrendously disfigured – and gendered female. Seduced by the language of the philosophical texts, the reader becomes entrapped not only in the labyrinths of his own mind but worse yet, in the baser parts of the female body. The elusiveness of language, like the mysteries of the female body, must be mastered by the male reader. The failure to assert control over the text engulfs the reader in a feminized confusion.

The turmoil in book 2 that originates in the womb of hell also seethes in Sin's womb or *chora*. She is thereby prevented both from leaving hell and from transcending her own depravity and physical anguish. Contemporary feminist theorists have appropriated the Greek concept of the *chora* as "an invisible formless being ... which is most incomprehensible" to convey the semiotic, ceaseless heterogeneity and the disruptive dimension of language (Roudiez 6). Read in this context, the birth of the grisly phantasm Death delivered by Sin is appropriately portrayed by the creation of echoes, images of voice, and signs by which Sin herself is also represented.[6] As Sin testifies, Satan, upon viewing the image of himself, became enamoured of his creation, and his pride turned to lust, Sin-oriented desire.[7] Death, the body of his defiled mother, and Sin's autobiographical narrative, which are all created out of rupture or rape, become the manifestations of the perversion of sexuality and language, linking, specifically, incest and tautology. Sin and her narrative originate in Satan; Sin in turn realizes that her fate is entwined with that of Death, her progeny, shadow, and echo.[8]

Engendered by Satan, Sin, her genesis story, and her child and lover Death become the formless, doubly formed creations of his depraved intellect. Whereas Sin's internal corruption is physically manifest in her own monstrous shape and the monsters she bears, and is represented in the account of her own prodigious history that she passionately narrates, Satan's sin is portrayed as intellectual. In book 2 the account of Sin's springing like Athena from the head of Satan-Zeus is recounted just after the description of the devils who become lost in vain speculations once Satan departs from hell. The allegory of Satan and Sin, then, is also continuous in *Paradise Lost* with a depiction of the fragmentation of language and the rupture between signified and signifier, which Milton and his contemporaries attributed to the abuses both of monarchical power and of intellectual philosophy.

The hybrid story of Sin is an account both of the prodigious birth of an imageless Death and of the echo that has no referent. In contrast to Eve, who is later created through dialogue, Sin, the product of Satan's monologue, can only attempt to confirm her origin in Satan and her end in Death's own destiny. Like her offspring and like Echo, who was also fated to haunt the caves, Sin is an image of voice, an echo, and a "Sign / Portentous" (2.760–1). Because of her strange birth, she is *portentuous*, unnatural or monstrous (Chambers 381). Nevertheless, she is at the same time a character who is "in ways too numerous and closely layered to spell out, a sign" (Quilligan 92). Philip Gallagher suggests that Sin signifies the commandment *noli me tangere!* and is the "'only sign of [the angels'] obedience left / Among so many signs of power and rule' (4.428–9)" (92). The rule, of course, is broken by Satan. Death, the by-product of the violation, becomes the sign of a sign, and is first identified by his mother: "I fled, and cri'd out *Death*; / Hell trembl'd at the hideous Name, and sigh'd / From all her Caves, and back resounded *Death*" (2.787–9). By providing the doubly formless and shapeless creature (2.667) with a name – echoed in the verses – Sin gives birth to a tautological language, one whose correspondence between word and meaning is lost. The echo from the caves or womb of hell continuously recalls the birth and naming of Death. As the son and the image of the narcissistic Satan, Death, like Satan, seeks to overshadow and destroy its creators. A parody of Narcissus, who fed on his own image to the point of death, the infernal trinity feeds on itself. Like the howling monsters that literally consume the bowels and womb of their mother, Death would devour her completely, Sin realizes, but "he knows / His end with mine involv'd" (806–7). The trinity's confusion of identities and denial of differences represented by the corruption of language, then, is oppressive – incestuous and demonic – rather than liberating, as we discover when comparing Sin's account with the book 3 portrait of the divine meritocracy, in which Milton celebrates the relationship between Father and Son, one based on difference, including a hierarchical and thus heretical difference.

Milton encourages us to interpret Sin as a sign of rebellion against divine authority, which is the meaning of the Hebrew word for Sin – *pesha*. In a mythological context the "double-form'd" Sin who acts as the gate-keeper is a Janus figure, whose open gates in book 7 of the *Aeneid* represent a state in upheaval. Satan's incestuous affair with rebellion foreshadows the tyrannical reign of the first postlapsarian monarch, Nimrod, the "rebel" of book 12 of *Paradise Lost*. In book 2 Sin "opens" the way further into confusion, which Satan, in turn, "penetrates." The "universal hubbub wild / Of stunning sounds and voices all confus'd" (951–2), anticipating the "hubbub strange" at Babel (12.60), is the afterbirth of Sin and the odious offspring created in Satan's image. The torment that Sin's monsters visit on her becomes archetypal for Satan's later anguish: the confused voices assault his ear "With loudest vehemence" (2.954), and his attempts at revenge likewise eventually "recoil" back upon him in book 9 (172). Similarly, Satan's encounter with "*Rumor* next and *Chance*, / And *Tumult* and *Confusion* all imbroil'd, / And *Discord* with a thousand various mouths" (965–7) in the Dantean intestines of hell adverts to the swarming of assembled devils in Pandemonium prior to the council in hell in book 1 (759–98). It also anticipates the noise of the war in heaven and, ultimately, the return of Satan to hell. In expectation of "high applause," the cursed Satan ironically would hear from the "innumerable tongues / A dismal universal hiss, the sound / Of public scorn" (10.507–9), as his own anatomy undergoes its involuntary metamorphic dissolution to snaky form.

The rhetoric of the divided body politic and of feminized changeability and irrationality used by pro-parliamentarians to discredit kingship was channelled into debates on state and church politics by pro-royalists of the seventeenth century. In their political dialogues, satirical pamphlets, and closet dramas, royalists staged mock trials and used imagery of grotesque physicality to portray female characters who recited false confessions and published their crimes by vomiting or bearing appropriately monstrous offspring. These satirical texts were aimed at prominent parliamentarians as well as at the producers of infernal pamphlet literature – the prodigious births and insubstantial creations of authors who were themselves labelled monsters. Towards the conclusion of his pamphlet, the author of "A Scourge for Pamphletizers" in *A Presse full of Pamphlets* laments that "this kind of new invented profession being grown to its last graspe, the substance and strength then being almost withered and decayed, the Occupations have turned the stream into another channell; and come new again to the proceedings of the Parliament." Thus the pamphlets multiply through the printing of "Diurnals" which allow the "Breeders" "at one prodigious birth, [to] bring forth fifteen at a time ... Besides, they have a corner, in their Venters to breed Conferences, Speeches, Petitions, Declarations, & C" (A4r-v).

The unregulated voices attributed to the pamphleteers and revolutionaries – the hybrid "Male-females" (*Presse* A4r) – and to "the Man-Midwives of the State" – the producers of parliamentary pamphlets and ordinances (*Mercurius Pragmaticus* no. 5) – were satirized in such royalist closet dramas as Samuel Sheppard's *The Committee-Man Curried* and the *Craftie Cromwell: or, Oliver ordering our New State*. Royalist texts parodying the "Lyurnalls" (*Craftie Cromwell* A3r) appeared in the form of ladies' diurnals, satirical pamphlets, and mistress-parliament dialogues, which mocked female-dominated societies and governments. The 1647 diurnals *An Exact Diurnall of the Parliament of Ladyes*, *The Ladies Parliament*, and *A Parliament of Ladies, with their Lawes newly enacted* and royalist Mercuries, particularly *Mercurius Melancholicus*, *Pragmaticus*, and *Elencticus*, ridiculed the sexual rapacity of parliamentary leaders and the ludicrousness of female jurors granting pardons to political traitors, while also publishing their own crimes.[9] Aristophanes' *Parliament of Women* provided a classical model for these satires, which were popularized in the seventeenth century by Henry Neville's *The Parliament of Ladies*. One of the four best-known mistress-parliament dialogues was *Mistress Parliament Brought to Bed of a Monstrous Childe of Reformation*, a quasi-dramatic political text labelled by W.W. Greg as the first act of a play of which *Mistress Parliament Presented in her Bed* – which opens with "Act Two" – is the sequel (Greg 1:xiv–vx, 2:677). The former political dialogue also serves, however, as the opening act for three 1660 female-parliament dialogues in which the post-1648 atrocities of Cromwell and the Rump are dramatized.

The royalist Restoration satires derived from the third edition of

*Mistress Parliament Brought to Bed* present the metamorphosis of parliament into a rump. These pamphlets were likely published by the main editor of *Mercurius Fumigosus,* John Crouch, who used the Restoration as an opportunity to rerelease the mistress-parliament dialogues. The texts mock the parliamentarians by portraying them as monstrous women whose entry into governmental affairs leads to feminized political anarchy. The broadsheet *Mris Rump brought to Bed of a Monster, with her terrible pangs* describes Mris Rump vomiting congealed clots of blood, votes and ordinances of parliament and bills containing "Jugglings, Cousenage, contradictions and Equivocations," as well as "Blasphemy, Treason and Tautalogies." In this pamphlet, dated 28 March 1660, Mris Rump produces a declaration written in terms that anticipate Sin's own confession to her father and paramour Satan in *Paradise Lost*. This declaration, in which Rump constantly undercuts herself, is presented on her behalf and takes the form of a mock plea for deliverance from hell, from tautologies, and from the child Reformation. Anticipating the prayer-like conclusion of Sin's appeal to Satan in book 2 (864–70), Mris Rump, in *"most grievous Pangs of Child-bearing,"* ends her plea with the words: "the severall Ministers within the Cities of London and Westminister, and the late Lines of Communications, are desired upon next *Good Friday* if I shall not be Delivered before, to keep a day of feined Humiliation, and Prating ... That so I may come in againe to Rule, Reigne, and Tyrannize over you, Rump everlasting, Impositions, Assessments and Taxations without end, *Amen.* Your despised Friend, *Rump.*" Mris Rump, who fails to recognize her mother – the Devils Arse – and denies her own "prodigious Birth," never succeeds in severing herself from her origin, her nature, or her destiny. No "deliverance" is possible: her vomiting culminates only in the very painful and eleven-year prolonged birth of the headless monster Reformation. Monstrous births are also featured in the 29 May 1660 *Famous Tragedie of the Life and Death of Mrs. Rump,* which resembles the 28 March broadsheet in form and content and, like the broadsheet, includes a verse epilogue that at once celebrates the restoration of Stuart monarchy while mocking the deliverance of the headless monstrosity by its whorish mother.

In the 2 April 1660 quarto pamphlet *The Life and Death of Mris Rump,* a freer adaptation of the 1648 political dialogue, Mris Rump figures even more obviously as the primary agent of political turmoil. Rump heads the council in hell that dissolves into an antimasque for murderers Vortiger, Etheldrid, Edricus, Cain, Oliver Cromwell, Reynolds, Pride, and Mulciber, who each claim responsibility for performing leading roles in the regicide. The late-born bastard child – the babe of Reformation created in the image of the Rump and Devils Arse – is described in greater detail as having, like Spenser's Errour, its stomach "full of false Oathes, Papers, and Engagements," which it in turn never has the opportunity to disgorge before it vanishes into a stinking vapour.

The strong enforcement of hierarchical distinctions between masculinity and femininity in seventeenth-century England, of which the feminization of social disintegration and tyranny was at once a cause and effect, betrays the shifting nature and mutability of those categories. Milton adopts the images of monstrous pregnancy and parturition used by classical and Renaissance writers and by pro-royalist pamphleteers, particularly in the mistress-parliament and rump dialogues, applying them against their original bias to discredit a monarchical figure grown tyrant, Satan himself. Satan's encounter with chaos is tautological and specifically allegorized as an encounter with his own feminine sinfulness and unruliness.[10] In the allegorical account the reader, then, discovers the dual nature of Satan. Sin embodies Scylla's physical deformation; her monstrous appearance is of females who violate their maternal, non-public, and non-political role. Satan is the intellectual, public, political component of this hybrid whose numerous metamorphoses we witness throughout the poem. By supplying us with "moly" – the gift of reason given by Hermes to Odysseus to enable him to withstand Circe's enchantment – Milton encourages us to penetrate the double-natured allegory that is the Snaky Sorceress's history (2.724). Sin's creation story, which she relates to her father/lover, addresses in a seventeenth-century context the issues of subject-formation and the restraint on female desire and self-fashioning by a code of gender relations established by a patriarchal society. The woman's desire for identity labelled as monstrous nevertheless displays to this male author his own Sin.

## 2 EVE'S NARRATIVE

After Sin delivers her narrative, Milton inverts the images of monstrosity and directs our attention away from the whore to the mother. Born out of soliloquy, Sin propagates the echo, shadow, and the "shapes" of Death, whereas Eve, created by Adam in a moment of sanctioned narcissism, is redefined by him as "Substantial Life" (4.485) and is cast in the role of the mother of life. But the shift from Sin to Eve in the narrative is not unproblematic; in the account of Eve we witness the female character's creation out of the chaos from which she is never wholly dissociated. In an extra-literary context the characterization of Eve is indebted to the contradictory and controversial received Genesis tradition, which offered on the one hand a hierarchical model derived from Augustine and Aquinas, who emphasized female deficiency and on the other an egalitarian portrait of the woman as a fully realized human in relation to man (J. Turner, chap. 3). In *Paradise Lost* Eve is situated between two worlds: she is the expression of Adam's interiority and is also the embodiment of substantial life, into which God and Adam make her. Eve's retrospective history is located in the middle of book 4 and thus, like Sin's story, interrupts and defers the relation of Satan's classic epic journey, to which the narrator returns at the conclusion of the book. Eve's creation account in the narrative is, however, by no means separate from the context out of which it arises; Satan is the voyeur and audience, roles in which we as fallen readers are also cast by violating the suspended lyrical moment.

Like Sin's autobiography, Eve's narrative is created out of the rupture of the autonomous space that the female character initially constructs. Since selfhood has always been modelled on the male, Western society has traditionally associated social disorder with female self-fashioning and changeability (B. Johnson 154), making the female's assertion of identity "unnatural" to the point of being monstrous. Eve's narrative is doubly unnatural: the presentation of her account is unauthorized, and it describes Eve's unauthorized self-encounter. According to the politics of conversation established in the poem, Eve's autobiographical account must be appropriated. In the official creation scenes throughout the epic, the female presence is actually repressed; God and Adam penetrate and colonize the private female sphere, and patriarchal voices impose order on the "vast Abyss" on which their own genesis stories become inscribed. "Bring forthe frute and increase upon the earth" becomes the colonial injunction and rationale.

The rupture or violation of the uninhabited space that Eve creates for herself causes it to become constituted by and interconnected with the outside or "public" world. Eve herself tells the story about her contract with Adam, indicating that her voice develops from her subjection to paternal law. The account of her submission to Adam is more controversial than Milton's recommendation for agreement between both spouses: "the first and more important point [in marriage] is the mutual consent of parties concerned, for there can be no love or good will, and therefore no marriage, between those whom mutual consent has not united" (*Prose* 6:368). While this passage in *The Christian Doctrine* presents the issue of marital politics and, by implication, gender relations, unambiguously, the poem does not. In *Paradise Lost* we must account not only for Adam's paradoxical act of seizing Eve with his gentle hand, but also for Eve's echoing of the two patriarchal voices to whose commands she submits and which make her aware of the double-formed nature of her identity.

After repeating the words by which Adam first defined her (4.440–3) – words she will pronounce again at the end of her story – Eve, at the beginning of her narrative, recalls her experience upon first awaking. She remembers that "a murmuring sound / Of waters issu'd from a Cave and spread / Into a liquid Plain, then stood unmov'd / Pure as th'expanse of Heav'n" (453–6). The syntax of the verses suggests that sound actually pours from the cave and then stands unmoved, thereby indicating its sterility and anticipating Eve's experience of the echoes and the reflections she reads uncritically. Her fancy blurs the distinction between the liquid plain and the sky; there is no reason for Eve to direct her attention upward or away from her image.

Like Sin's story, Eve's echoes the Narcissus myth in several ways. The reference to the cave (454) reminds us of the lonely caves in which the disembodied voice of Echo dwelt in the myth. Eve's portrait is reminiscent of Narcissus's while also recalling Echo's; Eve imitates the actions of both mythological characters. The imitation – regarded as narcissism in a postlapsarian context – is not simply visual but also "a representation activating various facilitations corresponding to the *sonorous* ones," as Julia Kristeva explains in "Freud and Love: Treatment and Its Discontents" (qtd in Silverman 118). In the lyrical space Eve recounts the experience of viewing the image:

> As I bent down to look, just opposite,
> A Shape within the wat'ry gleam appear'd
> Bending to look on me, I started back,
> It started back, but pleas'd I soon return'd,
> Pleas'd it return'd as soon with answering looks
> Of sympathy and love.   (4.460–5)

Difference – the awareness of alternative perspectives and the impetus to effect change – has been momentarily suppressed in the private sphere that Eve sentimentalizes.[11] Image and model express the same desire in the same fashion. The image becomes for Eve an acoustic mirror, one that responds with "answering looks" and thereby causes her assimilation with the reflection.

Self-fashioning is prevented by narcissism – that is, by the projection of an image or façade that cannot withstand interrogation;

inquiry begins with a form of self-consciousness that corresponds in this male-authored text with the entry into the patriarchal symbolic order. Subjectivity is from the very outset dependent upon the recognition of a distance separating the self from the other, an object whose loss is simultaneous with its apprehension.[12] Narcissus discovers that the image he loves is himself. This image becomes for him an absolute. Milton adds another scene to the Ovidian account in the portrayal of Eve's self-confrontation and encounter with difference. Eve is informed by the warning voice about the identity of the image she sees. By making her self-conscious, or by introducing her to subjectivity – certainly a gendered subjectivity[13] – the male voices situate and define Eve, who initially finds herself "much wond'ring where / And what [she] was, whence thither brought, and how" (451–2). The encounter requires her to acknowledge with "experienc't thought" that her original experience, her self-confrontation, is superficial.

The authority of her "fixt" eye or gaze is challenged by the divine voice that imposes order on her act of self-definition. Following the voice, as it requests, Eve becomes a kind of shadow while being shown that she is no echo. The voice identifies her as an image (472), in order that she might learn to distinguish herself from the "smooth wat'ry image" (480) that she must abandon, though reluctantly. The paternal voices of God and then Adam call her from being a desiring subject to becoming an object of desire. They also require her to participate in the symbolic order in which her lyrical story is reinscribed when Adam presents his creation account in book 8. Eve describes her experience in retrospect because she acquires language only upon leaving the imaginary order and entering the symbolic. The process of speech or the act of narrating the creation account causes a distancing effect, as well as a separation of the self and other and a shattering of the illusion of spontaneity.

Christine Froula and Janet Halley argue for the antifeminist nature of Eve's story by concluding that Eve's actions are conditioned by vain desire; compelled to yield to the dominating Miltonic voice, Eve is "indoctrinated" into her own "identity." In fact the colonization by the patriarchal authority is so successful that Eve, like Sin, literally becomes its voice, echoing the divine warning to abandon the reflected image (Froula 329; Halley 248). "What there thou seest fair Creature is thyself" (4.468), Eve repeats in her remembered account. The reflection is not *of* Eve, according to the voice; it *is* Eve, Halley announces, in agreement with Froula. The subsequent verses in the poem qualify this reading, however: "With thee it came and goes: but follow me, / And I will bring thee where no shadow stays / Thy coming" (469–71). If Eve is actually a reflection, then she is at the same time much more than that. Verse 469 distinguishes between "thee" and "it." In the subsequent line "it" is replaced by its referent "shadow," which Eve both identifies with and dissociates from the image she first sees. In the context of the larger narrative Eve is called away from the insubstantial object that she essentializes and is required to accept her inferior position in the chain of being that Milton essentializes.

The dialogue in which Eve engages with the voices of God and Adam is not much of an exchange, at least not in Eve's retrospective account. The two paternal authoritative voices interrupt her self-encounter. Her words speak of absence, regret, and desire that must be repressed: "What could I do, / But follow straight" (475–6), Eve asks, though her gesture of turning back indicates the possibility of an alternative action. She ends by acknowledging her submission; having begun her story by addressing Adam as "Guide" and "Head," Eve concludes on a similar note by acknowledging her status in relation to man's: "with that thy gentle hand / Seiz'd mine, I yielded, and from that time see / How beauty is excell'd by manly grace / And wisdom, which alone is truly fair" (4.488–91). Sin's "attractive graces" (2.762), which aroused Satan's self-love, provoked the seduction Sin recalls in her narrative. Eve's "sweet attractive Grace" (4.298) is distinguished from Adam's "contemplation" and "valor" (297) by the poet-narrator, and now from "manly grace" by Eve herself. The yielding is an act of submission, requiring Eve to address the dialectical nature of her identity and to redefine herself according to Adam's understanding of her role. Adam's command that she return to him is reminiscent of the Omnific Word's imposition of order on the Abyss, involving the division of the firmament from the waters – the "expanse of liquid, pure" (7.264), which Eve had naïvely characterized in her recollected, reflective account as being as "Pure as th'expanse of Heav'n" (4.456). The blurred definitions, repetitions, and echoes in Eve's story and the gesture that has her turning to look back all suggest that her experience is liminal, representing her disengagement from one role without the complete adoption of another.[14]

Eve's narrative is created in retrospect when she is required to differentiate between the private and public spheres and also between herself and Adam. The final verses of Eve's story, which speak of her redirection by God and Adam, reveal Eve's new vantage point gained by her act of submission: line 489 does not conclude with "yield" but with "see." Applying a hermetic reading of the passage, Davies argues that "The 'seizing' of Eve's hand leads to her 'seeing' a higher truth than she had known before. She is rapt, or enraptured" (*Idea of Woman* 216). However, in the context of gender politics established in the poem, what Eve's insight allows her to recognize is her inferior position in relation to Adam.

Deceived by her claims to autonomy, Eve is coaxed from her private sphere soon after her creation. Remaining in the imaginary is equivalent to becoming "unproductive" and incapable of living in human society. When she ignores Adam's warning voice in book 9, Eve falls prey to narcissism by again creating her own space in the garden. Her assertions of identity and independence eventually provoke her fall, which leads to her unwilling submission to Adam's governance. In Genesis 3:16 the sentence reads, "Unto the woman he said, I wil greately increase thy sorowes, & thy conceptiós. In sorowe shalt thou bring forthe childré, and thy desire *shal be subject* to thine housband, and he shal rule over thee." Though Milton's Eve recognized Adam as her head even in her prelapsarian state, her punishment after the Fall renders her more subordinate; in *Paradise Lost* God declares to Eve: "Thy sorrow I will greatly multiply / By thy Conception; Children thou shalt bring / In sorrow forth, and to thy Husband's will / Thine shall submit, hee over thee shall rule" (10.193–6). In the poem, "In sorrow forth" modifies both the manner in which children are brought forth and the terms of woman's domination by man. The conferred sentence redefines the politics of conversation and gender relations by compelling Eve to submit to her husband painfully and unconditionally. Postlapsarian submission is coercive, and Milton and his contemporaries perpetuate the coercive claims about the position of women on that basis.

From the perspective of seventeenth-century radicals, who foregrounded the Priestly creation account, Adam and Eve were created as equals, with "no such distinctions and differences as men do" make (Fox A2). Instead, writes another Quaker, "the government, rule & dominion was Joyntly and not apart, given to man & woman ... they were of one mind & soul & spirit, as well as one flesh, not usurping Authority over each other ... the woman was not commanded to be in subjection to her husband till shee was gone from the power" (Portfolio 1b140. 21–2). Milton does distinguish between the creations of Adam and Eve, while maintaining nevertheless that their difference is one of degree and not of kind. After their fall, the hierarchical nature of their relationship is emphasized even more through the subordination of Eve. Eve responds to Adam's lamentation on death and on the corruption of womankind (10.845–908) by accepting blame for the transgression and by offering to die for him, a gesture that qualifies her initial narcissism. When the proposal is rejected by Adam, Eve recommends abstinence, which, she suggests stoically, must be realized through death or suicide (992–1006). Adam again dismisses this death sentence and reminds Eve that co-operation and labour rather than wilful barrenness will defeat their enemy. The acts of labour, however, emphasize all the more clearly the distinctions between their gendered roles, particularly by revealing the double significance of Eve's act of submission. While Adam will till the earth to yield its fruits, Eve, in imitation of the boughs that once yielded fruits (4.332–3), the earth that yielded food (5.401), and the vines in Eden that yielded nectar (5.428), will yield, though in labour, the "Fruit of [her] Womb" (10.1053) – an act also foreshadowed by her reluctant submission to the male voices.

Eve's story of her enchantment with her own reflection, her dream about rapture and temptation at the beginning of book 5, and her aspirations for knowledge and advancement in book 9 – in which the connection between the sinful woman and the serpent reappears – are all interpreted in the larger narrative as vain attempts at self-assertion. In her discussion of Eve in "Eve and the Arts of Eden," Diane McColley argues that the character performs a great many of the acts in which Milton participated as a poet; her dreams, for example, represent the function of the imagination, and her songs the legendary Arcadian origins of poetry.[15] In both her pre- and postlapsarian state, however, "fruitful" creativity is defined in terms of maternity for Eve, whose body is the vehicle for the Word. In her story in book 4 Eve echoes Adam's definition of her: "hee / Whose image thou art, him thou shalt enjoy / Inseparably thine, to him shalt bear / Multitudes like thyself, and thence be call'd / Mother of human Race" (471–5). As a male author Milton celebrates feminine virtues and "unsung" heroism only in so far as he can appropriate them when he is increasingly denied access to the public sphere. At the end of the epic the poet restores the power of speech to Eve so that he might set his voice against hers. He allows her to speak not in "the conceptual language" of desire, art, or prophecy but in the "experiential language of motherhood" (Van Den Berg 364): "This further consolation yet secure / I carry hence ... / By mee the Promis'd Seed shall all restore" (12.620–1, 623). Eve is restored to the mother earth to ensure the fruitfulness of her yielding, like the poet-narrator who returns to the "Native Element" (7.16) to check his aspirations for flight. Ironically, however, substantial life and higher creativity do not originate in the female. The male bypasses the chaos of the womb by representing the superior act of giving birth as an intellectual, not a physical exercise. Moreover, the epic poet throughout invokes creative inspiration not from the female Muse but from the divine paternal voice; the mother's care is in fact an illusion and misconception he discovers in book 7 when recalling the abandonment of Orpheus by Calliope.[16]

## 3 ADAM'S NARRATIVE

After the dramatic history of the war in heaven in book 6, Raphael further responds to Adam's request to know what was done "before [his] memory" (7.637) by relating the Genesis creation story in book 7. Memory relies on images of voice by connecting the actions of showing and telling; the act of remembering also redefines the relationship between past and present. The angel's own account will be in turn "honor'd ever / With grateful Memory" (8.649–50), Adam responds at the end of book 8, which is dedicated to his own memory. By restructuring the 1667 epic to create the twelve-book edition of *Paradise Lost*, Milton provides more opportunities for Adam's interventions and more space for dialogue generally. Adam's remembered account in book 8 does not merely suspend the narrative process: it offers a different way of interpreting the official Genesis story and the creation accounts of Eve and Raphael: "at least in the case of human actions and changes, to know an event by retrospection is categorically, not incidentally, different from knowing it by prediction or anticipation. It cannot even, in any strict sense, be called the 'same' event, for in the former case the descriptions under which it is known are governed by a story to which it belongs, and there is no story of the future" (Mink 546).

Retrospection, here represented as an act of memory, involves an active engagement with past and present readings of events. Memory, not documentation, is in fact the recorder of history in *Paradise Lost*. Because the act of remembrance is never linear, it resists a chronological reading of historical events. Paul Ricoeur explains that memory "*repeats* the course of events according to an order that is the counterpart of time 'stretching-along' between a beginning and an end." Repetition is more than a reversal of future happenings: "it means the retrieval of our most basic potentialities inherited from our past in the form of personal fate and collective destiny" ("Narrative" 180). The recollection of events actually displaces the origin and the ur-history with the multiple, even "unauthorized," creation accounts in the poem. In this section I will examine Adam's development of his creation story, which adds another episode to the angel's account and which, in a narratological and historiographical context, at once ruptures and re-members Eve's.

Responding enthusiastically to Adam's offer to present his autobiography, Raphael explains that his knowledge of humanity's creation is limited, a comment that testifies to the incompleteness of the genesis story just recounted (7.519–47): "say therefore on; / For I that Day was absent, as befell, / Bound on a voyage uncouth and obscure, / Far on excursion toward the Gates of Hell" (8.228–31). While God was ordering the chaos, Raphael was pursuing a spy, who was bent on mixing "Destruction with Creation" (236). Raphael's remark confirms at once his own and Satan's absence on the sixth day of creation. Just as God's creation of humanity compensates for the loss of the rebel angels, so does Adam's personal creation story fill for Raphael the gap in the historical narrative left by Satan.

In the exchange of accounts between the historians Raphael and Adam, the relationship between speaker and listener is reversed. Raphael remarks on how the divine image has been manifested in Adam both inwardly and externally: "Speaking or mute all comeliness and grace / Attends thee, and each word, each motion forms" (8.222–3). According to this description, Adam's words are speech-acts, revealing the speaker's relationship to God; Raphael declares that the angels "inquire / Gladly into the ways of God with Man: / For God we see hath honor'd thee, and set / On Man his Equal Love: say therefore on" (225–8). The angel's subsequent remark, "for I attend, / Pleas'd with thy words no less than thou with mine" (247–8), and his emphasis in the passage on the eloquence and gracefulness of Adam's words suggest, nevertheless, that Adam has a greater ability to delight than to instruct his listener; his mode of expression is, therefore, inferior to Raphael's in the hierarchy of discourse.

Adam's retrospective narration suspends the dialogue between Adam and Raphael with which book 8 begins and ends. Still, the representation of the creation story is dialogic. Adam begins by mentioning that he expects a response from Raphael: "How subtly to detain thee I devise, / Inviting thee to hear while I relate, / Fond, were it not in hope of thy reply" (207–9). Moreover, Adam's narrative consists of dramatic monologues and of conversations between himself and God. When we return to the framing dialogue at the end of book 8, Adam's account is not relegated to history but spills over into a final exchange between the speakers, which I examine at the end of this chapter.

Adam's autobiographical narrative responds not only to Raphael's history but also to Eve's, which it, however, overshadows.[17] While Eve in her account peered into the smooth lake, Adam upon awaking gazes at the sky (8.258). The "murmuring sound / Of waters," associated symbolically with maternity in Eve's account (Nyquist, "Gynesis" 198), is also referred to by Adam, but Adam in his creation account clearly separates the "liquid Lapse of murmuring Streams" (8.263) from the land and sky. In Eve's narrative Adam's "gentle hand / Seiz'd" hers so that she might shift her "fixt" eyes and confront her repressed contradictory nature, thereby learning to "see" properly (4.488–9). Similarly, sleep paradoxically "with soft oppression seiz'd / [Adam's] drowsed sense" (8.288–9) to prepare him for his first encounter with his author. Intuiting the existence of the Maker, Adam desires to communicate with him but is first led into temptation (8.306–9), as Eve herself was in her dream in book 5. The disjunction between Adam's inquiries and God's explanations reveals a difference between the speaker and the addressee, a difference on which dialogue nevertheless depends. The belated reply contrasts with the reflecting, echoing shape or the acoustic mirror in Eve's account, which responds immediately "with answering looks / Of sympathy and love" (4.464–5), thus creating an artificial or "vain" exchange.

The voice of God in Adam's account identifies itself as the guide of the awakened Adam, who would otherwise have continued "wand'ring" (312). Overpowered by his colloquy with God, Adam swoons and dreams again, only to awake and discover that the imagined shapes have become substantial. Adam's identification with an other self, like Eve's enchantment with her image, has a narcissistic quality, though Adam's narcissism is condoned; it is "sparked, sanctioned, and then satisfied by his creator" and thus is distinguished from Eve's self-encounter, which is condemned (Nyquist, "Gynesis" 196). Adam, more than Eve, is imbued with the desire for self-knowledge that he acquires through and not at the expense of dialogue. His conversation with God culminates in the creation of Eve, "Substantial Life," the manifestation of his desire for an other self and the product of his masculine imagination.

His retrospective account follows Eve's in the ordering of the events in the narrative, but precedes and envelopes Eve's in the historical account of humanity's creation.[18] The conflict here is not only between narrative (the signifier and the textual disposition of events) and story (the signified, the narrative context, or supposed order of events) (Genette 27), but also between the different interpreters whose accounts constitute and reconstitute the arrangement of the narrated events. Adam's history completes Eve's but, at the same time, exposes its gaps. In fact, as Adam's hand seizes Eve's, so does his account rupture the suspended moment and lyrical space that is her story. Adam inscribes Eve's narrative into his own creation history, thereby imitating the historian who ruptures the lyrical space – the womb of historicism – in order to ensure its productivity.

A metaphor taken from historiography that emphasizes the connection between historical inquiry and sexual penetration clarifies Adam's role as a revolutionary historian. Anticipating the Foucauldean dismantling of the comprehensive view of "traditional history," which resists differences and prevents choice, Benjamin urges that the seductive power of the whore of homogeneous history, called "Once upon a time," be resisted and overcome. In *Theses on the Philosophy of History* Benjamin describes the historical materialist(-rapist) taking cognizance of a subject in order to "blast open the continuum of history" (264), thereby "blasting a specific life out of the era or a specific work out of the lifework" (265). Representing the act of interrogation in sexual terms, Benjamin declares that the construction of a homogeneous historical continuum from which all traces of rupture are expelled is comparable to the indifferent whore or inviolable virgin. The whore of history is a virgin, whose availability and barren emptiness suggest infertility. Reassessing the Lacanian theory that the imaginary offers a vital moment of relation to any object, Benjamin proposes, then, that the womb of historicism be transfigured by violence into an arrested moment of time and thereby forced to a revolutionary crisis.[19]

In the poem Adam appropriates Eve's account in the narrative of his creation. Individual attempts at expression are not self-sustaining, productive, or meaningful outside of conversation and dialectical thinking. Adam's genesis account is sanctioned because it is dialogic, co-authored, and expresses a desire for a companion. The terms "converse," "communication," "communion," "company," "collateral," "accompanied," and "colloquy" are employed by Adam in his primary request to God for "conversation," which refers to intercourse – that between two individuals speaking a common language – and to sexual intercourse (8.412–36). Adam establishes through reason and dialogue with God his need for conversation with an other self. The exchange mediates between unequals, but in doing so the "friendly condescension" – a term used to describe the conversation between Adam and Raphael (8.9) – also makes the human speaker acutely aware of his difference from the addressee; Adam is dissatisfied with his futile discussion with the animals, but cannot sustain an exchange with God in that "celestial Colloquy sublime" (8.455).

In the movement from verbal to visual communication – discourse to dream – in book 8, Eve is born; again she is situated between two worlds and is made both the subject and object of the male conversation. Though Eve momentarily vanishes, leaving Adam in the dark, she reappears at once as an embodiment of the fanciful shapes Adam experienced in his dream and as an incarnation of God's verbal promise to Adam (491–9). In the conversation between God and an unfallen Adam, a correspondence between individual desire and the articulation of desire, as well as between a creating fancy and a shaping reason, is achieved through the fashioning of Eve, who represents the first covenant between God and humanity. Her own conversations with the angels and God are filtered through dreams. Because they represent rather than distort reality, dreams, like inspiration, provide an alternative though inferior mode of communication. "God is also in sleep, and Dreams advise" (12.611), Eve announces to Adam, who, at the poem's conclusion, descends from the Visions of God to instruct her about her destined role as the mother of humanity.

At the end of his own creation story, Adam comments on the two different impressions of Eve that he has experienced. The first – derived from his conversations with God and Raphael – is of Eve's imperfect embodiment of the divine image (8.540–6). From another perspective, however, Eve appears perfect:

> yet when I approach
> Her loveliness, so absolute she seems
> And in herself complete, so well to know
> Her own, that what she wills to do or say,
> Seems wisest, virtuousest, discreetest, best.   (546–50)

Adam is misled by the outward image of Eve, from which Eve herself was initially called away by the voices of God and Adam. While relocating Eve's narrative in his own creation story and directing her into the symbolic order, Adam, by idolizing her, nevertheless situates her on the margins of that order between himself and the uncultivated imaginary sphere. In the dialogue with Adam that frames his story in book 8, Raphael encourages his pupil to adopt a hierarchical view of the relationship, believing that Adam's admiration of Eve is based exclusively on physical attraction to her. Adam corrects his initial interpretation and that of Raphael, to whom he has disclosed his inward feelings (607–8), and reassures his mentor that he has not after all forgotten Eve's difference from himself. Though for Adam the ladder of love includes physical love, his announcement that there is unity in diversity and that he and Eve are of one mind and soul, "Harmony to behold in wedded pair" (605), does not make them equals. As Eve's story is defined by the parameters of Adam's creation account, so is her identity determined by her marriage to Adam and by the gender hierarchy.

The book 8 exchange ends interestingly with an erasure of gender difference that Raphael describes at Adam's request: "if Spirits embrace, / Total they mix, Union of Pure with Pure / Desiring; nor restrain'd conveyance need / As Flesh to mix with Flesh, or Soul with Soul" (626–9). In instructing Adam about angelology, Raphael mixes material and spiritual terms to describe angelic relations and depict the ability of angels to move between polarities, a performance that does not exclude desire. In her analysis of the above verses Catherine Belsey remarks how strange it is that Renaissance culture, which polarized male and female stereotypes, should, in the poetry of Milton or in the paintings of the Italian Renaissance, represent a higher form of life as transgressive and endorsing of sexual indecisiveness (67). Examining Milton's portrayal of angels, Belsey concludes that the poet deliberately and entirely erased all gender differences and power differentials: "In Milton's heaven there are no gender stereotypes, no antithetical voices, masculine and feminine, no opposition affirmed as privilege. There can be no consequence, no sexual rule and no submission, no authority grounded in anatomy" (67).

In "Choreographies," Jacques Derrida produces a kind of "utopian utterance" (Moi 172) – a dance of voices that might speak to Raphael's lesson about angelic relationships. If one could "approach" a relationship to the other where discriminating codes of sexual marks were erased,

The relationship would not be a-sexual, far from it, but would be sexual otherwise: beyond the binary difference that governs the decorum of all codes, beyond the opposition feminine/masculine, beyond bisexuality as well, beyond homosexuality and heterosexuality which come to the same thing ... I would like to believe in the multiplicity of sexually marked voices. I would like to believe in the masses, this indeterminable number of blended voices, this mobile of non-identified sexual marks whose choreography can carry, divide, multiply the body of each "individual," whether he be classified as "man" or "woman" according to the criteria of usage. (76)

While gender may be less an issue in Milton's heaven than it is in Eden, even the hierarchical, heretical relationship between Father and Son reflects the gendered, politicized relationship between

Adam and Eve on earth.[20] Difference is a precondition for mutual development, so that the denial of differences is for Milton actually oppressive – even incestuous and demonic – rather than liberating. Adam's remembered narrative in book 8 is authorized by Raphael because the speaker is conscious of his historical role and of the place of his words in the hierarchy of discourse. In turn, Adam's appropriation of Eve and of her genesis story, which involves relocating and historicizing it in his own account, is likewise sanctioned by the politics of conversation established in the poem. For Milton an "ideal" community cannot exclude political, sexual, or cultural codes of difference, as Eve's story does and Raphael's example of angelic relations seems to do, thus rendering the former suspect and the latter unrealizable. Milton's garden is politically charged, and the voices he inscribes in the poem are politically and sexually marked, thus establishing the conditions for future conversation, my primary concern in the next chapter.

# 5 "Learning to Curse": Colonialism and Censorship in Paradise

After the Fall of *Adam*, there were two general Curses inflicted on Mankind: The one upon their *Labours*, the other upon their *Language*.   Wilkins, *Mercury: or the Secret and Swift Messenger*

>     till more hands
> Aid us, the work under our labour grows,
> Luxurious by restraint; what we by day
> Lop overgrown, or prune, or prop, or bind,
> One night or two with wanton growth derides
> Tending to wild.                           *Paradise Lost* book 9

As a symbol for England traditionally reserved for celebratory purposes, the edenic garden was lost to the nation's tragic history. Seventeenth-century writers, notably Andrew Marvell and Milton, appropriated and, more specifically, feminized Eden to represent the defeat of the nation in terms of the desecration of paradise.[1] The feminized garden is the site of political strife and cultural tensions; its openness and unruliness make it especially susceptible to exploitation.[2] "*England* is the Paradise of women": according to this proverb, all European women would gladly move to England if given the opportunity, John Ray concludes. Yet the English language itself, Ray realizes, spreads infection, particularly when it is deployed to advance the antifeminist's cause: "though in no Countrey of the world, the men are so fond of, so much governed by, so wedded to their wives, yet hath no Language [as the English] so many Proverbial invectives against women" (54).

In the received tradition of the Genesis account, Eve is conventionally associated with the earth and the garden; at the beginning of the seventeenth century Esther Sowernam distinguishes woman from man by announcing that the former, unlike the male worldling, was created in Paradise, thus making her a "Paradisian" (224). Defined by her maternal role in a biblical and literary context, Eve is called to obey God's command to "increase and multiply." In both pre- and postlapsarian worlds the command is justified as a colonial imperative.³ Yet in *Paradise Lost*, where Milton sanctions the imperative in ways I described in the previous chapter, the resistance to colonialism is also inscribed, in so far as the Fall is represented by the enclosure of the garden and the ravishment of both Eve and Adam. The restraint of natural growth and the retardation of historical progress lead to the couple's failed conversation and to their banishment from Eden to the "wild Woods forlorn" (9.910).

The book 12 account of Babel offers a political reading of the fall of the postlapsarian pastoral world attributed to Nimrod – the "mighty hunter against the Lord," "deceiver, oppressor, and destroyer of the animals of the earth" (Augustine 2:112–13). When Nimrod's followers build the tower of Babel, they oppress the pastoral society established after the destruction of Eden and fracture the "Native Language" (12.54) that originated in the garden.⁴ This chapter first examines the censorship of conversation and of "superfluity" in the garden, which leads to the fall of Adam and Eve into wildness, incivility, and linguistic confusion. Thereafter I discuss the gradual restoration of dialogue that inspires Adam and Eve to reemplot the event of their fall and that of the "woeful Race" they conceive (9.984). Part 2 of this chapter focuses on Michael's resistance to Adam's literalization of postlapsarian history and his reemplotment of the nation's tragic history in the double-voiced narrative of books 11 and 12. The poet, I argue, ultimately justifies the colonizing acts of the "fit ... though few," who christen the New World and in whose names providential history is rewritten.

## 1 LAPSED CONVERSATIONS

### Colonial imperatives

In book 9 Adam rejects Eve's proposal for divided labour by reminding her that absolute dominion over nature is not divinely mandated: "These paths and Bow'rs doubt not but our joint hands / Will keep from Wilderness with ease, as wide / As we need walk, till younger hands ere long / Assist us" (244–7). Though they occupy a privileged position in the hierarchy of creation, Adam and Eve cannot control nature's wild growth entirely because their world is processive and not product-oriented. Moreover, Adam reminds Eve that God never intended that they be prevented by their labour from engaging in conversation (235–9). Their dialogues on gardening in books 4, 5, and 9 complement the accounts of poetic creation described throughout the epic. In collections and works of verse of the Renaissance and seventeenth century, the art of poesy was in turn represented by the art of gardening; thus poetry, along with music and the visual arts, was intended to reproduce a "paradisal consciousness" (McColley, *Gust* 12). Like the process of tending the garden, the acts of poetic creation, criticism, and interpretation are interconnected activities in which the reader might engage for a limited time and then leave, the conversation "vitally still in progress," so that others may also intervene and resume the work.[5]

Milton represents paradise as dynamic and as accommodating of diversity and change; as such, Eden offers a model for the alternative political community that Milton proposes for the English nation. The application of an ecological metaphor, which is part of the conversation about environmental poetics and politics, provides a discourse for addressing the relationship between political representation and the orchestration of voices in the poem. To understand the make-up of an organic system, we must study the correspondence of the parts and their significance in the system they constitute. In the text the individual voices are heard in diverse collective expressions. Without making the protectionism absolute, the sovereignty of the individual voices must also be protected.[6] Just as the different species in the garden have distinct functions, so each voice contributes to the creation of a multifaceted truth. Ecology offers statements of unity in diversity, spontaneity, and complementarity. Such statements, however, are historically determined. In very general terms, the medieval world-view was hierarchical and hostile to reciprocity; it was represented by the scale of nature that upheld a vertical unity in the universe "from the Mushrome to the Angels." The contemporary model, by comparison, is built on democratic relationships: "ecology recognizes no hierarchy on the level of the ecosystem. There are no 'kings of the beasts' and no 'lowly ants.' These notions are the projections of our own social attitudes and relationships on the natural world. Virtually all that lives as part of the floral and faunal variety of an ecosystem plays its coequal role in maintaining the balance and integrity of the whole" (Bookchin 59–60). Milton mediates between the two perceptions of (social) ecology by developing a dynamic hierarchy – modelled on his proposed commonwealth – whose constituents differ not in kind but in degree from each other. Though individuals may be equal in the community, they may not possess the same amount of power or have the same ability to persuade. Eve in *Paradise Lost* is equal to Adam in the democracy of grace and original righteousness, but subordinate in the hierarchy of creation. Challenging the more fixed classical and Renaissance constructions of gender, Milton characterizes the difference between the sexes as one of degree – internal *homology* – rather than kind or internal difference. "Biology is just less important to Milton than hierarchy, than 'greater' or 'lesser'" (Guillory 72); while Milton spends considerable time in his portraits of Adam and Eve describing their make-up, he devotes more attention to their making. Both characters present individual creation stories, and both are reminded of their position in the chain of being and of the status of their accounts in the poem's official Genesis narrative.[7]

Because it has a potential for excessive growth and for disproportions, perversions, and aberrations (8.26–8), nature, like society, cannot be regarded as homogeneous; nor can it be defined by its clashes of opposites. While nature possesses dominant species just as society has its authoritative voices, the terms for exercising control in either realm are complicated, particularly in light of the significance attributed to even the "lowest" of God's creations. In his description of the garden the poet-narrator rejects the conventional representation of Eden as a *hortus conclusus*, a static bower of bliss, and offers instead a portrait of a fertile, regenerative garden that embodies "In narrow room Nature's whole wealth, yea more" (4.207). In book 4 he develops a loosely structured genesis narrative by detailing the geography and scenery in an Eden created out of and simultaneously a critique of biblical, mythological, historical, and literary gardens of various kinds.[8] In describing the plant life, he distinguishes between the different varieties of vegetation. As God's handiwork, even the smallest, least important life-forms are imbued with value. "In these thy lowest works, yet these declare / Thy goodness beyond thought, and Power Divine" (5.158–9), Adam and Eve announce in their "unmeditated" orison, thus anticipating Raphael's reference in the official creation account in book 7 to the parsimonious emmet, whose political significance I discussed in chapter 1. The individually named creatures (4.341–52) in the garden sport about the newly created human beings, whose differences were outlined earlier (4.295–311). Just as his presence permeates the whole of the narrator's account, so does the voice of Satan penetrate the description of Eden, suggesting that, like the divine act of creation, poetic composition is a creation not *ex nihilo* but out of chaos. Eve then narrates her own genesis story – another creation out of chaos – which is corrected and completed by Adam's book 8 narrative. Despite foregrounding the scale of nature, the poet-narrator in book 5 at the same time celebrates the harmony of all of nature: "they led the Vine / To wed her Elm; she spous'd about him twines / Her marriageable arms, and with her brings / Her dow'r th'adopted Clusters, to adorn / His barren leaves (5.215–19). This appropriated description of the first task mentioned in Virgil's *Georgics* is intended in these enjambed verses to suggest Adam's support of Eve's fruitfulness (McColley, *Gust* 190).

The poetic-ecological metaphor helps to explain how language works and meaning is created in the account of Eden. By employing the words "wanton," "wild," "erroneous," "eccentric," "voluble," "lust," "dart," "ardor," "play," "disport," "appetite," and "luxurious" – all which have sexual connotations – in both pre- and post-lapsarian settings, the text accommodates both the etymologies of the words and the meanings they acquire in different contexts. In *An Essay Towards a Real Character* Wilkins invented an alternative genesis account by systematically naming and taking inventory of nature. The preparation of his dictionary – an attempt at developing a "universal character" or restoring the Adamic language – involved classifying and drawing up tables of natural bodies in chapter 3, of plants in chapter 4, of animals in the subsequent chapter, and eventually of actions and human relations in chapters 9 and 10 respectively. In Milton's poeticized account of its evolution, language develops as organic signifying process through the unfolding of the creation story: similes arise on the third day, references to things crowd the fifth, and by the sixth we reach into Adam and Eve's consciousness, with all its attendant warnings (Broadbent 238–42). The formation of human consciousness, subjectivity, and voice is explored much more extensively in books 4 and 8, when Eve and Adam themselves present their respective genesis accounts.

In book 9 Eve herself for the first time initiates the dialogue between the couple[9] when she grows anxious about the great abundance of Eden, in which the work of Adam and Eve "outgrew / The hands' dispatch of two Gard'ning so wide" (9.202–3). Eve acknowledges that she is threatened by this excess. The terms "erroneousness," "eccentricity," "wildness," and "wantonness" – a word used to identify feminine unruliness that requires governance (4.306) – are applied by Eve in her definition of Eden:

> till more hands
> Aid us, the work under our labour grows,
> Luxurious by restraint; what we by day
> Lop overgrown, or prune, or prop, or bind,
> One night or two with wanton growth derides
> Tending to wild. (9.207–12)

Eve proposes that the couple separate for the sake of efficiency to control or restrain difference in the garden, which she eventually reduces to a "narrow circuit" (323). Because nature requires taming (215–19), the couple must divide its labour lest "th' hour of Supper comes unearn'd" (225). Offering her own way of governing the garden, Eve introduces a mercantile element into the theological equation to tend Eden (Christopher 154). Eve is not alone in her misreading of nature's overgrowth: Adam too expresses concern about the "disproportions" created by the "superfluous hand" of an otherwise "wise and frugal" nature (8.26–8). Raphael explains that the vastness and complexity of the universe do not undermine God's authority but, on the contrary, confirm it and ensure human freedom. Near the conclusion of Adam's dialogue with Raphael in book 8, nature's excessiveness is again characterized in feminine terms; while exalting Eve above her designated place in the scale of creation, Adam criticizes nature for its overgenerosity in bestowing "Too much of Ornament" on Eve (8.538). "Accuse not Nature, she hath done her part; / Do thou but thine" (561–2), Raphael advises, reminding Adam of his responsibility in exercising dominion in paradise.

The Fall of humanity coincides with and is depicted by the violation of the natural order and the politics of conversation. The latter is portrayed both by the separation of Adam and Eve and by the breakdown of the representational function of their language. The poet-narrator never actually describes the Fall; rather he represents it by signs, thus indicating that direct communication is one of the first casualties of the original transgression. The loss of linguistic innocence later occurs in a postlapsarian setting when God reduces the language of the builders of Babel to a "hideous gabble" (12.56). In book 9 the temptation takes place subtly, through the manipulation of voice, gesture, and perspective. Though the poet-narrator himself recounts Satan's encounter with the estranged Eve, we see Eve through the eyes of Satan, who becomes the focalizer in the passage:

> He sought them both, but wish'd his hap might find
> Eve separate, he wish'd, but not with hope
> Of what so seldom chanc'd, when to his wish
> Beyond his hope, Eve separate he spies,
> Veil'd in a Cloud of Fragrance, where she stood
> Half spi'd, so thick the Roses bushing round
> About her glow'd. (421–7)

The poet-narrator repeats the terms "hope," "wish," and "spies" in describing Satan's act of weaving a net of words to ensnare the veiled Eve. As Eve seeks to govern the garden, Satan attempts to dominate the woman through his speech and penetrating gaze. The syntax of the verses emphasizes both the extent of his control and the gradual fulfilment of his desire: "Eve" and "hope," which are at opposite ends in verse 422, are juxtaposed in the middle of verse 424 when Satan spies Eve. This passage anticipates the description in *Paradise Regained* of the disguised Satan's first gaze upon the Son, which signals the beginning of the temptation scenes (1.314–20).

Satan's corruption of Eve and edenic language in the temptation scene is anticipated by his violation of paradise upon his discovery of the New World (3.542–4). In book 9 Satan, whose gaze would be identified in a later period as an imperialist gaze, constructs an obsolete Ptolemaic view of earth (9.99–113) and transforms Eden into a *hortus conclusus*. The devil first climbs into the garden as a hunter, as "a prowling wolf / Whom hunger drives to seek new haunt for prey" (4.183–4). Satan's predaciousness foreshadows the tyranny of the mighty hunter Nimrod, who causes the confusion of tongues and oppresses the postlapsarian pastoral society, which had been organized into familial and tribal groups. By adopting various animal guises, "as their shape serv'd best his end / Nearer to view his prey" (4.398–9), the devil perverts their nature for his own intents (395–410). The first "Artificer of fraud" thereby moves down the chain of being until he is metamorphosed into a serpent, lowest of creatures. The degradation of Satan throughout books 4 to 10 has also been characterized in terms of his decline "from a rebel against authoritarianism and an indomitable laborer and builder in the wilderness to an imperialist policy maker and insatiably combative technocrat" (Stavely 90–1). If we read *Paradise Lost* even more specifically as a poem about empire, then Satan can be identified as "the diabolical deceiver who enslaves the inhabitants of the New World by cheating them out of their territory and replacing them with his own destructive plenipotentiaries" (Evans 232), as well as a buccaneer, pilgrim, and empire-builder who "rehearses virtually all the major roles in the repertoire of English colonial discourse" (234).[10]

The colonization of Eden and its inhabitants is achieved through the censorship of voices in the garden. Satan's soliloquy addressed to his own thoughts (9.473–93) signals the end of prelapsarian conversation between Adam and Eve and the start of the largely one-sided "exchange" between Satan and Eve. This temptation scene begins and ends in silence and consists of oratorical strategies, rhetorical play, and the restatement and perversion of the divine command. During the performance we recognize Eve's association with the garden, which Satan violates. Satan begins the temptation

"Proem" (549) after managing to attract attention to "His gentle dumb expression" (527). The "Serpent Tongue / Organic" (529–30) – "meaning as a tool" (A. Williams 116) – is actually an ineffective weapon: the "impulse of vocal Air" (530), which inspires the words of temptation, only creates more "unctuous vapor" (635). The words do provoke Eve to accept the serpent's "conduct" "Beyond a row of Myrtles, on a Flat, / Fast by a Fountain, one small Thicket past / Of blowing Myrrh and Balm" (627–9). Nevertheless, as she announces, "we might have spar'd our coming hither, / Fruitless to mee, though Fruit be here to excess" (647–8). The speaker of babble who fails at *conversation* is himself impotent. He attempts first to transform Eve back into that object-image from which the voices of God and Adam, now absent, called her away. The tempter develops his own scale of nature in the garden he encloses in order to seduce Eve, whom he defines with an arsenal of epithets: "sovran Mistress" (9.532), "A Goddess among Gods" (547), "Empress of this fair World" (568), "Sovran of creatures, universal Dame" (612), and "Queen of this Universe" (684). Extending his control, Satan repeats the words "beheld," "discern," "sees," "seen," and above all "gaze," a word that rhymes with "amaze" and with the description of Satan "blazing with delusive Light" (639). "Glozing" (9.549), the verbal counterpart to "gazing," prevents dialogue by appropriating and defining the subject. Eve's inability to read Satan's flattering words and gestures critically and to offer alternatives to his propositions results in the Fall. Satan's success is confirmed when his victim employs his own rhetoric, his demonic discourse, and his forms of argumentation.

The hypnotic effect of gazing at the serpent in book 9 recalls the state of rapture experienced by Eve and seemingly by the tempter who became fixed on the fair "Tree / Of interdicted Knowledge" (5.51–2) in her book 5 dream (47, 57). While the accounts of the temptation scenes both in the dream and in the garden in book 9 are rife with sexual overtones, they are also politicized. Sowernam, in describing the original Fall, explains that the woman was seduced by "a Serpent of the masculine gender"; "maliciously envying the happiness in which man was at this time, like a mischievous Politician, he practiced by supplanting of the woman to turn him out of all" (224). In *Paradise Lost* the devil likewise employs the rhetoric of a politician. Satan's temptation of Eve in the dream with the words, "Why sleep'st thou Eve? now is the pleasant time, / The cool, the silent, save where silence yields / To the night-warbling Bird" (5.38–40), anticipates his seduction of his cohort Beelzebub with words of rebellion: "Sleep'st thou Companion dear, what sleep can close / Thy eye-lids? and rememb'rest what Decree / Of yesterday, so late hath past the lips / Of Heav'n's Almighty" (673–6). Chronologically, the temptation experienced in dream actually takes place after the war in heaven, thereby lending Eve's first temptation an added political significance. When Satan seduces Eve in books 5 and 9, he glosses over the divine decree in order to make her forget it, thereby to provoke an act of disobedience. In addressing Beelzebub, Satan recalls the divine command in order to inspire rebellion in his next-in-command. The language that the poet-narrator uses in his descriptions of Satan's verbal assaults on Eve is appropriately militaristic, as I indicated in chapter 3.

Satan takes great pains in rehearsing his attacks, and the fact that Eve at first responds intelligently to the temptations confirms her knowledge and free will. Nevertheless, her speeches, while revealing the independence and empowerment of the speaking voice, also betray Eve's submission to the dominant discourse. Eve initially proves herself to be an active interpreter of Satan's words when she acknowledges that the exuberance of the garden ensures the freedom of its inhabitants while, at the same time, reminding them of their obligation to act responsibly: "in such abundance lies our choice" (9.620). Moreover, she suspects the oversimplification and flattery in the serpent's temptation speech: "thy overpraising leaves in doubt / The virtue of that Fruit" (615–16). Her rhetoric, even at this point, however, is infected: "overpraising" is Satan's word. The tempter thereafter evades the problems of interpretation by responding with further attempts at simplification. Satan smooths out or paves over the troubled way leading to the tree by ignoring the intricacies of language, the differences between God and his creation, and the theological and legal implications of violating the command. "Empress, the way is ready, and not long" (626), maintains the creator of short cuts; though rolling in tangles, Satan "made intricate seem straight" (632).

Eve's critical-reading skills lead her at first to suspect the falseness of Satan's premises and to realize that God's decree transcends human understanding: "God so commanded, and left that Command / Sole Daughter of his voice; the rest, we live / Law to ourselves, our Reason is our Law" (9.652–54). Unlike their other laws, this command is not subject to interpretation through discursive reasoning. The violation of this rigid interdiction – cited at several points, beginning 4.419–27 – is punishable by death, Adam remembers: "for know, / The day thou eat'st thereof, my sole command / Transgrest, inevitably thou shalt die" (8.328–30). These verses recall Genesis 2:16–17:"Thou shalt eat frely of everie tre of the garden, But as touching the tre of knowledge of good and evil, thou shalt not eat of it: for whensoever thou eatest thereof, thou shalt dye the death." In book 9 Satan quotes the divine mandate before Eve does, but restates it in an interrogative sentence (656–8). Eve in response echoes the interdiction, but supplies the clause left off by Satan: "Ye shall not eat / Thereof, nor shall ye touch it, lest ye die" (662–3), taken from Genesis 3:3. To Satan's partial recitation, Eve adds the condition "nor shall you touch it" and extenuates the command, replacing "inevitably thou shalt die" with "lest you die."[11] The extenuation, while leaving Eve "yet sinless" (659), provides Satan with similar opportunities for glossing. Employing his superior hermeneutic and oratorical skills, Satan rewords the interdiction in several ways until he abruptly rejects it: "ye shall not die" (9.685; Genesis 3:4). In the soliloquy after the Fall (10.720–844) Adam would also attempt to redefine the meaning of death to which the command refers. Adam, unlike Satan, however, is not able to dismiss the command, no matter how he interprets death.

Because she is more inclined to retard historical progress, natural growth, and the process of speech, Eve is Satan's easier prey. While Adam "still stood fixt to hear" the voice of Raphael following the narration of history (8.1–3), Eve is eventually rendered motionless after hearing the oratorical "preface" (9.676) of the tempter. All sense of contradiction and difference is lost: "Fixt on the Fruit she gaz'd, which to behold / Might tempt alone, and in her ears the sound / Yet rung of his persuasive words, impregn'd / With reason, to her seeming, and with Truth" (735–8). Whereas the dialogue between Adam and Raphael began after Adam's momentary suspension in book 8, the exchange between Eve and Satan ends with Eve's intoxication, resulting in her failure to recognize the tyranny of Satan's voice or to read his dramatic performance critically. Eve then soliloquizes, adopting the rhetorical strategies of the actor-orator himself. The "irrational" divine command is replaced by the seemingly rational language of the tempter, who is now characterized by Eve as an "Author unsuspect / Friendly to man, far from deceit or guile" (771–2).

After the Fall, Eve can no longer understand that liberty is not determined by one's rank in the hierarchy of creation, a paradox that Satan had contemplated in his confessional soliloquy (4.54–7). In her first postlapsarian speech Eve acknowledges a sense of disempowerment and weighs the advantages of concealing her knowledge from Adam "so to add what wants / In Female Sex" (9.821–2). Thus she proposes to invert the power differential she has discerned, a differential that renders her not only unequal but less than superior:

"for inferior who is free?" Eve adds, asking the satanic question (825). She decides at this point to involve Adam in her act of disobedience. By adopting the pose and words of a performer – "Prologue, and Apology to prompt" (853–4) – Eve imitates the oratory and theatricality of Satan (670–6). Believing that a "different degree / Disjoin[s]" her from Adam, Eve tempts Adam to embrace their "equal Lot" and "equal Joy, as equal Love" (883–4, 881, 882).

From one perspective, we cannot but read the Fall as a *felix culpa* and at once sympathize with and admire Eve for her inquisitiveness and aspirations to godhead, to which we were first attracted in books 1 and 2 of the poem. As fallen readers, we find ourselves more readily persuaded by Eve's curiosity and reasoning and the tempter's arguments than by the critical commentaries of the inspired narrator. Comic and parodic voices break up the tragedy. Eve's antiheroic actions, her desire for power, and her temptation speeches to Adam remind us of Satan's visual and verbal performances, by which we also were seduced; the devil's implantation of the demonic discourse in the paradisan and in her seed is thereby confirmed.

At the same time, however, though he was not the first to do so, Milton challenges the conventional patriarchal reading that charges Eve for humanity's original sin.[12] The soliloquies of Adam and Eve, which reveal the thoughts of the characters contemplating the temptation in book 9, come at parallel moments, thereby confirming their equal responsibility for the transgression. Breaking inward silence (9.895), Adam idolizes Eve, identifying her as the "fairest of Creation, last and best / Of all God's Works" (896–7), and he decides that he cannot forego conversation or love with her; nor can he ignore the "Link of Nature" that draws him (914). Ironically, conversation as verbal exchange and sexual intercourse is the first casuality of the Fall.

I return now briefly to this chapter's opening discussion of the garden's significance. In describing their postlapsarian condition, the narrator transports Adam and Eve to unhallowed ground. Their gestures and speech also distance them from the paradisal state; their internal corruption is conveyed by their incivility, their lust, their "guilty shame" about their nakedness, and by their silence, which speaks most loudly of their mutual guilt: "They destitute and bare / Of all thir virtue: silent, and in face / Confounded long they sat, as struck'n mute" (9.1062–4).[13] When Adam finally utters "words constrain'd," he laments, as does the poet-narrator in the fourth proem, that his barbarous language and displacement from Eden make communication with God or angel impossible (1080–2).

The poisoned conversation of Adam and Eve in *Paradise Lost* and their "learning to curse" dissociate them from the edenic community and relegate them to the wilderness, the "wild Woods forlorn" (910).[14] Milton imports the language of corruption and shame from the feminized East and the New World; reduced to a fallen and primitive state, they cover themselves with the leaves of the Indian fig or banyan tree:

> both together went
> Into the thickest Wood, there soon they chose
> The Figtree, not that kind for Fruit renown'd,
> But such as at this day to *Indians* known
> In *Malabar* or *Decan* spreads her Arms
> Branching so broad and long, that in the ground
> The bended Twigs take root, and Daughters grow
> About the Mother Tree, a Pillar'd shade
> High overarch't, and echoing Walks between;
> There oft the *Indian* Herdsman shunning heat
> Shelters in cool, and tends his pasturing Herds
> At Loopholes cut through thickest shade: Those Leaves
> They gather'd, broad as *Amazonian* Targe,
> And with what skill they had, together sew'd,
> To gird thir waist, vain Covering if to hide
> Thir guilt and dreaded shame.

As the narrator continues, he separates the lethal from the benign by dissociating the barbarous New World from the glorious biblical paradise:[15]

> O how unlike
> To that first naked Glory. Such of late
> *Columbus* found th'*American* so girt
> With feather'd Cincture, naked else and wild
> Among the Trees on Isles and woody Shores. (9.1099–1118)

In a gross approximation of India and America, a place that had been confused with India, Milton establishes a dramatic context for describing the original Fall. The Indian fig tree supplies Adam and Eve with a means of concealing their guilt. The allusion to Columbus's *recent* discovery of the "girt" American likewise invites the reader to judge Adam and Eve's proximity to shame. In the passage Milton mixes myth, science, and geographical place-names, glossing over their differences. At the same time he gestures towards scientific accuracy to remind us "that the Fall was history to him even though it may be mythology to us" (Rajan, "Banyan Leaves" 223).[16] The fallacies of Gerard's *Herball*, the standard Elizabethan work on botany, are left intact; Milton follows contemporary botanists in confusing the banyan, whose leaves are small, with the large leaves of the banana tree. Moreover, like the East and the New World itself, the tree is feminized not only by the description of the "Daughters [that] grow / About the Mother Tree" (1105–6) but also by the comparison of the broad leaves to the "*Amazonian* Targe." The allusion here is not to the giant leaves in the South American Amazon rain forest but to the target or "crescent-shaped shields" of the female warriors of Greek legend, identified by Virgil in the *Aeneid* (1.490). The confusion caused by the conscious and unconscious mixing of names is intended to reflect and compound the shame of the barbaric transgressors, but it also reveals the colonialist's violation of nature and of diverse peoples.

### *The restoration of dialogue*

If the violation of the interdiction results in the Fall, then the remembering of the Word through the restoration of dialogue leads to moral and social healing. Moreover, the act of narrating the Fall of Adam and Eve and then of humanity in the final books offers Milton a means of working through the tragedy and of repairing the conversations in the private and political spheres. In his treatises on marriage Milton treats the individual's private and public life as continuous within the institution of marriage, which is in turn subject to the same tensions as the body politic. In a social and political context, marriage transforms the private into a public self and, in turn, binds "the maried couple to all society of life, and communion in divine & humane things; and so associated" (*Prose* 2:448). Domestic discord has national consequences, Milton maintains, when, in the midst of his campaign for "true Reformation in the state" (*Prose* 2:229), he was struggling with a failed marriage. Justifying the right to divorce, Milton declares: "For no effect of tyranny can sit more heavy on the Commonwealth, then this household unhappines on the family" (*Prose* 2:229). "You are for *Divorce*, I see, as well of *Governours*, as *wives*," L'Estrange taunts in *No Blinde Guides* (10). The attacks on Milton's views by his opponents reinforced the connection between marital and state affairs in his own commentaries and in the minds of his contemporaries.[17] In the following section I will discuss Adam and Eve's gradual restoration of dialogue and the reemplotment of their tragedy; in the second half of this chapter I will examine these issues in the larger context of Michael's prophecy of human history.

The re-engagement in conversation occurs very slowly after the declaration of the sentence. Both Adam and Eve first voice their sad complaints, fallen modes of discourse that prevent communication but are at the same time important vehicles for self-examination. In his complaint Adam, believing that all he begets is "propagated curse" (10.729), turns on himself and on the event of his own creation, a birth he celebrated in his dialogue with Raphael. Now the poem is sustained by his meditation on death, whose "tardy execution" exposes a dialectic that feeds his torment: "But I shall die a living Death?" (788) "Can he make deathless Death?" (798) Adam agonizes, having cast himself into a self-made "Abyss of fears / And horrors" (842–3) resembling Satan's own inner hell. As the distorted vision of the devils increases their anguish by multiplying the images of the forbidden tree, so now Adam's conscience represents "all things with double terror" (850). The memory of the divine voice haunts him, just as the voices he formerly lent to nature now mock him: "O Woods, O Fountains, Hillocks, Dales and Bow'rs, / With other echo late I taught your Shades / To answer, and resound far other Song" (860–2).

Learning to curse, Adam thereafter verbally abuses Eve, the first born of dialogue, by transforming her verbally into the serpent. Having named her Eve, "Substantial Life" (4.485) and "Woman" (8.496), Adam offers a different etymological basis for the name; "Eve" was also thought to be cognate with the Hebrew term for serpent. The renaming contrasts significantly with the former use of epic epithets. By assigning Eve a name before the Fall rather than naming her after the transgression, Milton provides the female character with an identity and complexity that she lacked in the biblical Genesis story and qualifies the authority invested in Adam as a namer. In book 10 the fallen Adam reduces her to "a Rib / Crooked by nature" (884–5), thereby engaging in Satan's own acts of distortion and objectification. The literalization prevents both Adam and Satan from heeding the "mysterious terms" of the divine sentence, which, though unretractable, can be renegotiated. The partial recollection of the sentence by Adam recalls Faustus's cursory examination of Jerome's Bible: Faustus, who reads that "The reward of sin is death" (1.1.40), despairs and forgets the latter portion of the scriptural passage, namely that the gift of God is eternal life (Rom. 6:23). Likewise, Adam neglects that part of the judgment that promises retaliation against his enemy (10.179–81). The sentence itself is prophetic, and the poet-narrator includes a typological reference to Eve as Mary second Eve (183), who gives birth to the "Oracle."

However, Adam and Eve's fallen self-conception prevents them from seeing themselves in any kind of future role except one that propagates the curse.

Applying the psychoanalytic terms employed by Hayden White, I am arguing that both characters "overemplot" or overdetermine their tragedy by attributing so much importance to it that the tragedy continues to shape the characters' actions even after it should have become "past history." By articulating and publishing their experience and by emplotting and reemplotting their histories, Adam and Eve learn to "change the *meaning*" of the Fall and of its "*significance*" in relation to the complexly configured historical process (*Tropics* 87). In the poem the restoration after the Fall begins with the meditations of Adam and Eve, through which they achieve self-awareness and learn to recognize a salvational design in their story. By coming to terms with their sinful condition, Adam and Eve engage in a different kind of self-examination than did Satan after his tragic fall. Their confessions enable self-transformation; the recognition of their own salvation is the prerequisite for interpreting their roles in the meta-narrative of providential history and in the course of human history they develop. Milton himself had overemplotted the tragic events in the ten-book edition of the poem, in which the second half of the fourth "act" (book 8) dramatizes the Fall. In the composition of the twelve-book edition of the epic, the temptation scene is displaced from its location in the narrative by books 10 to 12, which provide additional space and time for working through the consequences of the Fall.

The reemplotment of the tragedy is achieved through Adam's acknowledgment of the various episodes and voices of which human history is composed. In response to the curse Adam invents for her and womankind (10.867–908), Eve, out of desperation, makes a plea for negotiation both with Adam and with God. Suggesting that they join forces against their common enemy, Eve takes the initiative by offering to return to the place of judgment and by requesting that the sentence be levied against her alone. Adam dismisses Eve's proposed gesture as futile but agrees to a truce between himself and Eve as they await "a long day's dying" (964). Having been deceived by Death, Eve proposes that she and Adam then attempt to deceive Death though abstinence from "Conversing, looking, loving" (993), a condition synonymous with death. Suicide is Eve's last desperate proposition for freeing both the couple and its progeny from an unending deathlike existence.

Eve's recommendation of suicide, a Roman solution, is unreasonable, Adam responds; self-destruction is an act of contumacy, or "Reluctance against God." Death will be conquered not by terminating but by sustaining conversation. Adam, therefore, argues against both "wilful barrenness" and violence, offering at the same time an alternative interpretation to the pronounced sentence. Conversation, in both senses, must continue. "To better hopes his more attentive mind / Laboring had rais'd" (1011–12), the poet-narrator explains, as he compares Adam's sudden hopefulness to Eve's despair. The "Labor" involves the recollection and re-engagement with the Word or with the terms of the conferred judgment. The larger implications of the sentence become gradually apparent to Adam:

> Then let us seek
> Some safer resolution, which methinks
> I have in view, calling to mind with heed
> Part of our Sentence, that thy Seed shall bruise
> The Serpent's head.   (1028–32)

The prophecy can only be fulfilled through the co-operation of Adam and Eve. For the first time Adam focuses on a different aspect of the sentence (1048–85). This epiphanic moment is difficult to account for.[18] Adam suggests it is inspired by his remembrance and his recasting of the events of the past, including the Son's merciful proclamation of the judgment (1046–8). But that does not adequately explain how the "hapless Seed" that he cursed in his previous lament (965) acquired for him this alternative significance. Adam's memories have served until this moment only to torment him.

Adam's interaction with Eve eventually leads to his renewed dialogue with God and informs his reading of the couple's role in the narrative of history. Eve performs an act of forgiveness and mercy that Adam soon after imitates. In this Christianized recasting of the tragic Fall, sympathy inspires sympathy rather than being extinguished by revenge. Eve's words and gestures of reconciliation move Adam to forget the curse that he has just pronounced on her and on their marital bond. Reunion is not immediate, though Eve is raised by Adam in a gesture of forgiveness that is later extended by God. Having been preoccupied with more optimistic thoughts, Adam is not persuaded by Eve's proposals for abstinence and suicide. Nevertheless, Eve's counsel is internalized rather than dismissed by Adam, who appropriates the female voice and reconstitutes the described events by telling another version of them. Eve asks that the sentence may be transferred on to her (932–6), and indeed it is: "thy Seed shall bruise / The Serpent's head," Adam remembers (1031–2). The Seed was first released into the conversational air by Eve, whose second complaint focuses on the "woeful Race." Her plotting the destruction of humanity, "both ourselves and Seed at once to free," is misguided. Yet again the liberation of humanity through the Seed is a possibility if Adam and Eve defeat rather than submit to death. If Adam, then, is inspired to reinterpret the sentence and the significance of the Seed, Eve is the one who implants the images and words within his mind; her narration provokes Adam's reemplotment and revision of the tragic history of the Fall.

Evidence of Eve's influence is also apparent in Adam's resolution that the couple should return to its judgment place to plead for mercy from God. Adam's words (1086–92) recall those of Eve (932–6), which Adam failed to heed beforehand (952–7). Eve's subsequent gesture of repentance, which causes Adam to lose his anger towards her, establishes the possibility of a reconciliation that also paves a way to heaven (1046–8). The poet-narrator repeats Adam's words first spoken by Eve in an abridged form (1098–104). The repetition is a classical convention, but at the same time the verses confirm in the context of this scene the temporary reassociation of words and meaning, and of speech and action, which Satan's false rhetoric and reasoning had severed.

The "sighs though mute" and the unsophisticated prayers offered by Adam and Eve (11.31–2) become the orisons of their fallen state. Whereas the prelapsarian orison was both unmeditated (5.149) and unmediated, dialogue between humanity and God now depends on intercession. In response to Adam's lament about the inefficacy of prayer (11.311–13), Michael, who is sent as a prophet of humanity's tragic history, announces that direct verbal exchange has been replaced by signs that continue to confirm God's presence in the world (351–4). Michael himself is one of those signs (355–8); his revelations and words, while requiring interpretation, serve a corrective and instructive function. Yet Michael's task of explaining the significance of the "Cov'nant in the woman's seed renew'd" (116) is accomplished through much trial. In the narrative of postlapsarian history, dialogue as rigorous exchange and criticism replaces the venial discourse between Raphael – the affable, "sociable Spirit" (5.221) – and an unfallen humanity.

## 2 THE COUNTER-NARRATIVE OF HISTORY

The revolutionaries themselves were guilty of attempting, even after their defeat, to bring about the end of history by raising Eden on English soil. Milton cast Michael, the warrior archangel and the trumpeter at the Last Judgment, as the prophet of the tragic postlapsarian history of humanity, which is restaged in seventeenth-century England. In book 11 Michael criticizes not only the Old Testament warmongers, who fought for fame, power, and wealth, but also their victims, who likewise acted out of self-interest:

> The conquer'd also, and enslav'd by War
> Shall with thir freedom lost all virtue lose
> And fear of God, from whom thir piety feign'd
> In sharp contést of Battle found no aid
> Against invaders; therefore cool'd in zeal
> Thenceforth shall practice how to live secure,
> Worldly or dissolute, on what thir Lords
> Shall leave them to enjoy; for th' Earth shall bear
> More than anough, that temperance may be tri'd:
> And all shall turn degenerate, all deprav'd,
> Justice and Temperance, Truth and Faith forgot. (797–807)

In the later years of the Interregnum the Puritans, who declared they were fighting the Lord's battles, competed for positions of power and profit. The glorious cause of the people of God was corrupted by the revolutionaries themselves, who manufactured new idols whereby they might "get themselves a name" (12.45).

Milton's earlier texts reveal his nostalgia for a golden age, which manifested itself in a prophetic political vision of a newly awakening nation (*Prose* 2:558). At the same time, the poet's belief in a dynamic historical process led him to distrust utopian constructions; in the *Areopagitica* Milton condemns a cloistered virtue and the sequestering of the self "out of the world into Atlantic and Eutopian polities, which never can be drawn into use" (*Prose* 2:526). While Milton's definition of engagement, particularly direct political intervention, changed considerably after the tragic fall of the nation, the poet did not regard the retreat to the private sphere or the development of a "paradise within" as an apolitical or atemporal action, as his royalist opponents who mocked and attacked his treatises themselves realized.

In the final books of *Paradise Lost* Milton challenges a coherent reading of history, reconstructing it as a dialectical process of "ceaseless change" (5.183), while still betraying an attraction to a teleological imperative and a typological interpretation. Typology reveals what was finished as embryonic, but by representing history as a movement from "shadowy Types to Truth" (12.303), it also establishes a pattern for historical development. In educating Adam, Michael assumes the roles of a tragedian and a prophet who expresses the poet's own desire to challenge the tragic design of postlapsarian history. Michael's corrections of Adam's reading of human history rupture the closed system he constructs as he knits together in a paradoxical, prophetic discourse the historical narrative with an emerging vision of providence in order to reemplot Adam's personal defeat and the tragedy of human history.[19]

The development of a meta-narrative of history is an act of censorship, one that is resisted by the recasting of the narrative in a paradoxical discourse. The malady of history must be interrogated to expose the verbal fictions and multiple voices of which the historical account is composed. In his presentation of the dialectic and prophetic narrative of history in the final books of the poem, Michael shows Adam how past events determine future occurrences and how images of the future dictate a reading and recasting of the episodes. Though Adam's own role as a historical interpreter appears insignificant in books 11 and 12, he is in fact responsible for the individual stories of social outcasts and unsung heroes in the narrative, which constitute the imagined political community and the postlapsarian Eden of the future. I now turn to the complexly configured, double-voiced account of human history in *Paradise Lost* by examining the exchange between Adam and Michael, who serves as both interpreter and critic of Adam's reading of his destined role.

In his reaction to the first "noble sight," which presents the murder of Abel by Cain, and to the multiple shapes of death that follow (11.466–95), Adam despairs as Eve did after the fall: "Better end here unborn ... who if we knew / What we receive, would either not accept / Life offer'd, or soon beg to lay it down, / Glad to be so dismist in peace" (502, 504–7). In an answer that recalls Adam's reply to Eve, Michael recommends that humanity learn to contend with its fallen condition while striving to redirect the course of history it has charted. Death is not the final destiny, but since it can be neither readily defined nor defeated as Adam later hopes (12.383–5), it remains an integral part of human experience. In this scene, then, Michael challenges Adam's literalization of the "bruise" referred to in the divine sentence first misread by Satan himself (10.499–500).

Undeniably, the voice of Michael is a censoring one that continually undercuts Adam's attempts at decoding the historical episodes. Nevertheless, though presenting his official view as fully developed, Michael suggests by the apocalyptic nature of the historical account that it is totalizing only for the time being and is open to counter-readings. Moreover, through his verbal corrections and critical interventions, Michael actually assumes the role of an iconoclast by dismantling the historical continuum and unsettling truths that Adam reifies by casting a blind eye on the visions he is shown. Michael's critical remarks can be detected even in those passages in which Adam serves as focalizer. The poet-narrator presents an account of the second vision:

> on the hither side a different sort
> From the high neighboring Hills, which was thir Seat,
> Down to the Plain descended: *by thir guise*
> *Just men they seem'd*, and all thir study bent
> To worship God aright, and know his works
> Not hid, nor those things last which might preserve
> Freedom and Peace to men: they on the Plain
> Long had not walkt, when from the Tents behold
> A Bevy of fair Women, richly gay
> In Gems and *wanton* dress; to the Harp they sung
> Soft amorous Ditties, and in dance came on:
> The Men though grave, ey'd them, and *let thir eyes*
> *Rove without rein*, till in the *amorous Net*
> Fast caught,*they lik'd, and each his liking chose*. (11.574–87, my emphasis)

Entranced by the postlapsarian pastoral scene west of Eden, Adam is, like the seemingly just men, deceived by what he sees. The enjambed verses describing Adam's vision, which also "roves without rein," link the scenes so as to discourage an extended examination of individual images. Michael's voice, though subtle, penetrates the vision and resonates in the poet-narrator's account. The references to the men, who by their guises seem just and whose studies are seemingly "bent" on knowing God's works "Not hid," as well as the description of the wanton dress of the women, which entrances the gazers, are misinterpreted by Adam, who responds enthusiastically to the scenes. According to the poet-narrator, the "bent of [human] Nature" is to admit delight (596–7); for that reason, Adam's idealization of "Nature" and his conclusion that "Here Nature seems fulfill'd in all her ends" (602) is particularly dangerous, Michael observes (603–6).

The prophet's account remains predominantly tragic throughout; Michael is guarded and cautious, and constantly advises Adam to contain his optimism. He also recommends a critical reading of the postlapsarian visions; exposing the dialectical nature of death, Michael warns Adam about the deceptiveness of "Nature," particularly human nature. Finally, he outlines various patterns of history to educate Adam about their complex configurations. His saddest task, however, is to describe Eden's destruction. The tragic effects of the Fall are perhaps best represented by the numerous descriptions of the violated pastoral landscape that fill the final books of *Paradise Lost*. Michael invites Adam to behold a field, "Part arable and tilth," the setting of the murder of Abel by Cain, "a sweaty Reaper" who originally worked the land (11.430, 434). The "bloody Fact," Michael explains, was committed out of envy for Abel's favour from heaven by Cain, who was unable to accept the terms of his brother's relationship to God. The crime anticipates the wars that turn the field – the one first defiled by Satan (4.186) – into a military battleground (11.646–55). The clamour and confusion of the "cruel Tournament" confirm that the earth is a shadow of heaven "and things therein / Each to other like" (5.575–6), as Raphael speculates in his preface to the war in heaven. God's iconoclastic act at the end of this book – which is also an attack on Renaissance theological commentaries that maintained the existence of paradise – anticipates the destruction of the tower of Babel at the opening of book 12. Traditionally reserved for celebratory purposes and associated with innocence and fecundity, the garden is stripped of its original significance and lost to history. God's transformation of Eden into a wasteland, "an Island salt and bare" (11.834), indicates that he "áttributes to place / No sanctity, if none be thither brought / By Men who there frequent, or therein dwell" (836–8). The iconoclastic act is a response to humanity's own irreverence for the garden and its origin.

Michael's narrative is interspersed with brief accounts of social outcasts and wild men, whose struggles in a barbarous age lead to their banishment to the wilderness. Like Abdiel and Enoch, Noah – the one just man of his time (818) – provides the only example of righteousness in a fallen world: "One Man except, the only Son of light / In a dark Age, against example good, / Against allurement, custom, and a World / Offended" (808–11). While in various Catholic commentaries Eden provided a place of refuge for Enoch and Elijah,[20] in *Paradise Lost* Enoch (11.665), Noah, Abraham (12.152), and Adam and Eve must internalize paradise. Anticipating the example of the Son in *Paradise Regained*, Eliah/Elijah in the second epic also inhabits the wilderness or desert, Eden's shadow (*Poems*, PR 1.353, 2.268, 277). As one who continues the fight against the barbarousness and barbarous dissonance of his (own) age, the prophet-poet locates in the history of the outcasts his genealogy and destiny. He and the other antiheroes of the postlapsarian world are world-weary; thus, in this scene of the tragedy, no "noble and puissant Nation [seems ready to rouse] herself like a strong man after sleep" (*Prose* 2:558).

The five opening lines of book 12 were added with the creation of the twelve-book edition. The archangel's pause "Betwixt the world destroy'd and the world restor'd" (12.3) marks the transition from book 11 to 12, draws added attention to the role of the narrators in shaping history, and provides Adam with the opportunity to interpose. This critical intervention recalls a similar interruption of the narrative at the start of book 8, which also became a separate book with the restructuring of the ten-book edition. Adam's creation story in book 8 is recontextualized in book 12, where his personal history becomes increasingly social and political. How that happens is one of Michael's primary lessons to Adam. That it happens is reflected in the double-voiced structure of the narrative: while Michael provides the verbal descriptions of the course of human history, the prophetic account is amplified by Adam's own readings of historical interveners and glimpses of historical promise, which constitute a counter-narrative in the tragic plot.[21]

The beginning of book 12 marks another transition: that from revelation to narration or vision to voice. Leonard Mustazza suggests that the move from image-narrative to verbal-narrative is progressive because it signals the start of the internalization process (110); this observation is confirmed by Michael's invitation to Adam to "behold" (12.142) and "See" (158). However, in changing to narration the angel is compensating for Adam's failed vision rather than expecting him to rely first and foremost on his insight: "I perceive / Thy mortal sight to fail; objects divine / Must needs impair and weary human sense" (8–10). In book 12 the translation from the visual to the verbal and also from meaning to word is imperfect. Adam's idolatry now wholly impairs his external vision and distorts his reading of history.

Adam's role as a reader of Michael's prophetic script makes us conscious of our subject position and the way we experience the historical account, which is remade in the image of its fallen and blind interpreters. Likewise, in the different scenes that constitute the final books, Michael reveals the episodic quality of history by drawing attention to the individuals who direct and redirect its course. Even providence operates through human agents, Michael explains, as he describes the world's antiheroes who unsettle the dominant narrative by developing their own stories and counter-narratives.

In a closer examination of Michael's account we discover that Adam, through his naïve inquiries and emotional reactions, is primarily responsible for the "human factor" in the tragic historical account. Among his responses to the prophetic visions and histories are: "But who was that Just Man? (11.681); "Let no man seek / ... what shall befall / Him or his Children" (11.770–2); "I rejoice / For one Man found so perfet" (11.875–6); "O execrable Son so to aspire /

Above his Brethren" (12.64–5); "say where and when / Thir fight, what stroke shall bruise the Victor's heel" (12.384–5); and "if our deliverer up to Heav'n / Must reascend ... who then shall guide / His people, who defend?" (12.479–83). Adam hungers for details, especially for information about exemplary humans who, like himself, fight for justice in the face of defeat. Thus, while we hear from Adam infrequently in books 11 and 12, his voice and his concerns are represented in the stories of the uncelebrated antiheroes whose individual narratives comprise Michael's palimpsest of history.

The desecration of Eden affects the intricate course of human history significantly in the final books. The ecological metaphor, which I adopted to describe the interrelationship of diverse lifeforms in the garden, applies to organic social development and to the complex construction of historical events. In book 12 the garden – the former origin and centre of creation – is displaced by the various accounts of the marginalized Israelite community, which continually falls into different hands and bears the scars of humanity's guilt. The history of paradise lost in the final books is, then, reconfigured as a narrative of the trials experienced by the "woeful Race" of Adam and Eve. Fearing an assault on his power, Pharaoh, "the lawless Tyrant" (12.173), oppresses the people of Abraham in a manner reminiscent of Nimrod, who earlier had "arrogated Dominion undeserv'd" (12.27) over the postlapsarian pastoral community. The Israelites are thereafter led by Isaac, an exemplary leader whose authority over the people is merited – his "worthy deeds / Raise him to be the second in that Realm / of *Pharaoh*" (161–3). Having been guided to Egypt, the people are left at Pharaoh's mercy after Isaac's death:

> there he dies, and leaves his Race
> Growing into a Nation, and now grown
> Suspected to a sequent King, who seeks
> To stop thir overgrowth, as inmate guests
> Too numerous; whence of guests he makes them slaves
> Inhospitably, and kills thir infant Males. (163–8)

The tyrant's opposition to the expansion of the Israelites is emphasized by the change from "Growing" and "grown" in line 164 to "overgrowth" in verse 166. Here we are reminded of Adam's and Eve's different responses to the abundant growth of the vegetation in the garden. In book 9 the poet-narrator recounts the couple's conversation on the subject of "how that day they best may ply / Thir growing work: for much thir work outgrew / The hands' dispatch of two Gard'ning so wide" (201–3). Again the references to "growing" at the beginning and "outgrew" at the end of verse 202 convey two opposing attitudes towards the idea of organic development. Superfluity proves to be a threat to absolutism and a blessing to the promoters of change. As we recall from the speech that introduces the separation scene, Eve decided that "excess" must be contained:

> the work under our labor grows,
> Luxurious by restraint; what we by day
> Lop overgrown, or prune, or prop, or bind,
> One night or two with wanton growth derides
> Tending to wild. (208–12)

Of course, governance of Eden is the primary duty of Adam and Eve, and yet nature's growth cannot be controlled absolutely. Individual efforts are meaningful only in relation to collective activities. Such is Adam's response to Eve's proposal for divided labour: "These paths and Bowers doubt not but our joint hands / Will keep from Wilderness with ease, ... till younger hands ere long / Assist us" (244–7).

The Israelites, descendants of Adam and Eve, inherit an empty garden and also find themselves continually dispossessed and persecuted. In his narrative Michael is provoked by Adam's comments to describe their chosen leaders and the models of government that they establish *en route* to the promised land. Guiding the Israelites out of bondage from Egypt is Moses, who serves as an intercessor for the people at a time when the voice of God had grown "dreadful" to the mortal ear. The "ordain'd Laws" establish a covenant between God and a fallen humanity and are given to the people "to evince / Thir natural pravity" (12.287–8). As an administrator of laws that apply to civil justice and to religious rites (230–1), Moses acts as both a political and religious leader. Though Milton challenges the connection between civil and ecclesiastical power in his political treatises, the example of Moses serves his greater purpose of applying religious statements on authority to political and civil issues both in and outside the poem. The kind of government that Michael describes at this point is a type for the commonwealth Milton proposes for the future of the nation.

Through Adam's questioning, we learn that the Old Testament laws are not ends in themselves but components of a larger process (280–4). He explains that the laws form a language of types and shadows for a new covenant "disciplin'd / From shadowy Types to Truth, from Flesh to Spirit," and from "works of Law to works of

Faith" (302–3, 306). The fulfillment of the covenant and the prophecies is accomplished by Christ, last of kings, through his "God-like act" of offering his life, which annuls the doom (427–8). Because his exemplary life and death prove inimitable, Christ is given relatively little coverage in Michael's account.[22] Or *perhaps* it was because Christ's martyrdom had too recently been staged by a corrupt king in a more contemporary drama of human history. Whatever the reason, Michael is eager to continue the narrative in order to relocate Eden in two other places – heaven (463–5) and the "paradise within" that Adam is instructed to create (587).

By the end of the narrative Adam moves temporarily into the private world, where he returns to awaken Eve. The connection between the private and public sphere is indicated by Eve's discovery that she possesses knowledge of human history that has been presented to her in the alternative, though inferior, medium of dreams. While having been confined to the imaginary world of dreams, Eve, to the ignorance of Adam and Michael, has participated vicariously in the public realm that she now suggests the couple enter together. Still Eve is defined by interiority and female creativity; at the conclusion of the poem, as I emphasized in the previous chapter, she prophesies her maternal function, repeating the words of promise delivered by Michael to Adam (12.327). Implanted in Eve is the Seed from which the Word will spring: "By mee the Promis'd Seed shall all restore" (623).[23]

There was "no restored Eden upon earth even while Milton lived and wrote" (Masson 6:652–3), and while Milton includes many different images of Eden throughout the poem, the poet could and would not intervene in literary history or in the political history of the nation to raise Eden in the wilderness. Nevertheless, when we reexamine those passages in the poem – and, as L'Estrange found, in treatises like *The Readie and Easie Way* – where Milton includes visions of future intervention or uses functionally ambiguous language, we discover the multiple episodes, interpreters, and actors that make up the narrative of history and also the possibilities for creating counter-narratives and alternative worlds within the existing one.

# 6 The Voices of Nebuchadnezzar in *Paradise Regained*

Recent twentieth-century critics have challenged traditional readings of *Paradise Regained* as a non-dramatic and apolitical text. Arthur Milner, who interprets the epic as a product of Milton's early Restoration pacifism, argues nevertheless that the endorsement of a withdrawal from politics should be regarded as a temporary strategy that is only part of a long-term solution. Other critics, from Arnold Stein to Joan Bennett and Christopher Hill, have attempted to dissuade us from reading *Paradise Regained* as an allegory of Milton's resignation to quietism by examining the brief epic in the context of the poet's continued commitment to the Good Old Cause after the defeat of the Revolution.[1] In this final chapter I will offer an interpretation of *Paradise Regained* as a multivocal and historically engaged text that interrogates dominant ideologies of political authority through its resistance to the single "negating" monarchical voice.

The debate in which Satan and the Son participate in *Paradise Regained* is not a substitute for political activism; rather, it relocates, without confining, that engagement in an intentionally ambiguous language that is at once political and prophetic. The Son renounces temporal force, but his verbal criticism of an absolute and centralized governmental power and his prophesied destruction of all monarchies are not the expressions of a quietist attitude. Moreover, the Son has only one lengthy internal monologue in *Paradise Regained*, one in which he speaks in several voices and in which others are also accommodated. Without dominating the debate, the

Son criticizes models of established governmental power and creates a language for a new Christian heroism, thus engaging in contra-censorship. In this chapter I first provide a political context for my reading of the poem by examining Milton's representations of Charles's negating voice and the "Stage-work" of his final performance (*Prose* 3:530). Thereafter I focus on highlights of the verbal contest, which becomes the forum for the development both of the Son's multifaceted identity and of the complexly configured narrative of history that Satan attempts to control. The final consideration of this chapter will be the temptation on the pinnacle, which I interpret as a tower of Babel scene – the site of contending voices and contested identities.

The confrontations between the epic's primary speakers are represented as verbal debates, initiated by Satan's attempts to test the divine status of the Son; Satan hopes to persuade the Son that he is a character in a plot or narrative – a poem of history – whose events continually offer new opportunities to validate his authority. Rather than presenting him with genuine possibilities, Satan, however, censors and gradually narrows the Son's choices in order to trap him. When he finally inquires, "What dost thou in this World?" (4.372), we recognize the limitations of his materialistic vision, which prevents him from discerning alternatives to his proposals. Censorship, like revenge, recoils back upon itself. Satan's temptations differ very little from each other and ultimately constitute an endlessly repetitive historical continuum. The Son in turn disrupts that continuum both by developing a language of paradox and prophecy[2] that challenges Satan's oratory and "smooth answers" and by offering alternative ways of acting in the world.

Though he resists the temptation to establish the kingdom in which he is prophesied to reign, the Son does not act outside of history, Providence, or the plot of the poem;[3] moreover, he can only participate in the narrative, whether historical or literary, rather than determine its outcome. "Thy coming hither ... I bid not or forbid" (1.494–5), he responds to Satan, who requests permission to engage him in verbal combat. The Son's limited knowledge of his destiny, his use of indirection, and his refusal to dominate the debate suggest that he is not an author, as the majority of critics have characterized him, but, like Satan, an actor in the poem and in the processive course of history. Since the Christian view of the narrative of history is that of a closed work, Satan may not in fact be out of order in demanding that the principles of closure be made known. If the Son writes the poem, he can write Satan out of it. But this is not the case; the directions of the debate and of the course of history are determined in different ways by both speakers. Whereas Satan remains interested in locating the Son in history, where he can be dealt with, the Son's use of prophecy and paradox in his verbal contest with Satan – a contest that replaces the military combat of the classical epics – allows him to resist Satan's censorship and to reemplot the events of the master-narrative authored by Satan.

No single voice assumes absolute control over the narrative of the poem. Milton includes, along with the dominant speakers, a number of dramatic voices that shape the prophetic course of history and the Son's historical role. A monological, hierarchical reading assigns a fixed status to the primary and secondary voices that must, then, achieve their identity within that context. A process-oriented view, by contrast, can leave the status of voices indeterminate, treating understanding as emergent and provisional rather than as the progressive inscription of a transcendental blueprint. Admittedly, the difficulty with talking about secondary voices in *Paradise Regained* is that hardly any are to be heard; with the exception of the prophetic voices of the fishermen and Mary,[4] the poem is overwhelmingly a debate between two principal speakers, thus making its format hostile to multivocality. However, in the context of this study I will argue that the poem's dialogism, its diverse representations of kingship and historical progress, and the Son's objections to the oppressive homogeneity of the opposing discourse all contribute to the multivocal quality of the text. In this unadorned brief epic the Son's voice is iconoclastic, breaking the visual and verbal icons Satan offers and creating a language for alternative forms of political engagement. The final scene, my primary consideration in part 2 of this chapter, is a dramatization of the account of Nebuchadnezzar's reconstructed tower of Babel. Satan's fall from the pinnacle represents, I argue, the silencing of the single negating voice and the symbolic collapse of monarchy.

## 1 IMAGES OF KINGSHIP

### *The negative voice of the monarch*

An examination of extra-literary seventeenth-century discourses that inform the agonistic composition of *Paradise Regained* offers insights into the ways in which political and cultural history is written and linguistically reconstructed in the period and the poem. Voicing their opposition to kingship, the parliamentarians not only denounced the idolatry of the royalists but also exposed the tyrannical power invested in the monarchical voice. Philip Hunton in *A*

*Treatise of Monarchie* demanded that the king "suspend the use of his *negative voice*, resolving to give his royall assent to what shall passe by the major part of both Houses freely voting, concerning all matters of grievance and difference now depending in the two Houses."[5] In *Observations upon some of his Majesties late Answers and Expresses*, Henry Parker urged parliamentarians to oppose the "negative voice" of the king, whose "meer breath ... blasts them in an instant" (213).[6]

Using exempla and the debate format to mock the kings and magistrates who had abused their political power, Milton, in *Eikonoklastes* – an iconoclastic text that provided in the aftermath of the regicide a critical response to the influential royalist treatise *Eikon Basilike* – also described the negative voice of Charles as one that discouraged political debate and dissent. The monarch "prevented all reply" (PL 2.467) in the parliamentary debates by assuming absolute power with his "negative voice." Addressing the rights of property that Charles instituted reluctantly or with "a negative will," Milton further accuses Charles both of using public rhetoric to mask private interests and of suppressing opposition by "smoothing" over contradiction and difference, as Satan would do in both of Milton's epics: "We expect therfore somthing more, that must distinguish free Goverment from slavish. But in stead of that, this King, though ever talking and protesting as smooth as now, sufferd it in his own hearing to be Preacht and pleaded without controule, or check, by them whom he most favour'd and upheld, that the Subject had no property of his own Goods, but that all was the Kings right" (*Prose* 3:574). Parliament, which attempted to preserve civil liberty and which "shal have labourd, debated, argu'd, consulted, and ... *contributed* for the public good *all thir Counsels in common*," is tyrannized by the negating voice: "nothing can be more *unhappy* ... [than to be] frustrated, disappointed, deny'd and repuls'd by the single whiffe of a negative, from the mouth of one wilfull man; nay to be blasted, to be struck as mute and motionless as a Parlament of Tapstrie in the Hangings; or els after all thir paines and travell to be dissolv'd, and cast away like so many Naughts in Arithmetick, unless it be to turne the O of thir insignificance into a lamentation with the people, who had so vainly sent them" (*Prose* 3:579). The monarchical voice ultimately prevents the reconstruction of the commonwealth: "the *Remora* of his negative voice, which like to that little pest at Sea, took upon it to arrest and stopp the Common-wealth stearing full saile to a Reformation" (*Prose* 3:501).

The proliferation of images of monarchy continued even after the regicide, when the royalists resurrected the king by casting him as martyr in the controversial *Eikon Basilike*.[7] Milton in turn attempted to break the spell of the king's words by which Parliament and the Commonwealth had been rendered mute and impotent. In supporting Parliament's cause in the pamphlet war, Milton at once severs the connection between civil and ecclesiastic power and locates the origin of governmental authority in the people themselves (*Prose* 3:211–12). The dominant voice of the treatise is accompanied by the voices of the readers and of the misguided people betrayed by monarchy who are enlisted to oppose the king; the denunciation of tyranny becomes thereby a consensual act of voice, a vote against censorship, and a rewriting of the monarchy's master-narrative of history.

In his attack on the widely circulated *Eikon Basilike*, allegedly authored by Charles, Milton observes that the self-referential inscription underwriting the king's negative voice discourages multiple interpretations of his final performance:

In which negative voice to have bin cast by the doom of Warr, and put to death by those who vanquisht him in thir own defence, he reck'ns to himself more then a negative *Martyrdom*. But Martyrs bear witness to the truth, not to themselves. If I beare witness of my self, saith *Christ*, my witness is not true. He who writes himself *Martyr* by his own inscription, is like an ill Painter, who, by writing on the shapeless Picture which he hath drawn, is fain to tell passengers what shape it is; which els no man could imagin: no more then how a Martyrdom can belong to him, who therfore dyes for his Religion because it is *establisht*. (*Prose* 3:575)

The revolutionary interprets the monarch's staged death not as one of self-denial but of self-aggrandizement. Throughout the treatise Milton encourages a critical reading both of Charles's final dramatic act and of his verbal performances: "For in words which admitt of various sense the libertie is ours to choose that interpretation which may best minde us of what our restless enemies endeavor, and what wee are timely to prevent" (*Prose* 3:342). With this proposal Milton urges a reinterpretation of Charles's text; empowered by its deluded readers, *Eikon Basilike*, according to Milton, rewrites history, specifically the early defeats of the royalists, to ensure that the martyred king could still perpetuate "that interest by faire and plausible words, which the force of Armes deny'd him" (343). A critical reading of the images and voices of monarchy is, then, an act of dissent and political intervention – a reaction to censorship and the royalist control of English history.

Milton actually betrays an earlier attraction to martyrdom in

"The Passion." However, he aborts the attempt to portray the heroic sacrifice of the crucified Christ in the poem, which focuses by the fourth stanza on the poet's own passion. Later, when the royal actor plays the part of the martyr,[8] Milton adds to his anti-Catholic sentiments strong political reasons for refusing to portray the Crucifixion as an act of deliverance. In *Eikonoklastes* Milton reminds his readers of Christ's testimony: "If I beare witness of my self, saith *Christ*, my witness is not true" (*Prose* 3:575). The poet-revolutionary denounces both the vainglorious martyrdom staged by the king and – though Samson's performance would prove to be an exception – inimitable feats of superhuman strength. In *Paradise Regained* the Son insists, "I seek not [my glory], but his / Who sent me, and thereby witness whence I am" (3.106–7). His response to Satan is an expression of self-denial anticipating both the Son's martyrdom, which the poem defers,[9] and his last speech-act, which, like Samson's own final speech and iconoclastic performance, "admitts of various sense" by inviting conflicting interpretations.

In *Paradise Regained* Milton portrays the Son as an exemplary political and moral leader[10] and as an alternative to both the classical epic hero and the Renaissance courtier. The establishment of effective leadership, like the re-membering of truth, depends, however, on debate, which both acts must continue to promote. The best way of approaching the truth through the perfection of knowledge is "by endeavouring after meetings of people to conferre and discourse together," not by preaching or delivering "long set speeches," William Walwyn explains in *The Vanitie of the Present Churches* (273). The model of debate, which Milton continued to defend even in his last pamphlet, is strategically employed in the epic. The verbal contest between Satan and the Son cannot, however, be reduced to a competition between opposites; Satan's propositions are at one level quite rational and rhetorically well argued. Moreover, the Son actually betrays a human attraction to the possibility of intervening in the nation's political affairs (1.216–20),[11] and even after the soliloquy, the psychological battle is not over: "such thoughts / Accompanied of things past and to come / Lodg'd in his breast" (1.299–301). Nevertheless, the Son undeniably remains largely unmoved by Satan's offers.[12] That is not to imply that there is no debate; nor does the Son's evasion of direct confrontation transform the poem into a Socratic dialogue or a rhetorical exercise.[13] Rather, the poem portrays a different kind of conflict represented by the verbal contest and the speakers' complex attempts at achieving expression and authority through language. Words incarnate the Son, and the verbal debate affords Satan an equal opportunity as a contender.

In the year of the Restoration the voices of resistance were again suppressed through the monarchy's reintroduction of censorship.[14] The Commons petitioned the king to issue a proclamation ordering the burning of Milton's two anti-royalist treatises by the common hangman. The ritual served as an extreme act of censorship, while confirming Milton's Areopagitican announcement that books are living things empowered by the advocates and, ironically, by the opponents of their ideas. Expressing his political views in his later poems, Milton in *Paradise Regained* represents Satan as the Master of Revels, the censor and monarchist, who attempts to provoke the Son to assert his godhead and fulfil the prophecy of his imminent reign and the end of worldly history. The temptations are dramatized in the debate in which Satan asks the Son to participate, and in which he tries to bring history to an end by demanding that the Son provide definitive responses to his offers. In effect, Satan tempts him to establish an earthly kingdom or to raise Eden in the wilderness, an Eden that God has destroyed in an iconoclastic act in book 11 of *Paradise Lost*. The Son's struggle, then, is to refuse to adopt the negating, characteristically monarchical voice and instead to develop an alternative mode of expression and voice of authority.

### The baptisms of the Son

The poem begins not with a panegyric on kingship or a cry of "Astraea Redux" but with the Baptist's announcement of the "new-baptiz'd" Son of God, who arrives unobtrusively: "From *Nazareth* the Son of *Joseph* deem'd / To the flood *Jordan*, came as then obscure, / Unmarkt, unknown" (23–25). The poet-narrator recalls how the Father heralded his Son while the Spirit descended upon him "in likeness of a Dove" (30–2). God's proclamation becomes a refrain in the poem, one that along with the descent of the Spirit is subject to various interpretations to highlight the multifaceted identity of the Son.

"Nigh Thunder-struck" by the divine voice (35–6), as he is as well at the end of the poem (4.627), Satan addresses the council of hell and recounts the scene of baptism and the devils' defeat in his own terms. The doom of the devils is imminent, Satan decides thereafter. As he misconstrued the significance of the "bruise" in *Paradise Lost* (10.498–500 ), so now Satan misinterprets the judgment pronounced on the devils. He fears that history is about to draw to a conclusion with the fulfilment of prophecy:

> that fatal wound
> Shall be inflicted by the Seed of *Eve*

> Upon my head. Long the decrees of Heav'n
> Delay, for longest time to him is short;
> And now too soon for us the circling hours
> This dreaded time have compast, wherein we
> Must bide the stroke of that long-threat'n'd wound,
> At least if so we can, and by the head
> Broken be not intended all our power
> To be infring'd. (53–62)

Satan repeats and also literalizes "wound" and "head," as the juxtaposition of "head / Broken" and even "head. Long" indicates. The circling hours mark the return of the past, which haunts Satan and simultaneously assures him that his temptation will produce results identical to those of the first seduction: "the way found prosperous once / Induces best to hope of like success" (104–5).

Satan's primary error in his reading of the scene is his conventional interpretation of kingship. Satan literalizes the testimony of both John the Baptist and God, failing to recognize the symbolic significance of the anointment:

> on his head
> A perfect Dove descend[ed], whate'er it meant,
> And out of Heav'n the Sovran voice I heard,
> This is my Son belov'd, in him am pleas'd.
> His Mother then is mortal, but his Sire,
> Hee who obtains the Monarchy of Heav'n,
> And what will he not do to advance his Son? (1.82–8)

Evidently Satan still believes in the divine right of kings. Having identified monarchy with absolute political power, Satan fears that the Son might usurp the dominion that he had claimed for himself (98–9, 124–5). The satanic council is amazed by the oratory of "their great Dictator" (113), to whom they unanimously entrust their fate. The response to Satan, however, comes not from the devils Satan addresses but from God, who has only one speech in *Paradise Regained*. By speaking of merit, God contradicts Satan's reading of the relationship between the Father and Son (82–8): "I have chose / This perfect Man, by merit call'd my Son, / To earn Salvation for the Sons of men" (165–7). In his exchange with Gabriel, God sets the stage for the psychological and political drama that will redefine the terms of kingship.

The angelic voices that sing thereafter in harmony of the Son's future trials give way to the solitary voice of the Son, whose "holy Meditations" are presented in a soliloquy (1.196–293).[15] The Son's account of his inner turmoil and swarming thoughts appears at first to resemble Satan's final soliloquy in *Paradise Lost* (9.473–93). Satan in the earlier epic addresses his own thoughts to assist him in forgetting the past, and thereby to justify his opportunism: "Occasion ... now smiles" (9.480), words repeated by the devil throughout *Paradise Regained*. The soliloquy is locked in word-play and leads to the seduction of Eve. Milton cautions us in both epics to be highly distrustful of monovocal speeches, the expressions of the divided self. The Son in his soliloquy in *Paradise Regained* speaks, however, of progress as he traces his life from his childhood. Moreover, his words complement the external struggle: "far from track of men, / Thought following thought, and step by step led on" (1.191–2). The rhythm of the verses imitates the forward motion of the Son's pilgrimage. The lines, then, are indicative of the processive course of history in which the Son participates. The soliloquy as a whole recalls the laments of Adam and Eve after the Fall in *Paradise Lost* in so far as it dramatizes a struggle of conscience, anticipates further actions, and is the means to the restoration of dialogue.

Though presented in seclusion, the Son's speech nevertheless accommodates other voices, among them that of Mary, which interrupts and divides the Son's soliloquy. Mary's words emanate from within the Son, and yet despite the Son's appropriation of her voice she seems to engage in conversation with him. Her recommendation is that he convert his thoughts to actions:

> High are thy thoughts
> O Son, but nourish them and let them soar
> To what height sacred virtue and true worth
> Can raise them, though above example high;
> By matchless Deeds express thy matchless Sire.   (1.229–33)

Framed by the soliloquy of the Son, the words of Mary – an otherwise marginal character in the poem – challenge that containment because they are prophetic and also invoke the prophets Simeon and Anna. In the subsequent book, which opens with various characters struggling to understand the Son's mysterious identity and destiny, we discover that Mary possesses more insight into her son's role than do the fishermen Andrew and Simon, who regard the Son's mission in terms of the military deliverance of Israel (2.42–8).[16] Mary's interpretation, however, is also derived from a secular understanding of kingship; she concludes that the "Private, unactive, calm, contemplative" life of the Son in Nazareth is "Little suspicious to any King" (81–2). Moreover, she offers a literal reading of Simeon's predictions that the Son will be responsible for the fall and rise of many Israelites and that her own end will be a violent one. Yet because she believes that her son is destined to fulfil "some great purpose he obscures," she chooses to wait, pregnant with anticipation: "I to wait with patience am inur'd; / My heart hath been a storehouse long of things / And sayings laid up, portending strange events" (102–4). Mary uses the language of enclosure and is portrayed as a vessel and bearer of the Word; yet because they are prophetic, like her son's, her words are authoritative. Both characters act as prophets and also opt for patient vigilance, and therefore the "unsung" heroism of both might be characterized as feminine.

In his soliloquy the Son constructs his history in relation to the various verbal and written accounts of the Messiah's destined role. Here as at the end of the poem, the Son's contested identity is the subject of contending voices. John the Baptist leaves the most powerful impression in the form of a prophetic announcement of the Son's arrival. Twice subject and object are juxtaposed in the Son's recollection of the declaration; the Baptist "with loudest voice proclaim'd / *Mee him* (for it was shown him so from Heaven) / *Mee him* whose Harbinger he was" (1.275–7, my emphasis). The baptism is described in different ways by several of the characters in the poem, thereby affording each the opportunity to confer an identity on the Son; every interpreter of the event rebaptizes him. The Son's multifaceted identity is rendered even more obscure by his own paradoxical discourse and by his open-ended reading of history, which begins with the event of the baptism. The descent of the Spirit in the form of a dove and the divine proclamation, which signal the commencement of his pilgrimage and growth toward self-awareness, are intended, he conjectures, to bring him out of obscurity (282–9). Nevertheless, the soliloquy ends with a note of uncertainty: "I am led / Into this Wilderness, to what intent / I learn not yet, perhaps I need not know; / For what concerns my knowledge God reveals" (290–3).

The wilderness is the site of contention, linguistic confusion, and the breakdown of hierarchical distinctions. The Son's soliloquy gives way to dialogue to mark the beginning of the temptation in the desert that precedes the Son's entry into public life. The Tempter confronts the Son in the guise of "an aged man in Rural weeds" (314), reminiscent of Spenser's Archimago and Milton's Comus. The sound patterns in the poet-narrator's description and the alliteration of "w's" in such words as "wild," "wither'd," "Winter," and "winds" (1.310–18) advance Satan's entrance.[17] The antagonist himself imitates the sounds of wildness in the speech that follows (321–34). As a desert inhabitant, Satan is at once a social outcast, a wild man who anticipates Nebuchadnezzar, and a *barbaros* or babbler.[18] But the "barren waste" is also the home of the marginalized, including Moses, Elijah (1.353–4), and Christ himself. Satan glosses over the differences between the desert's various inhabitants when he includes himself among the wretched: "But if thou be the Son of God, Command / That out of these hard stones be made thee bread; / So shalt thou save thyself and us relieve / With Food, whereof we wretched seldom taste" (342–5). The Son in response strips Satan of his disguise – "I discern thee other than thou seem'st" (348) – and then declares his godhead by refusing to declare it: "Why dost thou then suggest to me distrust, / Knowing who I am, as I know who thou art?" (355–6). Paradoxically, the Son's evasive statement actually exposes Satan. The scene foreshadows the "undisguising" and fall of Satan at the end of the epic. Moreover, the account recalls the discovery of the "Artificer of fraud" by Uriel in *Paradise Lost*. In the earlier epic the stripping is a visual act; in *Paradise Regained*, rhetoric at once reveals and veils Satan's pretence.

Once his identity is exposed, Satan makes a request to formalize and continue the debate: "Thy Father, who is holy, wise and pure, / Suffers the Hypocrite or Atheous Priest / To tread his Sacred Courts ... disdain not such access to me" (486–92). A rhetorical exchange would place the speakers on equal ground and render truth pliable and palatable: "Hard are the ways of truth, and rough to walk, / Smooth in the tongue discourst, pleasing to th' ear, / And tuneable as Silvan Pipe or Song" (478–80). The Son carefully avoids any definite answer here and throughout the epic: "Thy coming hither, though I know thy scope, / I bid not or forbid; do as thou find'st / Permission from above; thou canst not more" (494–6). An affirmative or negative response to Satan would prevent the exchange and challenge God's absolute authority.

Even before the end of the first book we realize that while the identity of the Tempter can no longer be concealed, the power invested in Satan as the original adversary and contender against God is not diminished, nor can its numerous manifestations be erased. In Satan's first soliloquy in book 4 of the earlier epic Milton alludes to Revelation 13:5, where John prophesies the tyranny of the beast that oppresses all peoples and nations. Milton contemporizes the reference in *The Tenure of Kings and Magistrates* in his condemnation of the magistrates who opposed the trial of Charles. Later in *A Defence of the People of England* Milton would appropriate an Old Testament passage and remark similarly on the authority granted to Nebuchadnezzar, to whom Charles is compared: "But God, you say, gave over many realms in slavery to Nebuchadnezzar. For a definite period, I confess, he did so (Jeremiah 27, 7), but I challenge you to show that he gave over the English as slaves to Charles Stuart even for half an hour; I would not deny that he permitted it, but I never heard that he gave them over. And on the other hand, if God enslaves a people whenever they have less power than a tyrant, why should he not also be said to liberate them when they have more power than a tyrant?" (*Prose* 4:387). This description of Charles, the seventeenth-century successor to Nebuchadnezzar, provides a context for interpreting the conferment of power on Satan, which the poet-narrator, Satan, and the Son in *Paradise Regained* all address. Offering to reveal to the Son the monarchies of the world that Michael had shown to Adam in *Paradise Lost*, Satan leads his opponent up the mountain, where he reproduces the scene; "(such power was giv'n him then)," the poet-narrator explains (3.251). In the subsequent book Satan tries to tempt the Son with the offer of Rome: "to me the power / Is given, and by that right I give it thee" (103–4). After the Son's response, he restates his claim: "The Kingdoms of the world to thee I give; / For giv'n to me, I give to whom I please" (163–4). The Son in turn confirms Satan's rightful possession of the kingdoms but criticizes his abuse of the right; he does so by drawing attention to the significances of the word "give," which Satan had been using indiscriminately:

> The Kingdoms of the world to thee were giv'n,
> Permitted rather, and by thee usurp't,
> Other donation none thou canst produce:
> If given, by whom but by the King of Kings,
> God over all supreme? If giv'n to thee,
> By thee how fairly is the Giver now
> Repaid?   (4.182–8)

Satan has denied the origin of his power and used the passive form of the verb "give" – "giv'n to me." Moreover, he demands gratitude and service from the Son when he offers the kingdoms: "worship me as thy superior Lord, / Easily done, and hold them of me" (167–8). The Son in the above quotation responds by reminding Satan of the terms of the original contract and identifying the "Giver."

Despite the seeming contrasts in the poem between Satan's seductive speeches and the Son's powerful counter-arguments, the contraries are interconnected. The poem dramatizes the duel between the Son and Satan in terms of a conflict of opposites; yet the language used by the speakers transforms "duel-ism" and dualism into duality. The difference between dualism and duality is difference itself: in dualism, difference is dichotomy, whereas for duality, difference is supplementary, so that the intelligible and the sensible, for example, could not exist in isolation.[19] Duality, then, assumes a dialectical relationship between opposites.

The Son's initial preoccupation with a multitude of swarming thoughts reveals that the setting of the poem is at one level the complex psyche of the Son himself: "with holiest Meditations fed, / Into himself descended" (2.110–11). The argument that the Son represents reason and Satan passion does little justice to the Son's struggles – expressed in his soliloquy and by his evasive language – or to the persuasiveness of Satan's arguments. Though the Son manages to resist Satan's temptations throughout the poem, he does not reject Satan's proposals absolutely. The possibilities of participating in the banquet, liberating the oppressed peoples, studying classical culture, or raising Eden "in the waste Wilderness" (1.7) are not directly dismissed, though Satan's proposals, offered for the purpose of self-advancement, are not accepted either. Yet rather than promoting non-action, the Son in his responses challenges the oppositional relationship between individual and state affairs, and identifies heroism and kingship with self-governance – the prerequisite for political reform (2.466–7).

To the psychological reading we can add a seventeenth-century political interpretation of the epic that addresses Milton's contribution to the revolutionary effort before and during the Restoration period. The instant solutions Satan proposes to liberate the oppressed and solve Israel's national problems are reminiscent of the revolutionaries' attempts at establishing the English Commonwealth, the kingdom of God on earth. Milton's prophecy in the *Areopagitica* of a nation awakening like a strong man after sleep (*Prose* 2:558) is one that the poet-revolutionary hoped would be realized through his commitment to the good old cause and ultimately through the fall of monarchy. It is, moreover, an allusion to the Book of Judges' description of Samson (16:6–14), a symbol of England for Milton (*Prose* 1:858–9). At the same time, the distinction between continuity and contiguity in the *Areopagitica* betrays the tentativeness of the proposal to found the ideal earthly paradise for which the revolutionaries fought. Satan's political strategies in the poem reflect a view of government and history espoused, ironically, by monarchists and revolutionaries alike during the Civil War. Both sides were guilty of attempting to control political and historical change. The experience of personal and political defeat revealed to Milton the presumptuousness of his aspirations and of Parliament's attempted appropriation of English history. The struggle to resist these political ambitions is represented in *Paradise Regained* by the Son's internal debate, his verbal contest with Satan, by the inclusion in the poem of various individual and national historical accounts, and by the staging of the final temptation on the temple pinnacle.

## 2 ANTI-IMPERIALISM

### Iconoclasm and prophecy

Since the confusion of tongues at Babel and the dispersion of the Word at Pentecost, language resists absolutes and takes revenge on those who would use it to argue for the lack of alternatives to a given thought or action. Satan's failure to read the Son's destined role critically is apparent in his rhetorical question: "Reign then; what canst thou better do the while?" Throughout the poem the Son manages through a paradoxical and prophetic discourse to offer differing points of view without denying Satan's right to speak. In turn he manages to thwart Satan's attempts at censoring his words and dictating his actions. In part 2 I will demonstrate that Satan's fall from the temple pinnacle – the tower of Babel in *Paradise Regained* – represents the silencing of the negating voice and, as Milton suggests in *Eikonoklastes*, the symbolic end of monarchy itself (*Prose* 3:405).

Satan denies the speakers' contest by glossing over their different motives and moral positions. The rejection of multiple viewpoints is again an act of censorship. Milton argued on the eve of the Restoration that the teaching and seduction by the false prophets – associated by the advocates of censorship with the Church of Thyatira in Revelation 2:20 – could be hindered by permitting the conflict of good and evil – that is, by "instant and powerfull demonstration to the contrarie; by opposing truth to error, no unequal match" (*Prose, Of Civil Power* 7:261). In response to Satan's temptation to embrace earthly glory and emulate "Great Julius" (3.39), the Son, then, restores competing definitions to the concepts whose various significances Satan had limited. He does so by repeating Satan's words and recontextualizing them in his answer:[20]

> Thou neither dost persuade me to seek wealth
> For Empire's sake, nor Empire to affect

> For glory's sake by all thy argument.
> For what is glory but the blaze of fame,
> The people's praise, if always praise unmixt?
> And what the people but a herd confus'd,
> A miscellaneous rabble, who extol
> Things vulgar, and well weigh'd, scarce worth the praise?
> They praise and they admire they know not what;
> And know not whom, but as one leads the other;
> And what delight to be by such extoll'd,
> To live upon thir tongues and be thir talk,
> Of whom to be disprais'd were no small praise? (3.44–56)

The repeated terms "Empire," "glory," "praise," and "extol," as well as the words "fame," "confus'd," "rabble," and "tongues," recall the *Paradise Lost* account of the tower of Babel, which Satan is in fact about to show to the Son in this scene (280–1). By seeking glory indiscriminately, "Regardless whether good or evil fame" (*PL* 12.47), the followers of the unnamed Nimrod in *Paradise Lost* anticipate both the "miscellaneous rabble" to which the Son refers (*PR* 3.50)[21] and the English nation under the tyranny of Charles I and his successor, whom Milton identifies with the king of Babylon.

The debate over competing definitions of glory, empire, and historical development displaces the military battles between warriors portrayed in the classical epics. In *Paradise Regained* the definitions themselves break down when the weapons prove ineffective. Book 4 opens with Satan momentarily silenced, not so much by the Son's response in book 3 to the temptation of the empires as by his realization that the "persuasive Rhetoric" (4.4) he used to seduce Eve is not producing like results on the Son.[22] Predictability is lost; the futility of Satan's temptations is suggested by the juxtaposition of several similes used by the poet-narrator in describing Satan's efforts:[23]

> But as a man who had been matchless held
> In cunning, overreach't where least he thought,
> To salve his credit, and for very spite
> Still will be tempting him who foils him still,
> And never cease, though to his shame the more;
> Or as a swarm of flies in vintage time,
> About the wine-press where sweet must is pour'd,
> Beat off, returns as oft with humming sound;
> Or surging waves against a solid rock,
> Though all to shivers dash't, th'assault renew,
> Vain batt'ry, and in froth or bubbles end;
> So Satan, whom repulse upon repulse

Met ever, and to shameful silence brought,
Yet gives not o'er though desperate of success,
And his vain importunity pursues.   (10–24)

The accumulation of images provides an effective alternative to the epic simile in this passage. While the comparisons imitate the collision of "repulse upon repulse," each is only an approximation, thereby undercutting the Tempter's absolutism. The comparisons of Satan to a spiteful overmatched wrestler, a swarm of flies, and then to the surging waves represent the devil's movement down the chain of being, while also mocking his concomitant belief in recurrent and repetitive patterns of history.

As the surging waves' battery produces only "froth or bubbles," so does the rhetoric of the temptations dissolve into what the Son calls "So many hollow compliments and lies, / Outlandish flatteries" (124–5). The empires that Satan displays also fragment. In response to this temptation and to Satan's appropriation of world history, the Son predicts that the end of time will witness not the establishment but the destruction of all monuments to power. In turn, the spiritual Jerusalem will rise from the fallen earthly monarchies:

> Know therefore when my season comes to sit
> On *David's* Throne, it shall be like a tree
> Spreading and overshadowing all the Earth,
> Or as a stone that shall to pieces dash
> All Monarchies besides throughout the world,
> And of my Kingdom there shall be no end:
> Means there shall be to this, but what the means,
> Is not for thee to know, nor me to tell.   (146–53)[24]

This passage is taken from the prophetic Book of Daniel (4:8).[25] Daniel describes Nebuchadnezzar's dream of the great tree, whose height "reached unto heaven, & the sight thereof to the ends of all the earth." According to Daniel's inspired reading, the biblical tree is a symbol for the king (4:19). It is cut down and destroyed at the command of a voice from heaven, which prophesies the end of Nebuchadnezzar's tyranny and the commencement of the purgation both of his kingdom and himself (4:20ff). While the Son also uses the tree to represent his future position as Israel's true King, he describes his kingdom as being "like a tree." To literalize the symbol is to accept Satan's prophecy of the imminent reign of the Son.[26]

The other comparison that the Son draws is between his future heavenly kingdom and a stone that destroys the world's monarchies. Again the Son alludes to the Book of Daniel (2:26–45), specifically to

Nebuchadnezzar's dream of the stone that breaks without cause from a mountain, shattering the gold, silver, bronze, iron, and earthenware statue that represents the world's kingdoms.[27] The dream is allegorical in Daniel's prophecy as well as in the Son's account. In the Book of Daniel, however, Nebuchadnezzar literalizes the dream by actually constructing the statue, which he in turn transforms into an idol (3:1–23). The defiance of Shadrach, Meshach, and Abednego – who are sent to the furnace for their refusal to venerate the statue and the king – eventually breaks the spell of tyranny. The act that Satan in *Paradise Regained* tempts the Son to perform is likewise an idolatrous one (4.166–9).

In comparing Charles and Nebuchadnezzar – who is identified as king of Babel in the Geneva Bible – Milton constantly addresses the subject of idolatry. To justify his defence of the regicide and attack the cult of martyrdom, Milton identifies the king and the *Eikon Basilike* with a heathen tradition.[28] Having reminded his readers of Charles's refusal to call on Parliament during his reign, Milton in *Eikonoklastes* rewrites the monarch's prophecy and casts him as Nebuchadnezzar: "Much [Charles] Prophesies, *that the credit of those men who have cast black scandals on him shal ere long be quite blasted by the same furnace of popular obloquie wherin they sought to cast his name and honour*: I beleive not that a Romish guilded Portrature gives better Oracle then a Babylonish gold'n Image could doe, to tell us truely who heated that Furnace of obloquy, or who deserves to be thrown in, *Nebuchadnezzar* or the three Kingdoms" (*Prose* 3:498). Like Nebuchadnezzar, Charles resisted change, dissent, and historical progress.[29] Charles was an idolator in another sense as well: his collections of art expressed his cultural and aesthetic elitism, as Nebuchadnezzar's statue reflected the narcissism of the Old Testament king. Charles's interest in the visual arts, particularly paintings that displayed the classical and Renaissance principles of uniformity and symmetry, influenced the life of the court. The king surrounded himself with a few art connoisseurs who could appreciate and afford his preferred tastes in Rubens and Van Dyck (whom he knighted) and in Titian, Raphael, Correggio, and Mantegna. Because Charles devoted more attention to the arts than to government and policy-making, his court became a social rather than a political centre, exposing his obsession with propriety and dominance: "the atmosphere encouraged the rather bland ideological consensus of the governing circle, and did a great deal to ensure that the latter was not political in any traditional or overriding way" (Reeve 195).

As an iconoclast, Milton in *Animadversions* urges the destruction of the "Babylonish gold'n Image," which he later replaces with alternative models of moral and spiritual leadership: "throw down your *Nebuchadnezzars* Image and crumble it like the chaffe of the Summer threshing floores, as well the gold of those Apostolick Successors that you boast of, as your *Constantinian* silver, together with the iron, the brasse, and the clay of those muddy and strawy ages that follow" (*Prose* 1:700–1). Milton here condemns the long tradition of empire-building as well as the idolatrous worship both of episcopacy and, more generally, of the body of ancient writings; he recommends that his readers arm themselves instead with the words and weapons of Scripture: "Why doe wee therefore stand worshipping, and admiring this unactive and livelesse *Colossus* ... Goe therefore, and use all your Art, apply your sledges, your levers, and your iron crows to heave and hale your mighty *Polyphem* of Antiquity to the delusion of Novices, and unexperienc't Christians. Wee shall adhere close to the Scriptures of God which hee hath left us as the just and adequate measure of truth, fitted, and proportion'd to the diligent study, memory, and use of every faithfull man" (*Prose* 1:699–70). The Son in *Paradise Regained* takes this criticism of antiquity further yet. In book 4 Satan shows the Son the monuments of Athens, which display the wisdom of the ancients, whose achievements he celebrates in the account (4.236–80). Satan's praise of the tragedians' art, however, is ironic, particularly because it recalls the poet-narrator's comic description in *Paradise Lost* of the devilish philosophers' aspirations (2.546–65); in the later epic, Satan maintains:

> what the lofty grave Tragedians taught
> In *Chorus* or *Iambic*, teachers best
> Of moral prudence, with delight receiv'd
> In brief sententious precepts, while they treat
> Of fate, and chance, and change in human life,
> High actions, and high passions best describing. (261–6)

Satan tempts the Son to adopt the ancients as a model first by inviting him to participate visually in the scene and then by recommending the use of Greek learning to "render [him] a King complete" (283). The Son in response insists that readers bring "A spirit and judgement equal or superior" to their texts (324) and applies his own judgment to the political literature Satan offers for his edification. Without affirming or denying his knowledge of the ancients (286–7), the Son resists Satan's attempts at casting him into the classical image of the philosopher-king by exposing the hollowness of the ancients' doctrines and language, which he replaces with the "majestic unaffected style" of his own "native Language" (359, 333) – his most effective weapon.

154   Barbarous Dissonance and Images of Voice

The Son's answer exhausts Satan's arsenal of arguments: "all his darts were spent" (366). Satan's remaining speeches consist of reiterated proposals that complement his cyclical view of history. In his address to the Son thereafter (368–93), Satan first recalls the failed temptations and then proposes to return the Son to the wilderness where he first discovered him. The false prophet does so, however, with a warning – "yet remember / What I foretold thee" (374–5) – in which he outlines the consequences of rejecting his offers. The Son is failing to take advantage of his opportunities, the devil warns; now is the moment "When Prophecies of thee are best fullfill'd" (381). The stars predict doom for the Son, Satan elaborates. Moreover, because the time when the Son will finally reign in the kingdom "Real or allegoric" cannot be determined, it is imperative to act now, Satan insists, failing to discern the kingdom within.

As the narrative moves towards its culmination with the temptation on the pinnacle, we become increasingly aware of the interrelationship between tyranny and anarchy in the portrayal of the adversary and in his speeches. Satan reveals his connection with wildness and babble – which confirms his identification both with Nimrod and Nebuchadnezzar, the wild man – when he imitates the voices of the wilderness, the tempest, the "Infernal Ghosts," "Hellish Furies," and "terrors dire."[30] Moreover, the devil speaks for the voices by explaining their significance: "They oft fore-signify and threaten ill: / This Tempest at this Desert most was bent; / Of men at thee, for only thou here dwell'st" (464–6).[31] He makes the Son acutely aware of his vulnerability at this point by suggesting that the elements are conspiring against him. Reminding him that he is unprotected and isolated in the wilderness, Satan observes that the Son is after all only human, as the juxtaposition of "men" and "thee" suggests (466). However, Satan's arguments are old and repetitive; thus he continues, "Did I not tell thee ... ?" (467). This speech summarizes his former arguments: the time and means for attaining the kingdom are indeterminable; the Son will be subject to numerous adversities in the meantime; and the many "terrors, voices, prodigies" (482) offer "a sure foregoing sign" to validate the devil's predictions. Satan's prophecy – the fulfilment of which he deems imminent – replaces the biblical prophecy of the Son's reign which remains open-ended.

### "A Pinnacle of Nebuchadnezzars Palace"

Interconnected biblical and historical discourses about political authority are encoded in Milton's treatises of the Civil War and

Interregnum years and in the epics, which both end with accounts of the fall of Babel. Chapter 5 of *Eikonoklastes*, in which Milton addresses the king's reluctant institution of the Triennial Act and a second bill for the settling of Parliament, concludes with a pinnacle scene: "*His letting some men goe up to the Pinnacle of the Temple was a temptation to them to cast him down headlong.* In this *Simily* we have himself compar'd to *Christ*, the Parliament to the *Devill*, and his giving them that Act of settling, to his letting them goe up to the *Pinnacle of the Temple.* A tottring and giddy Act rather then a settling. This was goodly use made of Scripture in his Solitudes. But it was no Pinnacle of the Temple, it was a Pinnacle of *Nebuchadnezzars* Palace, from whence hee and Monarchy fell headlong together" (*Prose* 3:405). Here Charles, a false Christ, is toppled along with monarchy by Parliament. In *A Defence of the People of England* Milton recalls how Nebuchadnezzar was likewise ousted by the people. In correcting his contemporary readers' misconceptions about their restricted role in governmental affairs, Milton turns to Old Testament history: "Daniel tells us that when King Nebuchadnezzar ruled too haughtily men drove him from their society and left him to the beasts. Their laws were not called those of the king but of the Medes and the Persians, in other words, of the people; and, since they were irrevocable, the kings too were bound by them" (*Prose* 4:435). The biblical precedent provides a model for the English to exercise their own political right to self-determination. Moreover, by addressing his readers directly and giving the people a voice in the treatise, Milton creates the illusion of dialogue with a supportive audience and, paradoxically, participates in a Christ-like act of self-denial.

In this chapter I have already noted several allusions to Nebuchadnezzar – successor to Nimrod – in *Paradise Regained*, including Satan's reference to the ruler and builder of Babylon who conquered Jerusalem (3.281–3). Babylon is associated with the tower of Babel in the previous verse, "*Babylon* the wonder of all tongues" (280), and the two are also connected in *Paradise Lost* (12.343). The political authority offered to Satan in *Paradise Regained* was given to Nebuchadnezzar, the successor of Nimrod, in Jeremiah 27, as Milton indicated in *A Defence* (*Prose* 4:387). The significance of the "pinnacle" and the temple on which Satan places the Son has received considerable attention from critics, who have identified the pinnacle as a tower or as the wing of a temple, specifically that of Herod in Josephus' *The Antiquities*: "the valley was so deep that a man could scarcely see the bottom of it. Herod built a Portico of so vast a height, that if a man looked from the roof of it, his head would grow giddy, and his sight not be able to reach from that height to the bottom of the valley" (15.11.5).³² Herod's temple stands on the place of Solomon's to which Milton refers in *Paradise Lost* (12.334). In *Paradise Regained* the unnamed temple can be associated with a variety of different historical and allegorical temples or towers. The juxtaposition of temples and towers occurs several times in the poem: 3.268, 4.34, and in 4.544–7, which reads: "underneath them fair *Jerusalem*, / The holy City, lifted high her Towers, / And higher yet the glorious Temple rear'd / Her pile." In his prose tracts Milton uses the towering structure to symbolize the prelates who conspired with the pope "to support one falling *Babel*" and to participate in the "Idolatrous erection of [exquisite] Temples" or "*spirituall* BABEL[s]" (*Prose* 1:528–9, 590). In this context the temple in the poem represents both the tower of Babel and Nebuchadnezzar's statue, as well as the height of ambition, pride, and confusion.³³

In the pinnacle scene Satan finally challenges the identity of the Son directly. The devil first remembers in various ways the refrain of the epic's first two books: "Of the Messiah I have heard foretold / By all the Prophets" (4.502–3); "I among the rest, / Though not to be Baptiz'd, by voice from Heav'n / Heard thee pronounc'd the Son of God belov'd" (511–13); "Therefore to know what more thou art than man, / Worth naming Son of God by voice from Heav'n, / Another method I must now begin" (538–40). The Son has managed to sustain the debate thus far by not conforming to any conventional – primarily classical – models of authority. Now Satan uses that against him: "The Son of God ... bears no single sense; / The Son of God I also am, or was, / And if I was, I am" (517–19), he declares, denying both his difference from God and the effect of historical change. The final temptation recalls the initial temptation to change the stones into loaves, in so far as Satan again demands a miraculous performance that would confirm the hero's divinity.

Satan's riddle can only be solved through the reassociation of word and image or deed, on which Satan himself has previously commented (3.9). The Son's final statement is effective not so much because it is a declaration of his godhead but because word and deed have joined for one intervening moment to alleviate all doubt about the Son's merit and status. Here at the climax on the pinnacle, quietism constitutes heroic action; simplicity is most potent, and silence speaks loudest. The Son's response to Satan is a speech-act in so far as the Son's words and actions demonstrate that he merits his title: "Tempt not the Lord thy God; he said and stood" (561). The speech-act brings together the traditionally oppositional terms of speech and action, an idea that is central to the temptation scenes in the poem. The Word is in the act of standing made flesh.

At the same time, the statement, which is subject to multiple critical interpretations, complicates both the Son's identity and performance. The Son responds to Satan, and the poet-narrator confirms the identity of the speaker both before and after the statement. "The Lord thy God" refers to the Son, whom Satan must not tempt. However, the Son is not directly declaring his divine status at this point because he is quoting Scripture, the authoritative Word of God and the ultimate weapon. According to the biblical reading, "the Lord thy God" can also refer to the Father, whom the Son quotes and whom the Son must obey by not casting himself from the pinnacle. The words in the latter case do not belong to the Son, and yet, when he utters them in the poem, they acquire an ironic and powerful significance that figuratively and literally overwhelms Satan. Speech, in this scene and throughout the poem, is a form of action, which can be either circular and subversive or engaging, paradoxical, and open-ended. The accounts of Babel and Pentecost meet at this point. Whereas Satan becomes trapped by tautologies and the doubleness of his language ("The Son of God I also am, or was, / And if I was, I am" [518–19]), the Son uses irony and paradox to resist temptation and definition, and to represent his dialectical relationship with God and the scriptural Word.

The final temptation is also the site of conflicting and *contending* voices. The Son's response to Satan recalls not only Matthew 4:7, Luke 4:12, and less directly Mark 1:13 but also a number of Old Testament passages that describe the Israelite community under Moses' leadership in contention with Yahweh – that is, in rebellion against the Lord (Num. 20:10). At Massah (place of testing) and Meribah (contention) in the desert, the Israelites quarrel with and rebel against Yahweh, challenging him to assert his identity (Exod. 17:7; Deut. 6:16; Psalm 95). Because they defied Yahweh, Moses and his followers are rendered unclean and unfit to enter the Promised Land. Barred from the community (Num. 14:23), they must remain in the wilderness and continue wandering. The testing of Yahweh reminds us of the construction of Babel by the followers of Nimrod, the rebel, and of the reconstruction of the tower by the English nation, whose "covetous and ambitious" acts (*Prose* 7:422) led to the defeat of the Revolution and the failure to complete the English Commonwealth.

"Unchang'd / To hoarse or mute" by the barbarous dissonance of Satan's many voices,[34] the Son triumphs over his opponent without resorting to his superior strength, to martyrdom, or to declarations of divine status. The one solution to the predicament in which the incarnated Son finds himself is to refuse to acknowledge his godhead and rely instead on his *man*hood. The answer to the riddle that brought the Sphinx down and saved the lives of the people is, amazingly, "man." On that basis, I find the reading offered by a number of critics that the Son speaks as God or that God speaks through his Son problematic. This is not the time for a *deus ex machina*.[35] Nevertheless, the Son at this point does reveal his godhead, though not in a manner expected by Satan. He offers instead a superhuman display of patience, endurance, and ultimately of trust, suggested by his last words of the poem (560–1). Rather than asserting his divine authority to defeat Satan or assuming the role of martyr, the Son indicates that he merits his position as Son of God by relying, paradoxically, only on human discourse. Disempowered as much by his own words as by the Son's responses, Satan, suffering from the confusion of tongues, falls like the Sphinx who "Cast herself headlong from th' *Ismenian* steep" (575).

In *A Defence of the People of England* Milton blamed the victimized English nation for its own fall, caused by its failure to resist the king's tyrannical rule. Obsessed with their glossary definitions and with the pompous publication of "laborious trifles," the people turned the Sphinx on themselves:[36] "You had better go and take Martin the cobbler and William the tanner, whom you so scorn, as your companions and guides in darkness; though actually they could teach you much and solve such foolish riddles of yours as: 'Is the people a servant in a democracy, when a king is in a monarchy? Is all of it, or but a part?' Then when they have acted as your Oedipus you should repay them by going to the devil as the Sphinx did; otherwise I can see no end to your foolish riddles" (*Prose* 4:389–90). Misguided by their wandering thoughts, speculative reasoning, and language games, the people became entrapped in their own labyrinths, thereby anticipating Satan's a*maze*ment prior to his fall at the end of the poem. Though Satan's reading of the Son throughout the poem cannot be characterized as naïve, when he finally asks, "What dost thou in this World?" Satan, rather than exhausting the Son's range of choices, indicates that his own perceptions of engagement in this world are limited:

> Since neither wealth, nor honor, arms nor arts,
> Kingdom nor Empire pleases thee, nor aught
> By me propos'd in life contemplative,
> Or active, tended on by glory, or fame,
> What dost thou in this World? (4.368–72)

The temptation is to resort to a particular kind of action, one that very much appealed to the Son in his earlier years and one that Satan here describes as "tended on by glory, or fame" (371), reminiscent of the construction of Babel. Satan's question suggests that the Son is involved in more than just acting out a destined role or countering Satan's arguments. *Paradise Regained* is not primarily a poem about negation or even endurance: it is about the redefinition of political action and intervention in a censored environment, and about creating alternatives where none seem possible.

In his last pamphlet, *Of True Religion*, written in 1673, Milton defended the need for debate as a way of challenging censorship and of developing a multifaceted image of truth. In *Paradise Regained* the verbal contest likewise promises to continue. Satan returns to his crew, which sits consulting, while the "meek" and human Son of God returns, as he entered the scene, "unobserv'd" to "his Mother's house" (4.636–9), having performed the previously "unrecorded" deeds "Above Heroic, though in secret done" (1.15). The real political arena in the end is the self and the discursive exchanges through which expression is achieved; the self, then, is also the base from which the composite interest takes effect.

# Conclusion

In this study of *Paradise Lost* and *Paradise Regained* I have presented a narrative of literary and historical development that resists the model of a "social text" to address the embodied reality of the voice. In the interrelated socio-political, linguistic, and narratological contexts I have examined, voice reconfigures itself as the embodied reality to which subjects in conversation and debate lend their own voices. By extending my investigation to an analysis of Milton's revolutionary conception of history as conversation, I have demonstrated that the view of history as exemplary and challenging to life coincides with and anticipates what will hardly be encountered again for over a century. Milton found precedent for this view in the ancients, but radically transformed and revitalized it. He accomplished this by restoring to our experience of the past the sense of its being constituted by a multitude of voices characterized by dissonances – "brotherly dissimilitudes" (*Prose* 2:555) – working towards a world-transforming counterpoint that is always just about to be achieved, like the song of the "Nativity Ode." Language and history, categories that seem as radically distinct from one another in human experience as they are in critical practice, are brought together for Milton through the mediation of the voice, so that the political interests of the various speakers provide a base for the commonwealth he designs. Most revolutionary thinkers of the seventeenth century locate the origin of legitimacy and power in the people; Milton locates it in the *voices* of the readers in the interpretive community whose conversations he at the same time orchestrates.

## Conclusion

My multivocal, transhistorical approach to Milton's texts is undeniably and self-consciously the product of a late twentieth-century perspective. This approach is also very much informed by the interpretation of "textuality" as existing in a circuit of conversation and connecting and equating canonical and non-canonical literary texts with the texts and voices of contemporary culture and politics, as well as with a range of discursive fields whose boundaries are constantly redrawn. It is a perspective shaped as well by current historical trends: the frustration with the single view, the influence of mass societies, and the desire for the expansion of political and ideological latitudes and for the diffusion particularly of institutional power. This approach has revealed that the seventeenth century, like the twentieth, found institutionality deeply suspect.[1] The case for a multivocal interpretation, then, is not simply that it is time to analyse Milton's texts in these terms because the univocal endeavour has gone on long enough. The case is rather that the injection of concepts such as multiple narrators and genres, open forms, strategic deferrals, and the exchanges between the poetic voices and discourses of the early modern period tells us something about how the poems were circulated to speak to their own time and how they may be recuperated to speak to ours.

# Notes

INTRODUCTION

1 The term "narrator" referred in the seventeenth and eighteenth centuries to a relater, declarer, or speaker of true stories or histories. The earliest examples of the verb "to narrate" (1656) are probably translations of the Spanish *narrar*. "To narrate" comes into English use only after 1750, according to the OED.
2 See Blackburne's account of critical responses to Milton by Restoration and eighteenth-century writers, who admired Milton's poetry while denouncing the political views expressed in his prose (1:135–53).
3 See Blake, *The Marriage of Heaven and Hell* 33–45; Shelley, "On the Devil, and Devils" 91–2; *A Defence of Poetry* 129–30. The Romantics were not the first to address the controversy of Satan's heroism; see, for example, Joseph Addison's criticism of "Mr. *Dryden*'s Reflection, that the Devil was in reality *Milton*'s Hero." Addison goes on to defend *Paradise Lost* as "an Epic, [or a] Narrative Poem" that does not require the kind of hero found especially in the tragedy (44). The critic nevertheless installs Christ in that position. Also see chap. 3, n 6, of this book.
4 Stein maintains that the ghostly presence of the narrative voice is responsible for wielding absolute authority over the characters' speeches and the poem's tone, themes, and structure (*Art of Presence* 7). Various critics who recognize the dramatic quality of the poem regard the poet-narrator as a stage-manager who produces and presents his own drama of inner conflict (Gardner 35). The dramatic role

that the "actor-priest" assumes unifies the whole poem (Rollin 29). Twentieth-century critics who dissociate Milton from the persona he creates include Rollin and also Ferry, who nevertheless affirms the autonomy of the represented voice and its control over the mood and meaning of the poem (49). Ferry argues that Milton creates in place of himself "an objectified voice with a distinct identity, tone, and manner, and the attitudes which the voice expresses are in keeping with that identity" (50). Rollin likewise distinguishes between Milton and the poet-narrator, identifies the latter as a controlling device, and declares his heroism (30).

Mulder refers to Milton's "tentative and faltering search for certitude" (145) and to the cast of characters in the poem who diffuse the narrative point of view. However, his essay is primarily indebted to and does not venture beyond two earlier studies of Milton's "persona," acknowledged by Mulder (n 9) and which I have cited – Ferry's *Milton's Epic Voice* and Riggs's *The Christian Poet*. Moreover, my study differs from Mulder's by locating the persona's struggles within a socio-political context.

5 Swaim discusses the pedagogical procedures of the two speakers and compares the reliance on the Book of Nature by Raphael to Michael's reliance on Scripture. Swaim then contrasts the emphasis on invention, illumination, and analogy in Raphael's narrative to Michael's concern with disposition and judgment and his interest in typology.

6 By *image* – which became increasingly more difficult to distinguish from *voice* as my study developed – I mean a visual representation or simulacrum, either textual or non-textual. Milton uses the term to refer both to the creation of humanity in the likeness or image of God and as well to the creation of images of worship or icons. A reader of the images can be either an idolator or an iconoclast. However, because the act of iconoclasm creates a void that must be filled by new interpretations, icon destruction and creation are inextricably bound. Institutions generally extend their power by arresting the play of meaning and by rejecting or reifying history. The response of a poet-revolutionary like Milton, who regards the world in terms of a text, is to encourage participation in the construction of meaning as well as in those establishments that create meaning. A critical reading of the images and voices of monarchy is an act of dissent and political intervention – a reaction to the monarchical control of culture and history. See Loewenstein, who identifies iconoclasm with a critical reading of the meta-narrative of history (63).

7 T.S. Eliot offers an analysis of some of the fundamental distinctions between the various poetic voices. The first kind of voice is that of the poet talking to himself or to nobody, yet inevitably being overheard.

The second is that of the poet addressing an audience irrespective of size, and this is the dominant voice of epic, though not the only voice (15). The third voice of the poet is heard when he attempts to create a dramatic character in verse. This voice becomes audible through the interaction of two or more characters in the poem.

8 Literary theorists of the 1970s and 1980s have challenged the definitions more explicitly and have also questioned the assumptions about the privileged position and controlling function ascribed to voice by New Critics and phenomenologists in particular. The phenomenological voice is situated within and pervades all discourse, according to Poulet, Croce, and Husserl; it is heard as transcending that discourse, and governs structurality without being governed or becoming subject to internal or external conditions. Writing, then, is a representation of acoustical images of speech or voice – a silent, unmediated, and logocentric meaning lodged in consciousness (Lentricchia 73).

9 I use the term "appropriation" in a literary sense to address the contested issue of the poet's use of narrative voices as "mouthpieces" (Cyr 309) and in a political context to define strategies for achieving political control. See London 4–5.

10 Burke redefines the oppositional relationship between scientific and poetic readings: "The body is an actor; as an actor, it participates in the movements of the mind, posturing correspondingly; in styles of thought and expression we embody these correlations – and the recognition of this is, as you prefer, either 'scientific' or 'poetic'" (*Philosophy* 130). Without glossing over the distinctions between scientific and poetic activity or dismissing the existence of different historical continuities, Burke insists that poetic history be given a status equal to that of extra-poetic history.

11 "To interpret means to react to the text of the world or the world of a text by producing other texts," Eco explains in applying a semiotic approach to the history of "the double metaphor of the world as a text and the text as a world" (23ff).

12 Howard recommends that critics break free from the formalist, humanist, and positivist assumptions that still inhabit them, which include claims to authorship and intentionalism (43). However, the death of the author, which Levin has called "bardicide," and the rejection of authorial intention that liberates the text, have actually left these critics not more but less free (502). Norbrook concludes that since, in the Renaissance, "authorial intention has a substantial and under-acknowledged political element, to ignore the intention is effectively to depoliticize" (8). Without returning to the old historicist conception of intentionalism, critics have reopened discussion of the subject once more; thus Lee Patterson contends that "simply to set

aside these intentions and purposes as unworthy of discussion is effectively to silence dissent" (66).
13 On this critical approach, see Howard 35ff.
14 Fletcher describes the formation, for perhaps the first time in English history, of what we may begin to call public opinion – not a united opinion, but a zone of discussion within the political nation of what the nature of the English state and church should be (99).
15 I analyse various models of history as conversation in chap. 2, part 2.
16 The discursive forms of nationhood in England's political forms and in the language and literature of poetry, law, antiquarian study, overseas travel, theatre, and church were mutually self-constituting, Helgerson demonstrates (11). My book treats the interaction of some of these discourses in investigating Milton's contribution to literary and political debates about the re-establishment of the Commonwealth.
17 "But if Babel is the verbal equivalent to the Fall," Entzminger observes, "Pentecost is the dispensation which counters the curse, converting the degeneration of language to a *felix culpa*" (89).
18 White defines emplotment as a mode of explanation: the act of "providing the 'meaning' of a story by identifying the *kind of story* that has been told" (*Metahistory* 7). The critic or historian is compelled "to emplot the whole set of stories making up his narrative in one comprehensive or *archetypal* story form" (8).
19 Voice and subjectivity developed in the seventeenth century through the recognition of political, cultural, and gender differences in a shared social world in which there was a sense of a being-for-otherness and a variety of perspectives (Bordo 50) that had to be read critically. At the same time, the conditions for identifying these cultural and social differences were themselves challenged. The various arguments of Daniel Rogers, William Secker, Margaret Fell Fox and George Fox, John Heydon, François Poulain de la Barre, and Thomas Goodwin eventually led to the theory that class and gender were culturally constructed rather than biologically given.
20 The regulation and cultivation of the unchecked, even perverse elements of nature, human nature, culture, and society became central concerns for medievalists and humanists alike, who attributed wildness both to moral iniquity and cultural difference. See chap. 5, n 2.
21 Unless we regard them as vain boasts intended to inspire false confidence in his compatriots, Milton's iconoclasm, his patterning of the new commonwealth, and his cry for continued action do little to support the belief that he ultimately resigned himself to accepting a quietist doctrine. Nevertheless, critics are divided on the subject of Milton's activism during the last quarter of his life. In contrast to O.B. Hardison and Fredric Jameson, to name two, who emphasize

Milton's retreat to the life of the imagination after his experience of defeat, Christopher Hill, Christopher Kendrick, Mary Ann Radzinowicz, and Joan Bennett defend Milton's political involvement in the Restoration years. Also see chap. 6, n 1. For an examination of the various contemporary critical readings of Milton's Civil War and Restoration political engagement, see chap. 5 of Rushdy's *The Empty Garden.*

22 Bal distinguishes between the narrator and the focalizer (118). Nevertheless, the act of narration involves elements of perception and subjectivity.

CHAPTER ONE

1 See "The Rebellion" in *Rump: or, An Exact Collection of the Choycest Poems and Songs ... to 1661.* Wilkins attributes the ballad to a "loyalist" author (1:32). Lamont quotes from Wilkins' edition and entitles the ballad "The Blessed Anarchie," also attributing it to an anonymous author (72–4). Thomas Jordan is identified as the ballad's author by Wedgwood (91) and Achinstein (86).

2 See "The Many-Headed Monster" in Hill, *Change* 181–204.

3 The beehive metaphor in Proverbs 6:6–8 was adopted by seventeenth-century royalists from Edward Simmons' *A Loyal Subjects Belief,* Griffith William's *Jura Majestatis,* and Godfrey Goodman's *The Fall of Man* (Milton, *Complete Poems,* Hughes, ed., 886 n 45).

4 Patterson suggests that authors build "*functional* ambiguity" into their texts in response to government censorship (*Censorship* 18). The development of this symbolic, necessarily evasive language becomes, then, an act of contra-censorship. I examine this strategy more extensively in chap. 2.

5 Similar offences had been committed, according to Luther in his *Lectures on Genesis,* by the pope who hypocritically adopted the title of servant to the people, and by kings who usurped God's authority and tyrannized his people. Milton comments on Luther's condemnation of the pope in *An Apology* (*Prose* 1:953).

6 According to Charles Stephanus's *Dictionarium,* cited by Starnes (267), "Nimrod" is a derivative of "marad," the Hebrew term meaning "rebellion."

7 On the received tradition of the Nimrod account, see A. Williams 160–3; Hardin; Schmidt.

8 For his account in *The Purgatorio* 12.34–6, Dante is indebted to Jerome's adaptation of Josephus' history of the building of Babel by Nimrod. However, the poet chooses to depoliticize the story and focus instead on the dispersion of languages caused by Nimrod. In

*The Inferno* he represents Nimrod as a giant, a gibbering beast, and a babbling fool (31.77–81). These descriptions culminate in Dante's commentary on the susceptibility of language to change and decay in *The Paradiso* 26.124–32.

9 Luther and Calvin both associated Nimrod with the fall of Babel, but Luther was more intent on condemning him outright: "he was the first Turk or pope on earth after the Flood" (2:197), and used tyranny to gain for himself a sovereignty to which he had no right, Luther announces in his *Lectures on Genesis*. Calvin, while also denouncing the papacy, which he compares to the Babylonian dispersion in *The Institutes of the Christian Religion*, is somewhat more reluctant to condemn monarchy. "It has not come about by human perversity that the authority over all things on earth is in the hands of kings and other rulers, but by divine providence and holy ordinance," he insists in his defence of the right of kingship (4.20.4a). As such, Calvin qualifies the part Nimrod as the first king plays in the construction of the tower. The tower was a work "not taken in hande by the counsell and will of one man; but ... all conspired together, insomuch that the fault and blame cannot be layde uppon one or a fewe" (*Commentarie* 248). Also see Edmund Spenser's *The Faerie Queene* 4.1.22, and Sir Thomas Browne's *Pseudodoxia Epidemica* 2.7.6. On the relationship of name, honour, and power or renown, see Pedersen 1:247–50.

10 In *Paradise Regained*, Nimrod is replaced by his successor Nebuchadnezzar, who conquered Jerusalem when he rebuilt Babylon – "the wonder of all tongues" (*Poems* 3.280).

11 Butler in "The Republican" accuses the Commonwealth builders of creating a utopian democracy, which he likens to "the Intelligible World, where the Models and Ideas of all Things are, but no Things; and 'twill never go further" (59).

12 The image of the whore is used in a different context by Butler to refer to the commonwealth itself. The Politician is ravished by the whore, who is characterized by her accessibility; the Politician "is wonderfully enamoured of a *Commonwealth* because it is like a common Whore, which every one may have to do with; but cannot abide *Monarchy*, because it is honest and confined to one" (61).

13 See *Prose, A Defence* 4:535–6; *Second Defence* 4:673–5; sonnet to Cromwell.

14 The proposition that authority (and ultimately any achieved identity) "always contains within itself the signs of its own subversion or loss" is made by New Historicists, particularly Greenblatt (*Self-Fashioning* 9).

15 Wilding interprets the passage as an assertion of Milton's radical egalitarian sentiments of 1649, which included justification of the

regicide (248), thereby contemporizing the story of Nimrod. Also see Radzinowicz, "Politics" 213, and Patterson, *Reading* 254–5.

16 Also see *Prose, The Readie and Easie Way* 7:436.

17 Harrington's definition of "the people" did not include the poor. Those who deserved the right to vote were property owners, who were sufficiently well off or free to make politically informed decisions. For Milton's definition of "the people," see *Prose* 3:337–49; Hill, *Milton* (160–2, 168–70). A more inclusive definition of the people is implied in Thomas Rainborough's defence of suffrage: "For really I think that the poorest he that is in England hath a life to live, as the greatest he; and therefore truly, sir, I think it's clear, that every man that is to live under a government ought first by his own consent to put himself under that government; and I do think that the poorest man in England is not at all bound in a strict sense to that government that he hath not had a voice to put himself under" (qtd in Morton 203).

18 I do not propose in this book to engage (re)surfacing debates about Milton's republicanism (one of the primary subjects of critical inquiry at the Fifth International Milton Symposium, Bangor, Wales), which are, incidentally, as much reactions to recent twentieth-century (British) political events as to revisionist readings of seventeenth-century Civil War history (Conrad Russell, J.C.D. Clark, John Morrill, J.C. Davis). See *Milton and Republicanism*, ed. David Armitage. I do, however, maintain throughout this study that Milton's orchestration of voices is informed by discourses of republican politics.

19 In Eva Figes' *The Tree of Knowledge*, a historically penetrating work of fiction about Milton's life told from the viewpoint of the prophetic character Deborah, the narrator criticizes and expresses admiration for her father's political optimism in the face of the Restoration: "I think he was much mocked for publishing a pamphlet at that time, which he did send to the General, in which he put forth a ready and easy way to keep the commonwealth, and stop the monarchy from coming back. Alas, had it been so easy, it should have been accomplished long since, and now it was too late. And yet, sir, though he dreamed still when others long had woken, I find in this a kind of hardiness that makes me love him, though I loved him not when I was at his mercy, and a child" (120).

20 Blackburne presents this anecdote: "It is recorded, that some royalists visiting Milton soon after the Restoration, at his house in Bunhill-Row, had the *humanity* to reproach him with his blindness, as a judgment upon him." In a note, Blackburne includes a response attributed to Milton: 'if you are so ready to apply judgments, how came your royal martyr to lose his head?" (1:136)

21 Milton's earlier attack on Salmasius in *A Defence* becomes ironic in the later years of the Interregnum, when Milton adopts a similar attitude to the people: "You must attack the populace as 'blind and brutish, without skill in ruling, the most fickle of men, the emptiest, the unsteadiest, and most inconstant.' This description best fits yourself" (*Prose* 4:471).

22 Aristotle defined this type of polity as a combination of oligarchy and democracy. The institution of rule by merit, whereby the government is in the hands of a select body of virtuous leaders, transforms the oligarchy into an aristocracy, according to Polybius.

23 Even the radicals' conception of the "people" did not include everyone, but that is not really the point, explains Hanson: "The medieval notion of the populus had been a fiction. The revolutionary idea, despite the fact that it embraced only about half the male population, was an operational principle. This is most apparent in the Levellers' constitutional schemes" (330). Independents, Presbyterians, and Levellers alike failed to include women in the franchise.

24 See, for example, "What it is which constitutes a mixed monarchy," 4.2 of *A Treatise on Monarchy* (Wooton 192–3).

25 The divine meritocracy described by Milton is a monarchy, aristocracy, and democracy according to the definitions provided by Cartwright. Milton's proposed commonwealth, however, divided its power between the aristocracy and the people and had no secular monarch. Monarchy as a form of government no longer fitted the facts of political life in the nation. God, the only legitimate king (*Prose* 7:445), governed both institutions, thereby connecting church and state governments once again. A model for the prospective commonwealth is provided by the meritocracy in heaven: the rhetoric of kingship is used by God, who elevates Christ as the anointed universal king, only once the merit of Christ (3.311) – which is reasserted in book 6.43 – is established. The provision for merit in heaven and in the governments of church and state assumes that the establishments are organic and allow for the advancement of individual members.

Hill addresses the conflict between the poet's republicanism and the royalist imagery used to describe God. God in *Paradise Lost* is at once different from the kings of the earth and precisely like them: in the end he will cease to be a king at all (*Milton* 343–4).

26 *An Apologeticall Narration* looks forward to the transformation of church and state, but is also very much concerned with repairing the damage done by the schismatic label: "*That* proud and insolent title of *Independencie* was affixed unto us, as our claime; the very sound of which conveys to all mens apprehensions the challenge of an exemption of all Churches from all subjection and dependance, or rather a

trumpet of defiance against what ever *Power, Spirituall* or *Civill*; which we doe abhor and detest" (Goodwin 331). The Quaker James Perrot likewise calls for "the *end* of all *distinctions* and *separations* by *Names*," particularly that of "Quaker"; "there are of the People called *Seekers, Baptists, Independents,* and *others* ... with whom I have *more Unity,* than with divers which are *called* by the Name *of Quakers"* (12–13).

## CHAPTER TWO

1 Anderson demonstrates that print-capitalism created a new social dynamic, making it possible "for rapidly growing numbers of people to think about themselves, and to relate themselves to others, in profoundly new ways" (40). Cf Helgerson, who develops the notion of the imagined community further in his discussion of the emergent forms of nationhood that account for changes in the corporate imagination in Tudor and Stuart England.
2 Dante explains, "In this form of speech Adam spoke, and in this form also all his descendants spoke until the building of the tower of Babel, which is by interpretation the tower of confusion; and this form of speech was inherited by the sons of Heber, who, after him, were called Hebrews" (*De Vulgari Eloquentia* 23–4). The Aramaic word balal ("confound") replaces the Hebrew term *Babili*. The displacement of Hebrew, the original language, is also attributed to the confusion of tongues (Leonard 55).
3 Satan refers to the tuneable "Silvan Pipe" in *Paradise Regained* when he flatters the Son by describing his language as one that "glozes" and smooths over all contradiction and the hard ways of truth (1.478–80). Ironically, Satan himself is at once the eloquent orator and the employer of an absolutist terminology, as I explain in chap. 6.
4 Shelley claims in the *Defence* that "no nation or religion can supersede any other without incorporating into itself a portion of that which it supersedes" (127). Burke contends that "The role of the opposition is by no means negligible in the shaping of society. The victory of one 'principle' in history is usually not the vanquishing, but the partial incorporation, of another" (*Counter-Statement* 71).
5 For a commentary on the threatened position of Latin by the vernacular tongues and its decline as a living language, see Anderson, chap. 3; Steadman, *The Hill and the Labyrinth* 90ff; Allen's "Some Theories"; chap. 1 of Davies' *Milton*.
6 The threat of linguistic mutability is discussed by Thomas Green 5ff. Steadman considers the effects of the "epistemological crisis" on language (126–8). He contrasts the philosophies of Agrippa, Montaigne, Pierre Charron, and Jean-Pierre Camus to those of Chillingworth,

Wilkins, Boyle, Locke, and Newton, who attempted to establish a middle ground between uncertainly and absolute certitude. Kahn characterizes the difference between deconstruction and humanist sceptical pragmatism, which ultimately transcends the epistemological dilemma (26). On the attempt to develop a universal language in the seventeenth century, see chap. 2 of Katz. The most helpful introduction to Renaissance linguistics is Charles Barber's *Early Modern English*. On the efforts by writers and philosophers from Renaissance humanists to Royal Society members and religious reformers to repair the ruins of Babel and the abuses of eloquence, see Entzminger 2–15. Also see chap. 2 of Markley's *Fallen Languages* and chap. 2 of another fine study, Achinstein's *Milton and the Revolutionary Reader*.

7 Though writing in an elevated style, Milton did choose to mark the distinction between speech and narrative description in his highly dramatic poem, as Corns explains: "We have, so far as I am aware, no direct evidence in the form of unmediated transcriptions of such dialogue, but it is, of course, absurd to imagine it to have been characterized by the sorts of traits we find in Milton. Modern oral modes of discourse – even quite structured kinds – are sharply differentiated from written modes: we may suppose that similar markers are contemporaneously obtained. Yet in the high incidence of short sentences, we have one formal differentiation, inscribed in the fabric of the poetry, of differences in discourse. Milton is not naturalistically simulating how men and women (and God and his angels, for that matter) speak: but he is formally marking off some parts of his poem as the (poetic, elevated, epic) representation of dialogue" (33).

8 In the *Apology* Sidney describes a hierarchy of kinds that ranges from the pastoral to the heroic, "the best and most accomplished kind of Poetry." Nevertheless, while characterizing the differences between genres and criticizing the mongrel tragicomedy of the English, who "mingle kings and clowns" and "match hornpipes and funerals," Sidney actually advocates (and creates) multigenre works. "If severed they be good, the conjunction cannot be hurtful," he maintains (42). Milton, a master of the *genera mixta*, later challenges the defined status of each genre and the prescribed hierarchical ordering.

9 See Love 188.

10 Christopher Hill explains that Milton was a marked man, fortunate to have escaped with his life; "censors would certainly be alert to anything written by him." He could not put his heresies or public opinions "into his last poems, except perhaps by a subterfuge wherein radically new interpretations are forged out of subtle reformulations of traditional materials" (*Collected Essays* 1:61). Also see *A Nation of Change,* in which Hill identifies early seventeenth-century

writers whose subjection to political censorship was reflected in the silences and paradoxes of their texts (40). Cf G. Hamilton on Milton's art of indirection (242–3) and Davies, *Milton* 59–63.
11 Also see Goldberg's *James I* 55–6.
12 Patterson's criticism of Hill is indebted to Radzinowicz's "The Politics of *Paradise Lost*," in which the author presents a "different picture of the poem than either the picture of political disengagement or of political encryption" by arguing that the poem is paideutic and constitutes a course in political eduction that serves the purposes a political program might play in another kind of work (Radzinowicz 205–6).
13 In *Censorship and Interpretation* Patterson declares that "functional ambiguity frees us somewhat from more radically skeptical conclusions about indeterminacy in language and its consequences for the reader or critic" (18).

   The stylistics of indirection can be explained in the same terms used by Love to account for the restricted circulation of certain texts: "While censorship was an important factor in the continuing vitality of scribal publication, it should not be forgotten that ... [various texts] were designed from the start for circulation within a particular circle or coterie within the governing class and drew their political character from this fact" (191).
14 Nietzsche also identifies the oppressive continuum in *The Will to Power*, where he offers an account of the merciless, cynical past (44). R. Williams in *Keywords* states that *Historie* refers mainly to the past, while *Geschichte* refers to a process that links past, present, and future (119).
15 Heidegger and Gadamer examine the notion of historical understanding as a conversation with the past.
16 Epic is not identified as an archetypal story form by White because it appears as the implicit form of the chronicle (Ricoeur, *Time and Narrative* 1:166).
17 "One's *Patria* is wherever it is well with one" (*Prose* 8:4).
18 Bennett criticizes the Marxist definition of Providence as applied to Milton by arguing that far from using literary means to mirror a doctrine or theoretical construct (named "Providence" by Jameson, conflated with "Predestination" by Kendrick, and roughly paralleled by "historical determinism" in Marxism), Milton uses literary means to capture, work through, and understand the same human experiences – "the ways of God to man" – that have been addressed less effectively by (competing) ideologies (32). After the Restoration, Milton qualifies his view of historical necessity and his belief in the possibility of action in the present, as well as in the predictability of Providence.

Dismissing its common associations with eschatology and teleology, Jameson defines Providence as the enabling presupposition of the historian. Providence is an ideology, governing the form with which historiography endows the events of the past (43). As such, the inscription of the self in the act of recounting historical events is unavoidable; see Bennett 84. At the same time, the identification of Providence with historical inevitability impedes self-expression.
19 Narrative was conventionally associated with kingship (Miner 7, 24 n 9), a subject Milton redefines and holds up to criticism throughout his dramatic epic narrative.
20 Grossman defines narrative as the working out of the story through the integration of the episodes, or as a kind of transitive discourse, a discourse that records a change from one state of affairs to another (25-6).

### CHAPTER THREE

1 Gilbert notes but provides no extended explanation for the inclusion of two Genesis stories in the poem (3.708-22 and 7.224-386), concluding that Uriel's brief account is better fitted to follow than precede Raphael's long narrative and that because the former implies knowledge of the latter, book 7 must have preceded book 3 in Milton's early arrangement of the poem (80). The relationship between the two stories, particularly the different descriptions of God's imposition of order upon chaos, deserves further consideration.
2 Hill also draws a parallel between heavenly and worldly history: "The War in Heaven and the Fall of Man were not different in kind from the historical events recorded in Books XI and XII. Events which occur in time – those revealed or related by Michael, classical legends or modern English history – are examples of the archetypal happenings in heaven and hell before history began" (*Milton* 344).
3 Verse (*versus* in Latin) suggests the idea of regular return; prose (*prosa; provorsa*) suggests a movement forward.
4 The creation of the poetic voice in Renaissance texts is connected with what Bordo has characterized as the "emergence of inwardness." Bordo attributes the "birth of subjectivity" to the recognition of cultural difference and a shared social world in which there is a sense of a "being-for-otherness" and a diversity of perspectives that must be taken into account. At one level, then, we are speaking not so much about the birth of subjectivity as the discovery of subjectivity: "the notion of influence proceeding from within the human being – not supplied by the world 'outside' the perceiver – which is capable of affecting how the world is perceived" (50). See Steadman on

the development of a literary self-consciousness in the sixteenth and seventeenth centuries (131–3).
5 On the soliloquy and monologue as fallen discourses, see Broadbent 80; Lewalski, *Rhetoric* 97–105; Kendrick 158; Grossman 71; Belsey 89. For a recent alternative reading of the soliloquy's purpose as a vehicle for the re-creation of selfhood, see Robertson.
6 The relationship between the poet-narrator and Satan has been extensively examined since Dryden. For some recent studies, see Carey's "Milton's Satan," Harada's "Toward *Paradise Lost*," Gross's "Satan and the Romantic Satan," and Yoon's "Satan's Gift to *Paradise Lost*." I will consider the relationship between the narrative strategies adopted by both characters.
7 Various critics have attempted to account for Milton's decision to begin the poem with Satan's history and then degrade Satan during the course of the narrative. According to Fish, the reader undergoes a moral reorientation (*Surprised* 38–56); Tayler in *Milton's Poetry* claims that the reader experiences a progressive unveiling of an essence there from the beginning (66–8). Kerrigan in *The Sacred Complex* argues that Satan represents the "origin, the original original sin, *Milton* turns away from" (170). For a more recent psychological-biographical study of Milton, see Shawcross' prize-winning *John Milton: The Self and the World*.
8 Comedy is based on a word meaning "revel": Gr. *komoida; komos*, revel.
9 The first edition of *Paradise Lost* was nearly suppressed, according to John Toland:

> I must not forget that we had like to be eternally depriv'd of this treasure by the ignorance or malice of the licenser; who, among other frivolous exceptions, would needs suppress the whole poem for imaginary treason in the following lines.
> – As, when the sun new ris'n
> Looks thro the horizontal misty air
> Shorn of his beams, or from behind the moon
> In dim eclipse, disastrous twilight sheds
> On half the nations, and with fear of change
> Perplexes monarchs. (121)

10 Satan is cast simultaneously as a champion (*certator*) and a dissembler (*hypokrites*) – the meanings of the epithet *agonistes*. Sellin explains that *agonistes* is most accurately defined not as "sport," "performance," or "mockery" but as "dissembling," "assuming a mask," or "playing a part" (157).
11 In *Rabelais and His World* Bakhtin defines the carnival as a second life

or counter-culture that opposes the official or high culture in literature and in public life, adding elements of indeterminacy, incivility, and inversion. Cf. Elle's comment on Satan (Morson 14).
12 Homer, *Iliad* 21.176–7, *Odyssey* 11.205–7; Virgil 6.700–1; Spenser 1.11.41.
13 Schwartz also examines the poet-narrator's "unseeing exhibitionism" (56–7).
14 See Toland 118. Coleridge addresses Milton's persecution during his latter days in the *Biographia Literaria* (1.2.37). Also see chap. 2, n 10 above and Milton, *Complete Poems*, Hughes, ed., 346 n 32–3.
15 Fowell and Palmer examine the history of this office and the ironic relationship between the Master of Revels, the Lord of Misrule, and the Abbot of Unreason (2ff). For a discussion of the transference of censorship duties from Sir Henry Herbert to Sir William D'Avenant and Thomas Killigrew, see G.M.G.'s *The Stage Censor* 56ff.
16 Kerrigan in *Prophetic Milton* lists interpretations of the phrase "an age too late" that include political explanations (78–80). Herodotus describes the Arabian identification of the gods Urania and Bacchus with religious ritual and inspiration (173). For Milton, Bacchus serves as a poetic muse; see, for example, "Elegia" 6, "Familiarum Epistolarum" 25. By calling on the meaning rather than the name of Urania in *Paradise Lost*, the poet, however, distinguishes the pagan Urania from the Christian Muse. Still, his inspired poetic creation continues to be threatened by (pagan) royalist bacchic dissonance and by the possibility that "all be mine, / Not Hers who brings it nightly to my Ear" (9.46–7)
17 Cf Addison's observation that Milton has in fact "finely observed" Aristotle's rule, in so far that in *Paradise Lost* "there is scarce a third part ... which comes from the Poet; the rest is spoken either by *Adam* and *Eve*, or by some Good or Evil Spirit" (46).
18 Kerrigan claims that though the poem begins with a dialogue between two narrative voices, they merge throughout the poem (*Prophetic* 140–2).
19 Minturno labelled the episodes of the classical epic as either "attached" – having some relation to the main fable or simultaneous with the action thereof – or as "outside," that is, comprising events that occur before or after the main action begins or ends. In his criticism of Milton, Samuel Johnson attributes some importance to the two episodes in *Paradise Lost*, that of Raphael and that of Michael: "Both are closely connected with the great action; one was necessary to Adam as a warning, the other as a consolation" (1:175.223). The difference between the narrators of the episodes in classical and Renaissance epics lies in their representation, their importance in relation to

the official voice, and in *Paradise Lost* specifically in the extent of their interaction and the self-consciousness of their narrations.

20 Coleridge refers to Milton to justify his own ventriloquism: "I regard truth as a divine ventriloquist: I care not from whose mouth the sounds are supposed to proceed, if only the words are audible and intelligible. 'Albeit, I must confess to be half in doubt, whether I should bring it forth or no, it being so contrary to the eye of the world, and the world so potent in most men's hearts, that I shall endanger either not to be regarded or not to be understood.' MILTON: *Reason of Church Government*" (BL 1.164).

21 Commenting on the submission required of married women, Mary Astell noted the discrepancy between Milton's anti-royalist politics and his displays of intolerance in the domestic sphere: "how much soever Arbitrary Power may be dislik'd on a Throne, not *Milton* himself wou'd cry up Liberty to poor *Female Slaves*, or plead for the Lawfulness of Resisting a Private Tyranny" (B. Hill 27).

CHAPTER FOUR

Special thanks to Janel Mueller for editing an earlier version of chap. 4, part 1, for my presentation at the Milton Society of America at the 1993 MLA.

1 Pronouncing him guilty of crimes against women by textual deed and by intellectual and cultural association, feminist critics of Milton over the past two decades have interpreted the poet's representation of gender and gendered voices as misogynous. These largely ahistorical studies by Marcia Landy and Christine Froula, among others, have been challenged by Barbara Lewalski, Joan Webber, Mary Nyquist, and Diane McColley. Nevertheless, what Mary Nyquist has identified as the predominantly North American liberal-humanist tradition of academic criticism, particularly on *Paradise Lost*, has neutralized hierarchical and ideological differences in the text ("Genesis" 99). The efforts by Joseph Wittreich, Stevie Davies, and Philip Gallagher to divest the poems of every vestige of antifeminism are, therefore, especially problematic.

2 Milton describes the dual nature of the marital conversation in *Colasterion*: "For this cannot but bee with ease conceav'd, that there is one society of grave freindship, and another amiable and attractive society of conjugal love, besides the deed of procreation, which of it self soon cloies, and is despis'd, unless it bee cherisht and re-incited with a pleasing conversation" (*Prose* 2:740). Like J. Turner, I analyse Milton's politics of "conversation," which Milton uses both as a general term for social intercourse and a legal and colloquial term for

copulation (204–5). But whereas Turner is primarily interested in the representation of sexual and marital conversations and relations in *Paradise Lost* and the received Genesis tradition, I focus more on verbal intercourse in the epics and their extra-literary contexts.

3 For recent studies of Milton's indebtedness to the Ovidian tradition, see DuRocher and also Browning, who examines Sin's narrative in reference to the myth of Circe. In *Mirrour de l'Omme* John Gower personifies Sin as the mother of Death, as does Serafino della Salandra in the episode of Sin, Malice, and Death in his *Adamo caduto*, published in 1647, though Milton may not have been familiar with the latter text. Phineas Fletcher made Sin the daughter of Satan and Eve. For an extensive list of criticism on the account of Milton's Sin in its classical, biblical, and Renaissance contexts, see Browning 155 n 4.

4 Milton is indebted to Echidna in Hesiod's *Theogony* 294–306 and to portraits of other similar hybrids. See A.C. Hamilton 253. In his edition of Spenser, Roche explains that the books and pamphlets represent theological treatises that debate the nature of the one true church, a theological controversy that locates the debaters – whom would Milton identify as infernal pamphleteers (*Prose* 7:452) – in Errour's den (1.1.20–1 n 206). Also see Milton's reference to the "new-vomited Paganisme" (*Prose* 1:520).

On the significance of the frogs, see Wisdom 19:10, Exodus 8:5–14, and Revelation 16:13.

5 See Stevens, *Imagination*, 120–1. Also see Gregerson's examination of the Satan-Sin-Death account in which she identifies linguistic confusion with the themes of imperialism and family romance (chap. 6).

6 *Chora* is derived from the Greek word for enclosed space or womb, defined by Plato in the *Timaeus* as "an invisible and formless being which receives all things and in some mysterious way partakes of the intelligible, and is most incomprehensible," as Roudiez states in his introduction to Julia Kristeva (6). Kristeva associates the chora with the semiotic, with ceaseless heterogeneity, and the disruptive dimension of language. For Milton, however, the creator must enter the symbolic order in which the *chora* is repressed. In this context the offspring of Sin's womb is associated with contradiction, meaninglessness, and perversion, and is contrasted with the poetic progeny of the poet-narrator (1.19–23) and the human creations of Eve. On Sin's violation of natural language, see Leonard 166–9.

On the multiple significances of the "womb" for Milton and the connection between "womb" and "mouth," see Adams 168–89. *Alvus* refers in Ovid both to belly and womb (Gregerson 207, 208–9). For an account of the Renaissance association of the womb with chaos, see Maclean, chap. 3. Burton explains that monstrous births, "moles, warts, scars, harelips, monsters," are produced "by force of a depraved phantasy" in the mother (1.2.3.2). In his list of the "Causes of Monsters" Paré offers both physiological and moral explanations for the births of deformed creatures. On ominous and monstrous births see Mack's "Prophets," Park and Daston in Spufford, and Bakhtin, *Rabelais* 329–31.

7 One cause of prodigious births, according to Paré, was the parents' intense gaze upon or imagining of monstrous things (40). In Satan's case, the devil gazes upon his own monstrous form and in turn conceives a monster, Sin.

8 "Milton associates custom with evil, and describes the relationship between the two in a tautological statement: "Custome [is] but a meer face, as Echo is a meere voice ... [who] accorporat[es] her selfe with error ... Error supports Custome, Custome count'nances Error" (*Prose* 2:223).

9 Written in defiance of government censorship, royalist closet dramas like *The Famous Tragedie of King Charles I*, in which Cromwell commits adultery with Lambert's wife on the night of the regicide, satirize the sexual rapacity of parliamentarians. See especially Lois Potter's *Secret Rites*. On female parliament political dialogues, see Potter's *"Mistress Parliament"* and Patton's "Women's activism." Also see Higgins for a list of satires of female parliaments and mock petitions (209–10, n 213–15). For a select list of Tudor and early Stuart satires on women, see the *Cambridge Bibliography of English Literature* 1:716–17.

10 Threatened by social and political disorder, men often exaggerated female unruliness; see N. Davis. By presenting women as unstable, men also had an opportunity to engage in linguistic game-playing and to create imaginative flights or mock social or political scenes, as evidenced in the pamphlet literature, including the ballad I quote in chap. 1. On the effeminate tyrant and on the anxiety about the fixity of the male self in political dramatic texts of the period, see Bushnell 20ff.

11 For a Marxist reading of the sentimentalization of the private sphere, see Nyquist, "Gynesis" 194; also see Van Den Berg, who explains that the mother was idealized as the sustaining alternative to the indifference and impersonality of emergent capitalism and the grasping anarchic individualism it fostered (358–9).

12 Silverman 78.

13 I am indebted to Nyquist's use of the phrase in "Genesis" 119ff.

14 Schwartz 18. Also see Victor Turner 97 and Bevington 3.

15 Lewalski's 1974 "Milton on Women – Yet Once More" anticipates McColley's argument about Eve in "Eve and the Arts of Eden" in so far as both critics present a largely sympathetic portrait of Eve. In *Milton's Eve*, for example, McColley claims that she intends to establish

a "regenerative reading" of Eve's role, that is, to demonstrate that Eve is "a pattern and composition of active goodness and a speaking picture of the recreative power of poetry itself" (4). My arguments about Eve's relationship to Sin, her construction of a lyrical voice and narrative, and her inferior creativity, along with my discussion of the politics of conversation and the development of a gendered subjectivity throughout chap. 4, complement and are indebted to the criticism of Mary Nyquist more than that of McColley and Lewalski.

16 On the Renaissance and early modern uses of trope of the birth of voice and poetry examined in interrelated literary, cultural, and feminist contexts, see Harvey's fine study, especially chap. 3.

In his psychological biographical study of Milton, Shawcross identifies the repression of the mother figure as one of the significant events in the psychic development of the poet: "The image of Orpheus and the inability of his mother Calliope, Muse of epic poetry, to save him are central to our understanding of Milton's newly conceived future and his perseverance, his rejection of Calliope as his Muse in *Paradise Lost*, and his hope and faith in himself" (188–9). The later "sublimation of demands of the Logos," the liberation from the father, involves, however, an embrace of the female principle (*John Milton* 189–90). Also see Kerrigan, *Sacred* 179–80.

17 Milton privileges the Yawistic over the Priestly Genesis creation story in Adam's account. In the Priestly story the two sexes come into the world simultaneously and equally, while in the former, the second biblical account, woman, less fully human than man, is described as the final creation. See Alter 141–6; Nyquist, "Gynesis" 151ff.

18 Nyquist in "Gynesis" provides an illuminating discussion on the recounting of Eve's story prior to Adam's in the poem (192ff).

19 Eagleton comments on the inappropriateness of the metaphor by asserting that the woman is not the whore of history, notwithstanding Benjamin's own fantasy, but in fact the exact image of the oppressed and the ultimate image of violation. The plight, particularly of the working-class woman, is evidenced in childbirth and child-rearing (*Benjamin* 47).

20 The relationship between Father and Son in various ways complements that between Adam and Eve. As I will suggest in chap. 6, the Son's voice and displays of unsung heroism can be characterized as feminine in so far as Milton displaces a masculine classical heroism for a feminized Christian resistance in the Restoration years. In their psychological studies of Milton, both Kerrigan and Shawcross discuss the redemptive female action of the Son, whom they compare with Eve (Kerrigan, *Sacred* 186–7; Shawcross, *Milton* 190–1). As I have

argued in this chapter, however, Milton celebrates female virtues only in so far as he can appropriate them for his male characters.

CHAPTER FIVE

1 Hill, *World Turned* 143-50, *Milton,* chap. 28; for Marvell, see "The Nymph Complaining," "An Horation Ode" 25-48, *Upon Appleton House* 321-8. See Waller's "A Panegyric to My Lord Protector: Of the Present Greatness, and Joint Interest of His Highness, and this Nation," in which the poet identifies England under Cromwell as a demi-Eden. For a similar theme, see Marvell's "First Anniversary of the Government under O.C."
2 See Stallybrass on the representation of the enclosed female body as a paradise, a symbolic map of "civilized" and colonized terrain (129-33). On the association of the natural, wild landscape with women, "the most unsettling segment of the mysterious Wild" (Roberts 23), see chap. 1 of *The Shakespearean Wild*.
3 On the interpretation of "increase and multiply" to justify female subordination, see J. Turner 118-19.
4 Augustine in *The City of God* identified Nimrod not as "a mighty hunter before the Lord" but rather as "a mighty hunter against the Lord" (2:112). As the original hunter, "deceiver, oppressor, and destroyer of the animals of the earth" (112-13), Nimrod perverted not only the natural order but also social order. The wildman lives on the margins or outside of the civil community. He is associated both with the wilderness or desert he inhabits and with the wildness he internalizes, and is himself "unnatural," even monstrous, in appearance. The rebel is responsible for the perversion of language – the confusion of tongues, as I discussed in chap. 2, has traditionally been interpreted as a cause and manifestation of barbarism. The contagion spreads, and conveniently the myth of the wild man provides an explanation for the existence of uncivilized peoples. According to Augustine, barbarous peoples were descendants of two other Old Testament rebels – Noah's sons, Ham and Japheth: "it ought not to seem absurd to us, that as in individual races there are monstrous births, so in the whole race there are monstrous races" (118). The regulation and cultivation of the unchecked, even perverse elements of nature, human nature, culture, and society became a central concern for medievalists and humanists alike, who attributed wildness both to moral iniquity and cultural difference. The relationship of wildness, incivility, and social and political unruliness is emphasized by Milton in the *Paradise Lost* accounts of Satan and Nimrod and of

humanity's fallen state. The best account of the myth of the wild man, destroyer of nature and of social and civil order, is Bernheimer's *Wild Men in the Middle Ages*.

5 Commenting on his relationship with the "great elder writers," who include Milton, Coleridge describes how he and his contemporaries carry on their work: "to us there remain only quiet duties, the constant care, the gradual improvement, the cautious unhazardous labours of the industrious though contented gardener – to prune, to strengthen, to engraft, and one by one to remove from its leaves and fresh shoots the slug and the caterpillar" (*The Friend*, no.4 [7 Sept. 1809]; qtd in Wittreich, *Romantics on Milton* 215).

6 Nor can protectionism be absolutely denied. To do so would allow no means of determining or correcting cultural types. This kind of liberalism, originating from the liberal-democratic philosophy that had its roots in the seventeenth century, cannot accommodate systematic relationships. It separates domains of experience and the private and public realms. It posits, furthermore – particularly in contemporary times – an adversarial and subversive relationship to nature. For Milton, the abuse of nature was represented by the kind of exorbitance of which Raphael warns Adam and Eve (7.126–30) and that is apparent in the descriptions of Comus.

7 My interpretation of pre- and postlapsarian gender relations emphasizes the hierarchical relationship between Adam and Eve more than McColley's does, particularly in such statements as: "If paradisal consciousness is not precisely egalitarian, but appreciates differences without pride or envy, neither is it in practice patriarchal" (*Gust* 208); "Milton is not always egalitarian, but he always questions stereotypes and false hierarchies" (212).

8 On the representation of paradise from the classical to the Christian tradition, see Giamatti. For Renaissance commentaries on paradise, see A. Williams. On the symbolic landscape, with reference to Milton's garden – his *locus amoenus* – and its relationship to its nearest literary analogues, see Lewalski, *Rhetoric*, chap. 7.

9 Milton, *Poems of John Milton*, Carey and Fowler, eds., 868 n 9.204; Nyquist, "Reading the Fall" 210.

10 Evans argues that *Paradise Lost* is a poem about empire in which Satan, Raphael, Adam, and Michael are featured as colonists in a "colonial drama" (232). I would add that the primary imperial voice is that of the poet-narrator.

11 See Fresch 83–90.

12 See J. Turner 108–13. Sowernam also attributes the fall to both Adam and Eve (224).

13 A *barbaros* was for the Greeks anyone who did not speak Greek – one who babbled. The babbler's human potential remained unrealized, thus making him unfit for participation in the life of the political community. The barbarous language of Adam and Eve relegates them to the wilderness of the New World (9.1099–118). Also see Greenblatt, "Learning to Curse: Aspects of Linguistic Colonialism in the Sixteenth Century" and *Learning to Curse: Essays in Early Modern Culture*. The wilderness of the postlapsarian world must be dissociated from the desert in which the few just men are exiled after the Fall, as I discuss in 5.2. On the isolation of the sinner from the Israelite community and the erasure of the transgressor's name from the Book of Life, see Pedersen 2:450–2. Also see PL 1.362–3 in reference to the fallen angels and the nameless Nimrod.

14 In the *Antiquities* Josephus describes Adam's reluctance in receiving God after the Fall. When God inquires why he "that before delighted in that conversation" now avoids him, the ashamed Adam remains mute. "Thy silence is not the sign of virtue, but of thy evil conscience," God judges (16). In response, Adam blames Eve, who in turn accuses the serpent. The narrator's own description of the "mutual accusation" of the couple after the Fall (9.1187) as "fruitless" suggests that a conversation that gets out of hand is as counterproductive as one that is silenced or censored. After the Son's declaration of the sentence, the narrative gives way to the voices of Sin and Death (PL 10.235–71).

Sowernam in the seventeenth century offers a feminist interpretation of the incident: Adam compounds his original sin (224) by arguing with God and attacking the woman; his accusation of God and Eve is "fruitless," as is Eve's blaming of the serpent (162).

15 The linguistic assimilation and colonization of a new environment were achieved through the adaption of terms from the colonizer's language and the semantic adjustment of those terms to cover the new phenomena at hand (Tuttle 597). The invention of botanical terms, which allowed the colonialists to distinguish the benign from the lethal, was a prerequisite for survival, but in general the naming of nature was the means of colonizing the New World for economics and conversion.

16 This discussion of the feminization and infernalization of the tree is developed in "Banyan Leaves" 222–4. Also see Stevens' "Leviticus" and Gregerson 217–30.

17 For Milton's scandalous reputation among his contemporaries as an Independent and "Divorcer," also see *Anarchia Anglicana*, in which Walker characterizes the author of *The Tenure of Kings and Magistrates*

as "a Libertine that thinketh his Wife a Manacle, and his very Garters to be Shackles and Fetters to him" (199); the anonymous *The Character of the Rump* mocks the poet-revolutionary who "would shake off his Governours as he doth his Wives, foure in a Fourtnight" (A2v-3r); G.S.'s *The Dignity of Kingship Asserted* accuses Milton of having thrown aside his wife and embracing atheism (H8r). Also see Haller, ed., *Tracts on Liberty* 1:128–39.

18  See Georgia Christopher for corresponding epiphanic moment in the *Aeneid* (172).

19  Criticism directed at books 11 and 12 is considerable since the time of Addison, who faults Milton for the shift from the visions of book 11 to the plain style of book 12 (144). Waddington provides a bibliography of critical studies of the final books (9 n 3). Also see Loewenstein 177 n 3; Entzminger 73; Grossman chap. 8. I defend books 11 and 12 in my analysis of their presentation of a double-voiced and revolutionary narrative of history.

20  Though many Catholic as well as Protestant writers assumed the destruction of Eden, Protestants were ready to assail the views of those writers – Sixtus of Siena, Cardinal Bellarmme, Leonardus Lessius, and Marius of Cologne – who still maintained its existence and its occupation by Enoch and Elijah as examples of popish error (Duncan 190–3).

21  See Loewenstein, who examines Milton's conflict between a tragic vision and a typological interpretation of history with implications of promise (95–125).

22  However, *Paradise Regained* takes for its subject the heroism of Christ, which I will examine in the next chapter.

23  In "'John, John, I blush for thee!'" Wittreich, who declares that Milton speaks with various voices and composes a poem that accommodates multiple discourses – patriarchal, misogynous, and feminist (22) – develops a largely sympathetic portrait of a prophetic Eve in books 11 and 12. Comparing Adam's discursive with Eve's intuitive thinking, Wittreich explains that Adam's visions are mediated by Michael while Eve's come directly from God and thus require no correction or supplement (37–40). I would emphasize, however, that Eve remains excluded from the main conversation in the final books. Moreover, despite John Smith's suggestion in *Of Prophecy* that "the representation of Divine things by some Sensible images or some Narrative voice" is included in dreams and visions (182), Milton associates the dream with irrationality and even amorality (though not with unreality) at the beginning of book 5. Wittreich's claim that Adam and Eve at the end of the poem submit mutually "to *their* manifest destiny" (38) disregards the hierarchical relationship between the two characters that is emphasized throughout the poem

and even in Eve's closing sonnet, the five final lines of which refer three times to her inferior status and fallen condition (12.619–23).

CHAPTER SIX

1 By "political" I do not mean that the poem promotes active engagement in state affairs but rather that, as a multivocal text, it interpretively and theoretically resists absolutism while also redefining the oppositional relationship between individual and collective concerns. See Rushdy (345–437). Critics making a case for the apolitical content of *Paradise Regained* include Milner, Rapaport, Jameson, and Wilding. Shawcross claims in *Paradise Regained: Worthy T'Have Not Remain'd So Long Unsung* that *Paradise Regained* has not been read as a political poem except by Arnold Stein (116). See Stein's *Heroic Knowledge*. Shawcross himself provides a political and dramatic interpretation of the poem; he reminds us that 75.5 per cent of the verses are full lines of speech (37). Also see Fish on the dramatic quality of the poem in "The Temptation to Action in Milton's Poetry." For a discussion of *Paradise Regained* as a political text, see Hill in *Milton*, Bennett, and Quint.

2 As Campanella remarked in the *Poetica* about Tasso, "the true prophet is one who not only says future things, but who scolds princes for their wickedness and cowardice and peoples for their ignorance, for sedition, and for bad behaviour" (1068). For Milton, prophecy is political, multivocal, and historically engaged. In the same year that *Eikonoklastes* was published, Eleanor Douglas prophesied the breaking of Charles/Belshazzar's image (A4r), which signalled the liberation and redemption of the nation. The iconoclasm paradoxically contributed, however, to a renewed idolatry after the regicide: the creation of images of monarchy that celebrated martyrdom. The composition of *Paradise Lost* and *Paradise Regained* was, I suggest, a response to royalists' celebration of monarchy and martyrdom and to their reading of the Restoration as the fulfilment of English history. Also see chap. 6, "A Nation of Prophets," in Hill's *The World Turned*.

3 Fish claims that what defeats Satan finally is "the Son's inability or unwillingness (they amount to the same thing) to recognize the fact that there is a plot at all" ("Things and Actions Indifferent" 166).

4 Prophecy offered a means of empowerment, particularly for the seventeenth-century English radicals, who created origins and genealogies for themselves and often made claims to inspiration. Prophecy moves history out of the control of the dominant regime by challenging both its closure and the subject of the historical account itself. In

*Paradise Regained*, the Son, the fishermen, and Mary, as well as Simeon and Anna, provide various different interpretations of history and prophecy. The language used by the Son and by the secondary characters in their oral histories is necessarily inventive and paradoxical. The oral histories have an oracular reach or are functionally ambiguous; they may include, but not necessarily so, references to specific events of the future.

5 Collins 159. Also see Wolfe 182–3.
6 Confidence in the word of the king was a major concern for parliamentarians: "The distrust of the few at the helm is not to be smoothed away. No one has so much eloquence as to persuade them to show confidence" (Gardiner 1:81).
7 The regicide was characterized as a second crucifixion by writers including Abraham Cowley, Bishop Henry King, and Clarendon. Wedgwood claims that "Many, if not most, thinking men then in England felt the earth shake under them when a king was executed on a public scaffold" (102). While many of the royalists' poems and ballads celebrating the king's reign had to be circulated in manuscript because censorship by Parliament had restricted printing, royalists managed to appropriate the historic event. On the day of the execution advance copies of *Eikon Basilike* were already circulating. The book, probably written by John Gauden, Bishop of Worcester, comprised what were claimed to be Charles I's reflections on his rule. Within about six weeks, twenty editions were produced; by 1650 the number reached thirty-six.
8 Milton also gathers suppport for his iconoclastic argument by paganizing the speaker who possesses the negative voice. Royalists had branded the revolutionaries "barbarians" and compared them to the Huns and Saracens who threatened the Christian empire. The revolutionaries in turn labelled the king the great oppressive Turk. In *Eikonoklastes* Milton criticizes Charles for "fettering" the people with a "presumptuous negative voice, tyrannical to the Parlament, but much more tyrannical to the Church of God" (*Prose* 3:492; also see 3:498), thus conferring on them no privilege "above what the *Turks, Jewes,* and *Mores* enjoy under the Turkish Monarchy" (3:574). Milton appropriates images of barbarism to describe further the current enslavement of the people who enjoy as much political freedom as "Turkish Vassals enjoy ... under *Mahomet* and the Grand Signor." The Turk represented an imperialist and autocratic government in which absolute rule by the one begot servile acquiescence in the many (Davies, *Images of Kingship* 51–5).
9 Georgia Christopher states that the Son's self-denying language is indicative of his later surrender of life (209).

10 The poem is also indebted to, yet significantly deviates from, the Renaissance humanist tradition of conduct books written to fashion gentlemen and instruct and socialize the courtier, aristocrat, and prince. Such texts included *The Prince, The Mirror for Magistrates, The Book of the Governor,* and *The Book of the Courtier.*

11 The Son's humanity has received much critical attention, particularly (and predictably) from Bennett 176, Hill, *Milton* 419, and Milner 168–9. Also see Samuel.

12 Fish lists a series of adverbs and adjectives that indicate that the Son is unmoved by Satan's offers: "unalter'd," "temperately," "patiently," "calmly," "Unmov'd," "unmov'd," "with disdain," "sagely," and "In brief" ("Things and Actions" 166).

13 Sloane argues that *Paradise Regained* has no sense of opposition or debate because "Jesus refuses to debate. His mode of thought and the narrator's are an escape from and an alternative to controversy" (230). Cf Rushdy, who responds convincingly that the Son combines intuitive and suprarational thought with "contraversal discourse" wrought out of debate (252–3).

14 The Act of Uniformity, which required all in ecclesiastical office to use *The Book of Common Prayer,* silenced Puritan ministers and nonconformists on St Bartholemew's Day, 24 August 1662. The Corporation Act and the Conventicle Act of 1670, "An Act to Prevent and Suppress Seditious Conventicles," sought to detain those contemplating revolution. See Cragg. Kendrick suggests that poetry served Milton as a libidinal reservoir into which political desires could be deposited when the poet was silenced in the Restoration (90–1).

15 A second, though brief soliloquy spoken by the Son is found in 2.245–59.

16 The fishermen are guilty of incarnating history, as Adam had mistakenly done (*PL* 12.384–5) and Satan persists in doing: "Duty to free / Thy Country from her Heathen servitude; / So shalt thou best fullfil, best verify / The Prophets old" (3.175–8). But unlike Adam and Satan, who literalizes prophecy, the fishermen are prepared to wait (49) and manage to derive hope from the idea of historical progress and possibility (49–57).

17 Unlike the primary speaker of *Paradise Lost,* the poet-narrator of *Paradise Regained* remains relatively unobtrusive throughout the poem. Critics have associated the poet-narrator's unobtrusiveness with the Son's own "meditative lesson in self-removal" (Cunningham 217). Fish and Mustazza both directly connect silence with obedience and self-denial (Fish, "Inaction and Silence" 38; Mustazza 214). However, the Son and the poet-narrator are not silent in the poem. The poet-narrator invokes the Muse out of fear of muteness:

"By proof th' undoubted Son of God, inspire, / As thou art wont, my prompted Song, else mute" (1.11–12). Satan himself is not only rendered mute at various times throughout the poem but continually attempts to end the dialogue.

18 A *barbaros* was for the Greeks anyone who did not speak Greek and thus was labelled unfit for the political community, as I discuss in the previous chapter.

19 Shoaf 2.

20 In the poem, the suggestion of combat is presented through patterned verbal duels in which a variety of figures of repetition are employed. The most common include *ploce* (repetition of the same word with some words interspersed) and *traductio* (repetition of the same root word in different grammatical forms). See Lewalski, *Brief Epic* (349). Rhetorical figures are as prominent in the language of the Son as in that of Satan. In the speeches of the Son they serve an iconoclastic function. The Son, for example, follows Satan's repeated use in his speech of "glory" and "inglorious" by incorporating in his answer repeated uses of "glory" and "glorious" (3.44–120).

21 Marxist critics in particular have had a difficult time explaining the seemingly undemocratic announcements by the Son. Christopher Hill jumps to Milton's defence: "Such words fit John Milton in post-revolutionary England better than they fit the Jesus of the gospels ... The violence of the outburst is also evidence of disillusion – with Parliaments which had failed in the forties, fifties and sixties, especially in respect of religious toleration, and with the electorate which had brought back kings, bishops and intolerance" (*Milton* 426). By the time of the Restoration, when the confusion caused by the reconstruction of the tower of Babel had spread extensively, Milton's enthusiasm for multivocality, represented especially in his Areopagitican arguments, had waned considerably (*Prose* 7:365–6).

22 The poet-narrator often introduces Satan's speeches by drawing attention to his use of language: 1.319–20, 1.465–67, 2.115–20, 3.5–6, 3.265–6. While Satan's words smooth over any sense of tension or contradiction between the speakers, the narrator signals Satan's entries in the debates by drawing attention to the divorce of meaning from words. The attention given to the language rather than to the content of Satan's speeches makes language itself the content. None of the Son's answers is introduced in a like manner. The contrast distinguishes Satan's speeches from the Son's and suggests that the significance of the Son's words extends beyond their immediate status as words to speech-acts.

23 Reeve 176.

24 In *Of Reformation* Milton announces: "*most Christian People* at that day

when thou the Eternall and shortly-expected King shalt open the Clouds to judge the severall Kingdomes of the World, and distributing *Nationall Honours* and *Rewards* to Religious and just *Commonwealths*, shalt put an end to all Earthly *Tyrannies*, proclaiming thy universal and milde *Monarchy* through Heaven and Earth" (*Prose* 1:616).

25 Despite the Son's repudiation of classical ideals, this passage (*PR* 4.146–53) shows how he adapts the visionary language of the Book of Daniel to the form of a classical simile in which he manages a pair of linked similes. The Old Testament tree has classical counterparts in Homer and Virgil, which the Son defamiliarizes but does not reject (Forsyth 207–11).

26 Lewalski, *Milton's Brief Epic* 278; Weber, *Wedges and Wings* 33.

27 For further significances of the stone see Lewalski, *Milton's Brief Epic* 278–80.

28 See Sandler 181; Davies, *Images of Kingship* 53–4. Milton also claimed that Charles's plagiarism of Sidney's Pamela prayer confirmed his heathenness (*Prose* 3:362–3).

29 This is not to suggest that right-wing Puritanism was not in various ways equally as resistant to multifaceted truths as Charles's philosophy and politics were.

30 Like Nimrod, the first postlapsarian hunter, Nebuchadnezzar is portrayed as a wild man in medieval and Renaissance iconography. The rebel, from which the name Nimrod is derived, is responsible for the perversion of language; the confusion of tongues has traditionally been interpreted as a cause and sign of barbarism. See Bernheimer's description of Nebuchadnezzar's insanity and wildness (12–13).

31 Hill also speaks for the voices by suggesting that they represent royalist propaganda (*Milton* 419).

32 *Poems of John Milton*, Carey and Fowler, eds., 1161–3; also see Weber, *Wedges and Wings* 62–3, and Shawcross, *Paradise Regained: Worthy T'Have Not Remain'd* 89–91.

33 The pinnacle scene has been interpreted in numerous ways. Satan's fall from the temple represents a final spiritual defeat corresponding to Satan's original fall; it is then a test of identity (Allen, *Harmonious Vision* 115; Lewalski, *Brief Epic* 315–16), and a moral trial according to Elizabeth Pope 80–3. Weber argues that the scene is both a test of identity and morals, and that the fall indicates that Satan's values are contrary to the nature of the universe and to the Son's temperance, justice, and holiness (*Wedges and Wings* 107–8). Carey and Fowler claim in reference to 4.538–40 that "Satan's words suggest that the pinnacle episode is to be an attempt to discover Christ's identity, not a temptation to vainglory or presumption" (1161). The temptation cannot, however, be entirely characterized according to Satan's final

words. Satan in fact does presume to test the obedience as well as the identity of the Son by offering him no alternative to casting himself off the pinnacle. Without denying the validity of those previously suggested, I am offering a reading of the passage as a recast account of the fall of Babel.

34 Laskowsky 11–13.
35 Frye argues that the Son's successful standing on the pinnacle means "that his human will has been taken over by the omnipotent divine will at the necessary point" ("The Typology of *Paradise Regained*" 227). My reading of the scene also differs from that of Lieb, who claims that while Oedipus's answer to the Sphinx is "man," the Son's is necessarily "God" (107).
36 Milton uses the Sphinx elsewhere to represent the monarchists (*Prose* 3:413), and also to convey the elusiveness of identity, as we find in *A Second Defence*, where Milton mocks his anonymous opponent, More, for not identifying himself on the title page of *Clamor* (*Prose* 4:592).

CONCLUSION

1 The seventeenth-century theological equivalent would be the church securely installed as the decisive institution. Right-wing Puritanism, nascently absolutist, is also the enemy. The gathered church proposes in response a democracy of reading, a multivocal communal text in which the truth is immanent and always provisional rather than a transcendental blueprint that history struggles to inscribe in itself.

# Works Cited

**PRIMARY SOURCES**

Addison, Joseph. *Criticism on Milton's Paradise Lost.* Ed. Edward Arber. London 1868.
Augustine, Bishop of Hippo. *The City of God. Works.* Trans. Marcus Dods. 15 vols. Edinburgh 1934. Vol. 2.
Bacon, Francis. *The Works of Francis Bacon.* Ed. James Spedding et al. 5 vols. London 1858–61; rpr Stuttgart: Frommann-Holzboog 1963.
*Be Merry and Wise ... shewing the Cause ... of our present Distempers.* London 1659.
Blackburne, Francis, comp. *Memoirs of Thomas Hollis, Esq.* 2 vols. London: Printed by J. Nichols 1780.
Blake, William. *The Marriage of Heaven and Hell.* In *The Complete Poetry and Prose of William Blake.* Ed. David Erdman. Berkeley: U of California P 1982.
Browne, Sir Thomas. *The Works of Sir Thomas Browne.* Ed. Geoffrey Keynes. 4 vols. London: Faber & Faber 1964. Vol. 2.
Burton, Robert. *The Anatomy of Melancholy.* Ed. Floyd Dell and Paul Jordan-Smith. London: Routledge 1931.
Butler, Samuel. *Characters.* Ed. Charles W. Daves. Cleveland: P of Case Western Reserve U 1970.
Calvin, Jean. *A Commentarie ... Upon Genesis.* Trans. Thomas Tymme. London 1578.
–. *Calvin: Institutes of the Christian Religion.* Ed. John T. McNeill. Trans. Ford Lewis Battles. 2 vols. Philadelphia: The Westminister P 1960. Vol. 2.
–. *Sermon on Pentecost. John Calvin: Selections from His Writings.* Ed. John Dillenberger. Garden City, NY: Anchor Books 1971.

Campanella, Tommaso. *Poetica: A History of Literary Criticism in the Italian Renaissance*. Trans. Bernard Weinberg. 2 vols. Chicago: U of Chicago P 1963. Vol. 2.

*The Character of the Rump*. London 1660.

Clarke, John. *An Essay Upon Study. Wherein Directions are given ... in all the several Parts of Learning*. London: Printed for Arthur Bettesworth 1731.

Cleveland, John. *The Poems of John Cleveland*. Ed. Brian Morris and Eleanor Withington. Oxford: Clarendon 1967.

Coleridge, Samuel T. *Biographia Literaria*. Ed. James Engell and W.J. Bate. Princeton: Princeton UP 1983.

–. *Table Talk*, 12 May 1830. In *The Romantics on Milton: Formal Essays and Critical Asides*. Ed. Joseph Anthony Wittreich. Cleveland: P of Case Western Reserve U 1970.

*Craftie Cromwell: or, Oliver ordering our New State. A Tragi-Comedie. Wherein is discovered the Trayterous under-takings and proceedings of the said NOL, and his Levelling Crew*. Mercurius Melancholicus. London 1648.

Dante, Alighieri. *De vulgari eloquentia*. Trans. A.G. Ferrers Howell. London: The Rebel P 1973.

–. *The Divine Comedy*. Trans. John Ciardi. New York: Norton 1977.

Derrida, Jacques, and Christie V. MacDonald. "Choreographies." Interview. *Diacritics* 12, 2 (1982): 66–76.

Douglas, Lady Eleanor Audeley. *Strange and Wonderfull Prophesies ... and other wonderfull Predictions*. London: Printed for Robert Ibbitson 1649.

Dryden, John. *Essay on Satire*. *The Works of John Dryden*. Ed. Walter Scott. 18 vols. London: James Ballantyne 1808. Vol. 13.

Du Bartas, Guillaume de Saluste. *The Divine Weeks & Works of Guillaume de Saluste Sieur Du Bartas*. Trans. Joshuah Sylvester, ed. Susan Snyder. 2 vols. Oxford: Clarendon 1979. Vol. 1.

Edwards, Thomas. *Gangraena, or, A Catalogue ... of the errours, heresies ... of the ... sectaries of this time ... together with ... corollaries from all the fore-named premisses*. London: Printed for Ralph Smith 1646.

*Eikon Basilike: The Portraiture of His Sacred Majesty in His Solitudes and Sufferings*. Ed. Philip Knachel. Publ. for The Folger Shakespeare Library. Ithaca: Cornell UP 1966.

Eliot, T.S. "Little Gidding." *The Complete Poems and Plays 1909–1950*. New York: Harcourt, Brace & World 1962.

–. *The Three Voices of Poetry*. London: Cambridge UP 1953.

Elyot, Sir Thomas. *The Book named The Governor*. Ed. S.E. Lehmberg. London: Dent 1962.

Erasmus, Desiderius. *The Education of a Christian Prince*. Trans. Neil M. Cheshire and Michael J. Heath. *Collected Works of Erasmus*. 86 vols. Ed. A.H.T. Levi. Toronto: U of Toronto P 1986. Vol. 27.

*The Famous Tragedie of the Life and Death of Mris. Rump ... As it was presented*

... *May, 1660*. London: Printed for Theodorus Microcosmus 1660.
*The Famous Tragedie of King Charles I*. [London] 1649.
Fox, Margaret Fell. *Womens Speaking Justified ... and how women were the first that preached ... etc*. London 1667.
Freud, Sigmund. *Civilization and Its Discontents*. Ed. James Strachey, trans. Joan Riviere. London: Hogarth P 1975.
G.S., a Lover of Loyalty. *The Dignity of Kingship Asserted: In Answer to Mr. Milton's Ready and Easie way ... Proving that ... Obedience thereto is ... the only way under God to restore ... these ... almost ruined Nations*. London: Printed by E.C. for H. Seile 1660.
*The Geneva Bible: A Facsimile of the 1560 Edition*. Intro. Lloyd E. Berry. Madison: U of Wisconsin P 1969.
Gildon, Charles. *To Mr. T.S. in Vindiction of Mr. Milton's Paradise lost*. In *Critical Essays of the Seventeenth Century*. Ed. J.E. Spingarn. 3 vols. London: Oxford UP 1957. Vol. 3.
Goodwin, Thomas, Philip Nye, et al. *An Apologeticall Narration Humbly Submitted to the Honourable House of Parliament*. 1644. In *Tracts on Liberty in the Puritan Revolution 1638–1647*. Ed. William Haller. 3 vols. New York: Columbia UP 1933. Vol. 2.
Hall, Joseph. *An Humble Remonstrance to the High Court of Parliament*. London 1640. New York: Da Capo P 1970.
Haller, William, ed. *Tracts on Liberty in the Puritan Revolution 1638–1647*. 3 vols. New York: Octagon 1965.
Harrington, James. *The Censure of the Rota Upon ... "The Ready and Easie Way to Establish a Free Commonwealth."* London: Printed by Paul Giddy 1660.
–. *Works; the Oceana and Other Works*. Aalen, Germany: Scientia Verlag 1963.
Herodotus. *Herodotus: A New and Literal Version ... with a Geographical and General Index*. Ed. Henry Cary. New York: Harper 1860.
Hobbes, Thomas. *Leviathan*. In *The English Philosophers from Bacon to Mill*. Ed. Edwin Burtt. New York: Random House 1939.
Homer. *Iliad*. Trans. Martin Hammond. Harmondsworth: Penguin 1987.
–. *The Odyssey of Homer*. Trans. Richmond Lattimore. New York: Harper and Row 1965; rpr 1977.
Johnson, Samuel. *Milton*. In *Lives of the English Poets*. Ed. George Birkbeck Hill. 2 vols. New York: Octagon Books 1967. Vol. 1.
Jonson, Ben. *Ben Jonson*. Ed. C.H. Herford and Percy and Evelyn Simpson. 11 vols. Oxford 1925–52. Vol. 8.
Jordan, Thomas. "The Rebellion." In *Rump: or an Exact Collection of the Choycest Poems and Songs Relating to the Late Times ... from Anno 1639 to Anno 1661*. London: Printed for Henry Brome and Henry Marsh 1662. 1:291–4.
Josephus, Flavius. *The Works of Josephus*. Trans. William Whiston. Peabody, Mass.: Hendrickson 1987.

King James I [C. Philopatris]. *The True Lawe of free Monarchies: or, The Reciprock ... Betwixt a free King, and his naturall Subjectes*. Edinburgh 1598.

L'Estrange, Roger. *No Blinde Guides*. London 1660.

*The Life and Death of Mris Rump and the Fatal end ... whence this ... Monster had its Nativity*. London: Printed for Theodorus Microcosmus 1660.

Luther, Martin. *Luther's Works: Lectures on Genesis, Chapters 6–14*. 54 vols. Ed. Jaroslav Pelikan and Daniel E. Poellot. St Louis: Concordia 1960. Vol. 2.

Lydgate, John. *Lydgate's Fall of Princes*. Ed. Henry Bergen. London: Oxford UP 1967.

Marlowe, Christopher. *The Tragical History of Doctor Faustus*. Ed. Paul H. Kocher. Arlington Heights, Ill.: AHM Publishing 1950.

Marvell, Andrew. *The Complete Poems*. Ed. Elizabeth Story Donno. Harmondsworth: Penguin 1972.

Masson, David. *The Life of John Milton*. 7 vols. Gloucester, Mass.: Smith 1965.

*Mercurius Pragmaticus*. London 1648

Milton, John. *Complete Poems and Major Prose*. Ed. Merritt Y. Hughes. New York: Odyssey 1957.

–. *Complete Prose Works of John Milton*. Ed. Don Wolfe et al. 8 vols. New Haven: Yale UP 1953–82.

–. *Facsimile of the Manuscript of Milton's Minor Poems Preserved in the Library of Trinity College Cambridge*. Ed. William Aldis Wright. Cambridge: Cambridge UP 1899. BM MS Facs. 133.

–. *The Poems of John Milton*. Ed. John Carey and Alastair Fowler. London: Longmans 1968.

–. *The Poetical Works of John Milton, with Notes of Various Authors*. Ed. Henry John Todd. 7 vols. London 1809. New York: AMSP 1970.

Monk, George. *Treason Arraigned. In Answer to Plain English ... directed to the Lord General Monck ... &c*. London 1660.

*Mris. Rump brought to Bed of a Monster, with ... the great misery she hath endured by this ... Monster of Reformation, with the great care of ... Mris London the Midwife*. London: Printed for Theodorus Microcosmus 1660.

Neville, Henry. *The Ladies Parliament*. London 1647.

Nietzsche, Friedrich. *On the Advantage and Disadvantage of History for Life*. Trans. Peter Preuss. Indianapolis: Hackett Publ. 1980.

–. *The Will to Power*. Ed. and trans. Walter Kaufmann. London: Weidenfeld & Nicolson 1968.

Pareus, David. *A Commentary Upon the Divine Revelation of the Apostle and Evangelist John*. Trans. Elias Arnold. Amsterdam 1644.

Parker, Henry. *Observations upon some of his Majesties late Answers and Expresses*. In *Tracts on Liberty in the Puritan Revolution 1638–1647*. Ed. William Haller. 3 vols. New York: Octagon 1965. Vol. 2.

Peck, Francis. *New Memoirs of the Life and Poetical Works of Mr. John Milton:*

*With An Examination of Milton's Stile, & Explanatory & Critical Notes on divers Passages of Milton & Shakespeare*. London 1740.

Perrot, John. *An Epistle for the most Pure Amity and Unity ... to all ... that desire ... God's Truth ... for Ever*. London: Friends House 1662.

Plato. *Republic*. Trans. Paul Shorey. *The Collected Dialogues of Plato*. Ed. Edith Hamilton and Huntington Cairns. Princeton: Princeton UP 1961.

Portfolio 1b. 140. "Concerning the Authority & Dominion in the Church & in the outward Creation." London: Friends House [ca 1650s]. In *Collection of ancient MSS illustrating the early times of the Society of Friends*. Comp. James Dix. Bristol 1876.

*A Presse full of Pamphlets: Wherein, Are set Diversity of Prints ... Composed into Books fraught with Libellous and Scandalous Sentences ... 1642*. London: Printed for R.W. 1642.

Puttenham, George. *The Arte of English Poesie*. Ed. Gladys Doidge Willcock and Alice Walker. Cambridge: Cambridge UP 1936.

Raleigh, Sir Walter. *The marrow of historie ... to the end of the last Macedonian War*. London: Printed by W. Du-gard, for J. Stephenson 1650.

Ray, John. *A Collection of English Proverbs ... Whereunto are added Local Proverbs ... and Scottish Proverbs*. Cambridge 1670.

Richardson, Jonathan. *Explanatory Notes and Remarks on Milton's Paradise Lost*. New York: Garland Publ. 1970.

Sackville, Thomas. "The Induction." *The Mirror for Magistrates*. Ed. Lily B. Campbell. Cambridge: Cambridge UP 1938; rpr Barnes & Noble 1960.

Sandys, George. *Ovid's Metamorphoses*. Ed. Karl Hulley and Stanley Vandersall. Lincoln: U of Nebraska P 1970.

Shelley, Percy Bysshe. *The Complete Works of Percy Bysshe Shelley*. Ed. Roger Ingpen and Walter E. Peck. 10 vols. New York: Gordian P 1965. Vol. 7.

Sheppard, Samuel. *The Committee-Man Curried. A comedy presented to the view of all Men*. London 1647.

Smith, John. *Of Prophecy*. In *Select Discourses*. Ed. Henry G. Williams. 4th ed. Cambridge 1859.

Sowernam, Esther. *Esther hath hanged Haman*. In *Half Humankind: Contexts and Texts of the Controversy about Women in England, 1540–1640*. Ed. Katherine Usher Henderson and Barbara F. McManus. Urbana: U of Illinois P 1985.

Spenser, Edmund. *The Faerie Queene*. Ed. Thomas Roche. New Haven: Archon Books 1984.

Sprat, Thomas. *The History of the Royal-Society of London, For the Improving of Natural Knowledge*. London: Printed by T.R. for J. Martyn 1667.

Toland, John. *The Life of John Milton ... with Amyntor ... and Various Notes Now Added*. London: Printed for John Darby 1761; rpr Folcroft P 1969.

Tooke, Andrew. *The Pantheon*. London 1713; New York: Garland Publ. 1976.

Virgil. *The Aeneid*. Trans. John Dryden. Ed. Robert Fitzgerald. New York: Macmillian 1965.

Voltaire [François-Marie Arouet]. *Voltaire's Essay on Epic Poetry: A Study and an Edition.* Ed. Florence Donnell White. New York: Phaeton P 1970.

Walker, Clement. *Anarchia Anglicana: or, The History of Independency. The Second Part ... By Theodorus Verax.* 1649.

Waller, Edmund. *The Poems of Edmund Waller.* Ed. G. Thorn Drury. 2 vols. London: G. Rutledge 1893.

Walton, Izaak. *The Compleat Angler, 1653–1676.* Ed. Jonquil Bevan. New York: Oxford UP 1983.

Walwyn, William. *A Whisper in the Eare of Mr. Thomas Edwards Minister ... Occasioned by ... Gangraena.* In *Tracts on Liberty in the Puritan Revolution 1638–1647.* Ed. William Haller. 3 vols. New York: Octagon 1965. Vol. 3.

–. *The Vanitie of the Present Churches.* In *The Leveller Tracts 1647–1653.* Ed. William Haller and Godfrey Davies. Gloucester, Mass.: Peter Smith 1964.

Welsted, Leonard. *Epistles, Odes, &c. Written on Several Subjects ... To which is prefix'd, A Dissertation concerning the Perfection of the English Language, the State of Poetry, & c.* London: Printed for J. Walthoe and J. Peele 1724.

Wilkins, John. *An Essay Towards a Real Character, And a Philosophical Language.* London: Printed for Sa: Gellibrand, and for John Martin 1668.

–. *Mercury: or the Secret and Swift Messenger. Shewing How a Man may with Privacy and Speed communicate his Thoughts to a Friend at any distance.* 2nd ed. London: Printed for Rich. Baldwin 1694.

Wilkins, W. Walker, ed. "The Anarchie, or The Blessed Reformation Since 1640." In *Political Ballads of the Seventeenth and Eighteenth Centuries.* 2 vols. London: Longman et al. 1860. Vol. 1.

Wilson, Thomas. *The Arte of Rhetorique.* 1553. A Facsimile Reproduction. Intro. Robert Hood Bowers. Gainsville, Fl.: Scholars' Facsimiles & Reprints 1962.

Wooton, David, ed. *Divine Right and Democracy: An Anthology of Political Writing in Stuart England.* Harmondsworth: Penguin 1986.

SECONDARY SOURCES

Achinstein, Sharon. *Milton and the Revolutionary Reader.* Princeton: Princeton UP 1994.

Adams, Mary. "Fallen Wombs: The Origins of Death in Miltonic Sexuality." *Milton Studies* 29 (1992): 165–79.

Allen, Don Cameron. "Some Theories of the Growth and Origin of Language in Milton's Age." *Philosophical Quarterly* 28 (1949): 5–16.

–. *Harmonious Vision: Studies on Milton's Poetry.* New York: Octagon Books 1979.

Alter, Robert. *The Art of Biblical Narrative.* New York: Basic Books 1981.

Anderson, Benedict. *Imagined Communities: Reflections on the Origin and Spread of Nationalism.* London: Verso 1983.

Appelbaum, David. *Voice.* Albany: SUNY P 1990.

Armitage, David, ed. *Milton and Republicanism*. Cambridge: Cambridge UP 1995.
Bakhtin, M.M. *Problems of Dostoevsky's Poetics*. 1963. Ed. & trans. Caryl Emerson. Minneapolis: U of Minnesota P 1984.
–. *Rabelais and His World*. 1965. Trans. Helene Iswolsky. Cambridge, Mass.: MIT P 1968.
–. *The Dialogic Imagination*. 1975. Ed. Michael Holquist. Austin: U of Texas P 1981.
Bal, Mieke. *Narratology: Introduction to the Theory of Narrative*. Toronto: U of Toronto P 1985.
Barber, Charles. *Early Modern English*. London: Deutsch 1976.
Barthes, Roland. *S/Z*. 1970. Trans. Richard Miller. London: Cape 1975.
–. *Sade, Fourier, Loyola*. 1971. Trans. Richard Miller. Berkeley: U of California P 1989.
–. *Image, Music, Text: Essays*. 1977. Trans. Stephen Heath. New York: Hill and Wang 1977.
Belsey, Catherine. *John Milton: Language, Gender and Power*. New York: Blackwell 1988.
Benjamin, Walter. *Theses on the Philosophy of History*. In *Illuminations*. Ed. and intro. Hannah Arendt, trans. Harry Zohn. New York: Harcourt, Brace & World 1968.
–. *Charles Baudelaire: A Lyric Poet in the Era of High Capitalism*. Trans. Harry Zohn. London: NLB 1973.
Bennett, Joan S. *Reviving Liberty: Radical Christian Humanism in Milton's Great Poems*. Cambridge, Mass.: Harvard UP 1989.
Bernheimer, Richard. *Wild Men in the Middle Ages: A Study in Art, Sentiment, and Demonology*. Cambridge, Mass.: Harvard UP, 1952.
Bevington, David M. *Action Is Eloquence: Shakespeare's Language of Gesture*. Cambridge, Mass.: Harvard UP 1984.
Bloom, Harold. *The Anxiety of Influence: A Theory of Poetry*. New York: Oxford UP 1973.
–. *Agon: Towards a Theory of Revisionism*. New York: Oxford UP 1982.
Bookchin, Murray. *Toward an Ecological Society*. Montreal: Black Rose Books 1980.
Booth, Wayne. *The Rhetoric of Fiction*. 2nd ed. Chicago: U of Chicago P 1983.
Bordo, Susan. *The Flight to Objectivity: Essays on Cartesianism and Culture*. Albany: SUNY P 1987.
Bouchard, Donald F. *Milton: A Structural Reading*. Montreal: McGill-Queen's UP 1974.
Brisman, Leslie. *Milton's Poetry of Choice and Its Romantic Heirs*. Ithaca: Cornell UP 1973.
Broadbent, John Barclay. *Some Graver Subject: An Essay on Paradise Lost*. New York: Schocken Books 1967.
Brooks, Peter. *Reading for the Plot: Design and Intention in Narrative*. New

York: Knopf 1984.

Browning, Judith E. "Sin, Eve, and Circe: *Paradise Lost* and the Ovidian Circe Tradition." *Milton Studies* 26 (1990): 135–57.

Burke, Kenneth. *Counter-statement*. 2nd ed. Los Altos, Calif.: Hermes Publications [1953].

–. *The Philosophy of Literary Form: Studies in Symbolic Action*. 2nd ed. Baton Rouge: Louisiana State UP 1967.

Bushnell, Rebecca W. *Tragedies of Tyrants: Political Thought and Theater in the English Renaissance*. Ithaca: Cornell UP 1990.

*Cambridge Bibliography of English Literature*. Ed. Frederick Wilse Bateson. 5 vols. London: Cambridge UP 1940.

Carey, John. "Milton's Satan." In *The Cambridge Companion to Milton*. Ed. Dennis Danielson. Cambridge: Cambridge UP 1989.

Chambers, A.B. "Sin and Sign in *Paradise Lost*." HLQ 26 (1963): 381–2.

Christopher, Georgia. *Milton and the Science of the Saints*. Princeton: Princeton UP 1982.

Collins, Stephen. *From Divine Cosmos to Sovereign State: An Intellectual History of Consciousness and the Idea of Order in Renaissance England*. New York: Oxford UP 1989.

Corns, Thomas N. *Milton's Language*. Cambridge, Mass.: Blackwell 1990.

Cragg, Gerald R. *Puritanism in the Period of the Great Persecution 1660–1688*. Cambridge: Cambridge UP 1957.

Culler, Jonathan D. *The Pursuit of Signs: Semiotics, Literature, Deconstruction*. Ithaca: Cornell UP 1981.

Cunningham, Merrilee. "The Epic Narrator in Milton's *Paradise Regained*." *Renaissance and Reformation* 25 (1989): 215–29.

Cyr, Marc. "The Archangel Raphael: Narrative Authority in Milton's War in Heaven." *Journal of Narrative Technique* 7 (1987): 309–16.

Davies, Stevie. *Images of Kingship in Paradise Lost: Milton's Politics and Christian Liberty*. Columbia: U of Missouri P 1983.

–. *The Idea of Woman in Renaissance Literature: The Feminine Reclaimed*. Lexington: UP of Kentucky 1986.

–. *Milton*. London: Harvester Wheatsheaf 1991.

Davis, Natalie Zemon. "Women on Top." *Society and Culture in Early Modern France*. Stanford, Calif.: Stanford UP 1975.

DiSalvo, Jackie. *War of Titans: Blake's Critique of Milton and the Politics of Religion*. Pittsburgh: U of Pittsburgh P 1983.

Duncan, Joseph Ellis. *Milton's Earthly Paradise: Historical Study of Eden*. Minneapolis: U of Minnesota P 1972.

DuRocher, Richard J. *Milton and Ovid*. Ithaca: Cornell UP 1985.

Eagleton, Terry. *Walter Benjamin, or Towards a Revolutionary Criticism*. London: Verso 1981.

–. *Literary Theory: An Introduction*. Minneapolis: U of Minnesota P 1983.

Eco, Umberto. *The Limits of Interpretation*. Bloomington: Indiana UP 1990.
Entzminger, Robert L. *Divine Word: Milton and the Redemption of Language*. Pittsburgh: Duquesne UP 1985.
Evans, J. Martin. "Milton's Imperial Epic." In *Of Poetry and Politics: New Essays on Milton and His World*. Ed. P.G. Stanwood. Binghamton, NY: Medieval & Renaissance Texts and Studies 1995.
Ferry, Anne D. *Milton's Epic Voice: The Narrator in Paradise Lost*. Cambridge, Mass.: Harvard UP 1963.
Figes, Eva. *The Tree of Knowledge*. London: Sinclair-Stevenson 1990.
Fink, Z.S. *The Classical Republicans: An Essay on the Recovery of a Pattern of Thought in Seventeenth-Century England*. 2nd ed. Evanston, Ill.: Northwestern UP 1962.
Fish, Stanley. *Surprised By Sin: The Reader in Paradise Lost*. New York: St. Martin's 1967.
–. "Inaction and Silence: The Reader in *Paradise Regained*." In *Calm of Mind: Tercentenary Essays on Paradise Regained and Samson Agonistes*. Ed. Joseph Anthony Wittreich. Cleveland: P of Case Western Reserve U 1971.
–. "The Temptation to Action in Milton's Poetry." ELH 48 (1983): 516–31.
–. "Things and Actions Indifferent: The Temptation of Plot in *Paradise Regained*." *Milton Studies* 17 (1983): 163–85.
Fletcher, Anthony. *The Outbreak of the English Civil War*. London: Arnold 1981.
Fokkelman, J.P. *Narrative Art in Genesis: Specimens of Stylistic and Structural Analysis*. Assen/Amsterdam: Van Gorcum 1975.
Forsyth, Neil. "Having done all to Stand: Biblical and Classical Allusion in *Paradise Regained*." *Milton Studies* 21 (1985): 199–215.
Foucault, Michel. "Nietzsche, Genealogy, History." In *Language, Counter-Memory, Practice: Selected Essays and Interviews*. Ed. Donald F. Bouchard, trans. Sherry Simon and Donald F. Bouchard. Ithaca: Cornell UP 1977.
Fowell, Frank, and Frank Palmer. *Censorship in England*. New York: B. Franklin 1970.
Fresch, Cheryl. "Milton's Eve and the Problem of Additions to the Command." *Milton Quarterly* 12 (1978): 83–90.
Froula, Christine. "When Eve Reads Milton: Undoing the Canonical Economy." *Critical Inquiry* 10 (1983): 321–47.
Frye, Northrop. "The Typology of *Paradise Regained*." *Modern Philology* 53 (1956): 227–37.
G.M.G. *The Stage Censor; an historical sketch, 1544–1907*. London: S. Low, Marston 1908.
Gadamer, Hans-Georg. *Truth and Method*. Trans. Garrett Barden and John Cumming. New York: Seabury P 1975.
Gallagher, Philip. *Milton, the Bible, and Misogyny*. Ed. Eugene R. Cunnar and Gail L. Mortimer. Columbia: U of Missouri P 1990.

Gardiner, Samuel R. *History of the Great Civil War*. 4 vols. New York: AMS P 1965. Vol 1.
Gardner, Helen. *A Reading of Paradise Lost*. Oxford: Clarendon 1965.
Genette, Gérard. *Narrative Discourse*. Trans. Jane E. Lewin. Ithaca: Cornell UP 1980.
Giamati, A. Bartlett. *The Earthly Paradise and the Renaissance Epic*. Princeton: Princeton UP 1966.
Gilbert, Allan. *On the Composition of Paradise Lost*. New York: Octagon Books 1972.
Goldberg, Jonathan. *James I and the Politics of Literature: Jonson, Shakespeare, Donne, and Their Contemporaries*. Baltimore: Johns Hopkins UP 1983.
–. *Voice Terminal Echo: Postmodernism and English Renaissance Texts*. New York: Methuen 1986.
–. "Dating Milton." In *Soliciting Interpretation: Literary Theory and Seventeenth-Century English Poetry*. Ed. Elizabeth D. Harvey and Katharine Eisaman Maus. Chicago: U of Chicago P 1990.
Green, Thomas M. *The Light in Troy: Imitation and Discovery in Renaissance Poetry*. New Haven: Yale UP 1982.
Greenblatt, Stephen. "Learning to Curse: Aspects of Linguistic Colonialism in the Sixteenth Century." In *First Images of America: The Impact of the New World on the Old*. Ed. Fredi Chiappelli et al. 2 vols. Berkeley: U of California P 1976.
–. *Renaissance Self-Fashioning: From More to Shakespeare*. Chicago: U of Chicago P 1980.
–. *Learning to Curse: Essays in Early Modern Culture*. New York: Routledge 1990.
Greg, W.W. *A Bibliography of the English Printed Drama to the Restoration*. 4 vols. London: Oxford UP 1939–59.
Gregerson, Linda. *The Reformation of the Subject: Spenser, Milton, and the English Protestant Epic*. Cambridge: Cambridge UP 1995.
Gross, Kenneth. "Satan and the Romantic Satan: A Notebook." In *Remembering Milton: Essays on the Texts and Traditions*. Ed. Mary Nyquist and Margaret Ferguson. New York: Methuen 1987.
Grossman, Marshall. *"Authors to Themselves": Milton and the Revelation of History*. Cambridge: Cambridge UP 1987.
Guillory, John. "From the Superfluous to the Supernumerary: Reading Gender in *Paradise Lost*." In *Soliciting Interpretation: Literary Theory and Seventeenth-Century English Poetry*. Ed. Elizabeth D. Harvey and Katharine Eisaman Maus. Chicago: U of Chicago P 1990.
Halley, Janet E. "Female Autonomy in Milton's Sexual Politics." In *Milton and the Idea of Woman*. Ed. Julia Walker. Chicago: U of Illinois P 1988.
Hamilton, A.C., et al. *The Spenser Encyclopedia*. Toronto: U of Toronto P 1990.
Hamilton, Gary D. "*The History of Britain* and Its Restoration Audience."

In *Politics, Poetics, and Hermeneutics in Milton's Prose*. Ed. David Loewenstein and James Grantham Turner. Cambridge: Cambridge UP 1990.
Hanson, Donald. *From Kingdom to Commonwealth*. Cambridge, Mass.: Harvard UP 1970.
Harada, Jun. "Toward *Paradise Lost*: Temptation and Antichrist in the English Revolution." *Milton Studies* 22 (1986): 45–78.
Hardin, Richard. "Milton's Nimrod." *Milton Quarterly* 22 (1988): 38–44.
Harding, David. *Milton and the Renaissance Ovid*. Urbana: U of Illinois P 1946.
Hardison, O.B. *Toward Freedom and Dignity: the Humanities and the Idea of Humanity*. Baltimore: Johns Hopkins UP 1972.
Harvey, Elizabeth D. *Ventriloquized Voices: Feminist Theory and English Renaissance Texts*. New York: Routledge 1992.
Heidegger, Martin. "Onto-theo-logical Constitution of Metaphysics." *Identity and Difference*. Trans. Joan Stambaugh. New York: Harper & Row 1969.
Helgerson, Richard. *Forms of Nationhood: The Elizabethan Writing of England*. Chicago: U of Chicago P 1992.
Higgins, Patricia. "The Reaction of Women, with special reference to women petitioners." In *Politics, Religion and the English Civil War*. Ed. Brian Manning. London: Arnold 1973.
Hill, Bridget, ed. *The First English Feminist: Reflections on Marriage and Other Writings by Mary Astell*. New York: St Martin's 1986.
Hill, Christopher. *God's Englishman: Oliver Cromwell and the English Revolution*. New York: Dial P 1970.
–. *The World Turned Upside Down: Radical Ideas during the English Revolution*. London: Temple Smith 1972.
–. *Change and Continuity in Seventeenth-Century England*. Cambridge, Mass.: Harvard UP 1975.
–. *Milton and the English Revolution*. London: Faber and Faber 1977.
–. *The Experience of Defeat: Milton and Some Contemporaries*. London: Faber and Faber 1984.
–. *The Collected Essays of Christopher Hill*. 2 vols. Brighton: Harvester P 1985–86.
–. *A Nation of Change and Novelty: Radical Politics, Religions and Literature in Seventeenth-Century England*. New York: Routledge 1990.
Hollander, John. *The Figure of Echo: A Mode of Allusion in Milton and After*. Berkeley: U of California P 1981.
Howard, Jean E. "The New Historicism in Renaissance Studies." ELR 16 (1986): 13–43.
Jameson, Fredric. "Religion and Ideology: A Political Reading of *Paradise Lost*." In *Literature, Politics and Theory: Papers from the Essex Conference 1976–84*. Ed. Francis Barker et al. New York: Methuen 1986.
Johnson, Barbara. *A World of Difference*. Baltimore: Johns Hopkins UP 1987.

Kahn, Victoria. *Rhetoric, Prudence and Skepticism in the Renaissance*. Ithaca: Cornell UP 1985.
Katz, David S. *Philo-Semitism and the Readmission of the Jews to England 1603–1655*. Oxford: Clarendon 1982.
Kendrick, Christopher. *Milton: A Study in Ideology and Form*. New York: Methuen 1986.
Kermode, Frank. *The Genesis of Secrecy: On the Interpretation of Narrative*. Cambridge, Mass.: Harvard UP 1979.
Kerrigan, William. *The Prophetic Milton*. Charlottesville: Virginia UP 1974.
–. *The Sacred Complex: On the Psychogenesis of Paradise Lost*. Cambridge, Mass.: Harvard UP 1983.
Kress, Gunther, and Terry Threadgold. "Towards a Social Theory of Genre." *Southern Review* 21 (1988): 215–43.
LaCapra, Dominick. "Rethinking Intellectual History and Reading Texts." *Rethinking Intellectual History: Texts, Contexts, Language*. Ithaca: Cornell UP 1983.
–. *History and Criticism*. Ithaca: Cornell UP 1985.
Lamont, William M. *Politics, Religion, and Literature in the Seventeenth Century*. Totowa, NJ: Rowman and Littlefield 1975.
Landy, Marcia. "Kinship and the Role of Women in *Paradise Lost*." *Milton Studies* 4 (1972): 3–18.
Laskowsky, Henry. "A Pinnacle of the Sublime: Christ's Victory of Style in *Paradise Regained*." *Milton Quarterly* 15 (1981): 11–13.
Lawry, Jon S. *The Shadow of Heaven: Matter and Stance in Milton's Poetry*. Ithaca: Cornell UP 1968.
Lentricchia, Frank. *After the New Criticism*. Chicago: U of Chicago P 1980.
Leonard, John. *Naming in Paradise: Milton and the Language of Adam and Eve*. New York: Oxford UP 1990.
Levin, Richard. "The Poetics and Politics of Bardicide." PMLA 105 (1990): 491–504.
Lewalski, Barbara K. *Milton's Brief Epic: The Genre, Meaning, and Art of Paradise Regained*. Providence: Brown UP 1966.
–. "Milton on Women – Yet Once More." *Milton Studies* 6 (1974): 3–20.
–. *Paradise Lost and the Rhetoric of Literary Forms*. Princeton: Princeton UP 1985.
Lieb, Michael. *The Sinews of Ulysses: Form and Convention in Milton's Works*. Pittsburgh: Duquesne UP 1989.
Loewenstein, David. *Milton and the Drama of History: Historical Vision, Iconoclasm, and the Literary Imagination*. Cambridge: Cambridge UP 1990.
London, Bette. *The Appropriated Voice: Narrative Authority in Conrad, Forster, and Woolf*. Ann Arbor: U of Michigan P 1990.
Love, Harold. *Scribal Publication in Seventeenth-Century England*. Oxford: Clarendon 1993.
McColley, Diane Kelsey. *Milton's Eve*. Urbana: U of Illinois P 1983.

—. "Eve and the Arts of Eden." In *Milton and the Idea of Woman*. Ed. Julia Walker. Chicago: U of Illinois P 1988.

—. *A Gust for Paradise: Milton's Eden and the Visual Arts*. Urbana: U of Illinois P 1993.

Mack, Phyllis. "Women as Prophets during the English Civil War." *Feminist Studies* 8 (1982): 19–45.

—. *Visionary Women: Ecstatic Prophecy in Seventeenth-Century England*. Berkeley: U of California P 1992.

Maclean, Ian. *The Renaissance Notion of Woman*. Cambridge: Cambridge UP 1980.

Macpherson C.B. *The Political Theory of Possessive Individualism: Hobbes to Locke*. Oxford: Clarendon 1962.

Madsen, William G. "Earth the Shadow of Heaven." *PMLA* 75 (1960): 519–26.

Manning, Brian. "Puritanism and Democracy, 1640–1642." In *Puritans and Revolutionaries: Essays in Seventeenth-Century History Presented to Christopher Ricks*. Ed. Donald Pennington and Keith Thomas. Oxford: Clarendon 1978.

Markley, Robert. *Fallen Languages: Crises of Representation in Newtonian England, 1660–1740*. Ithaca: Cornell UP 1993.

Martz, Louis Lohr. *The Paradise Within; Studies in Vaughan, Traherne, and Milton*. New Haven: Yale UP 1964.

Mascia-Lees, Frances E., Patricia Sharpe, and Colleen Ballerino Cohen. "The Postmodern Turn in Anthropology: Cautions from a Feminist Perspective." *SIGNS* 15.1 (1989): 7–33.

Milner, Andrew. *John Milton and the English Revolution: A Study in the Sociology of Literature*. Totowa, NJ: Barnes 1981.

Miner, Earl. "The Reign of Narrative in *Paradise Lost*." *Milton Studies* 17 (1983): 3–25.

Mink, Louis. "History and Fiction as Modes of Comprehension." *New Literary History* 1 (1970): 541–58.

Moi, Toril. *Sexual/Textual Politics: Feminist Literary Theory*. Methuen 1985; rpr New York: Routledge 1986–90.

Morson, Gary Saul. "Who Speaks for Bakhtin?" In *Bakhtin: Essays and Dialogues on His Work*. Ed. Gary Saul Morson. Chicago: Chicago UP 1986.

Morton, A.L. *The World of the Ranters: Religious Radicalism in the English Revolution*. London: Lawrence & Wishart 1970.

Mulder, John R. "The Lyrical Dimension of *Paradise Lost*." *Milton Studies* 23 (1987): 145–63.

Mustazza, Leonard. "Language as Weapon in Milton's *Paradise Regained*." *Milton Studies* 18 (1983): 195–216.

Norbrook, David. *Poetry and Politics in the English Renaissance*. Boston: Routledge 1984.

Norris, Christopher. *Deconstruction, Theory and Practice*. New York: Methuen 1982.

Nyquist, Mary. "Reading the Fall: Discourse and Drama in *Paradise Lost*." *ELR* 14 (1984): 199–29.

—. "The Genesis of Gendered Subjectivity." In *Re-membering Milton: Essays on the Texts and Traditions*. Ed. Mary Nyquist and Margaret Ferguson. New York: Methuen 1987.

—. "Gynesis, Genesis, Exegesis, and the Formation of Milton's Eve." *Cannibals, Witches, and Divorce*. Baltimore: Johns Hopkins 1987.

Ong, Walter. *Ramus: Method, and the Decay of Dialogue: From the Art of Discourse to the Art of Reason*. Cambridge, Mass.: Harvard UP 1958.

Paré, Ambroise. *On Monsters and Marvels*. Trans. Janis L. Pallister. Chicago: U of Chicago P 1982.

Patterson, Annabel. *Censorship and Interpretation: The Conditions of Writing and Reading in Early Modern England*. Madison: U of Wisconsin P 1984.

—. *Reading Between the Lines*. Madison: U of Wisconsin P 1993.

Patterson, Lee. *Negotiating the Past: The Historical Understanding of Medieval Literature*. Madison: U of Wisconsin P 1987.

Patton, Brian. "The Women Are Revolting? Women's Activism and Popular Satire in the English Revolution." *JMRS* 23, 1(1993): 69–87.

Pearson, A.F. Scott. *Church and State: Political Aspects of Sixteenth Century Puritanism*. Cambridge 1928.

Pechter, Edward. "The New Historicism and Its Discontents: Politicizing Renaissance Drama." *PMLA* 102 (1987): 292–303.

Pedersen, Johannes. *Israel: Its Life and Culture*. 4 vols. London: Oxford UP; rpr 1946, 1954.

Pope, Elizabeth. *Paradise Regained: The Tradition and the Poem*. New York: Russell & Russell 1962.

Potter, Lois. "The *Mistress Parliament* Political Dialogues." *Analytical and Enumerative Bibliography* 1 (1987): 101–70.

—. *Secret Rites and Secret Writing: Royalist Literature, 1641–1660*. Cambridge: Cambridge UP 1989.

Quilligan, Maureen. *Milton's Spenser: The Politics of Reading*. Ithaca: Cornell UP 1983.

Quint, David. "David's Census: Milton's Politics and *Paradise Regained*." In *Re-membering Milton: Essays on the Texts and Traditions*. Ed. Mary Nyquist and Margaret Ferguson. New York: Methuen 1987.

Radzinowicz, Mary Ann. *Toward Samson Agonistes: The Growth of Milton's Mind*. Princeton: Princeton UP 1978.

—. "The Politics of *Paradise Lost*." In *The Politics of Discourse: The Literature and History of Seventeenth-Century England*. Ed. Kevin Sharpe and Steven Zwicker. Berkeley: U of California P 1987.

Rajan, Balachandra. "Osiris and Urania." *Milton Studies* 13 (1979): 221–35.

—. "Surprised by a Strange Language: Defamiliarizing *Paradise Lost*." Colloquium paper. University of Western Ontario, Jan. 1988.

—. "Banyan Leaves and Fig Trees: Some Thoughts on Milton's India." In *Of Poetry and Politics: New Essays on Milton and His World*. Ed. P.G. Stanwood. Binghamton, NY: Medieval & Renaissance Texts and Studies 1995.

Rapaport, Herman. *Milton and the Postmodern*. Lincoln: U of Nebraska P 1983.

Reeve, L.J. *Charles I and the Road to Personal Rule*. Cambridge: Cambridge UP 1989.

Ricoeur, Paul. "Explanation and Understanding: Some Remarkable Connections among the Theory of the Text, Theory of Action, and Theory of History." *The Philosophy of Paul Ricoeur*. Ed. Charles Reagen and David Stuart. Boston: Beacon P 1978.

—. "Narrative Time." *Critical Inquiry* 7 (1980): 169–90.

—. *Time and Narrative*. Trans. Kathleen McLaughlin and David Pellauer. 3 vols. Chicago: U of Chicago P 1983. Vol. 1.

Riggs, William. *The Christian Poet in Paradise Lost*. Berkeley: U of California P 1972.

Roberts, Jeanne Addison. *The Shakespearean Wild: Geography, Genus, and Gender*. Lincoln: U of Nebraska P 1991.

Robertson, David. "Soliloquy and Self in Milton's Major Poems." In *Of Poetry and Politics: New Essays on Milton and His World*. Ed. P.G. Stanwood. Binghamton, NY: Medieval & Renaissance Texts and Studies 1995.

Rollin, Roger. "*Paradise Lost*: Tragical-Comical-Historical-Pastoral." *Milton Studies* 5 (1972): 3–37.

Roudiez, Leon. Introduction to Julia Kristeva, *Desire in Language: A Semiotic Approach to Literature and Art*. Ed. Leon Roudiez, trans. Alice Jardine, Thomas Gora, and Leon Roudiez. Oxford: Blackwell 1980.

Rushdy, Ashraf. *The Empty Garden: The Subject of Late Milton*. Pittsburgh: U of Pittsburgh P 1992.

Said, Edward. *Beginnings: Intention and Method*. New York: Basic Books 1975.

Samuel, Irene. "The Regaining of Paradise." In *The Prison and the Pinnacle: Papers to Commemorate the Tercentenary of Paradise Regained and Samson Agonistes 1671–1971*. Ed. Balachandra Rajan. London: Routledge, 1973.

Sandler, Florence. "Icon and Iconoclast." In *Achievements of the Left Hand: On the Prose of John Milton*. Ed. Michael Lieb and John T. Shawcross. Amherst: U of Massachusetts P 1974.

Schmidt, A.V.C. "Chaucer's Nembrot: A Note on 'The Former Age.'" *Medium Aevum* 47 (1978): 304–7.

Schwartz, Regina M. *Remembering and Repeating: Biblical Creation in Paradise Lost*. Cambridge: Cambridge UP 1988.

Sellin, Paul R. "Milton's Epithet Agonistes." SEL 4 (1964): 137–62.

Shawcross, John. *Paradise Regained: Worthy T'Have Not Remain'd So Long Unsung*. Pittsburgh: Duquesne UP 1988.

—. *John Milton: The Self and the World*. Lexington: UP of Kentucky 1993.

Shoaf, R.A. *Milton, Poet of Duality: A Study of Semiosis in the Poetry and Prose*. New Haven: Yale UP 1985.
Sidney, Sir Philip. *An Apology for Poetry*. Ed. Forrest Robinson. Indianapolis: Bobbs-Merrill 1970.
Silverman, Kaja. *Acoustic Mirror: The Female Voice in Psychoanalysis and Cinema*. Bloomington: Indiana UP 1988.
Sloane, Thomas O. *Donne, Milton, and the End of Humanist Rhetoric*. Berkeley: U of California P 1985.
Spufford, Margaret. *Small Books and Pleasant Histories: Popular Fiction and Its Readership in Seventeenth Century England*. Athens: U of Georgia P 1981.
Stallybrass, Peter. "Patriarchal Territories: The Body Enclosed." In *Rewriting the Renaissance: The Discourses of Sexual Difference in Early Modern Europe*. Ed. Margaret W. Ferguson, Maureen Quilligan, and Nancy J. Vickers. Chicago: U of Chicago P 1986.
Starnes, DeWitt. *Classical Myth and Legend in Renaissance Dictionaries*. Chapel Hill: U of North Carolina P 1955.
Stavely, Keith W.F. *Puritan Legacies: Paradise Lost and the New England Tradition 1630–1890*. Ithaca: Cornell UP 1987.
Steadman, John M. *The Hill and the Labyrinth: Discourse and Certitude in Milton and His Contemporaries*. Berkeley: U of California P 1984.
Stein, Arnold. *Heroic Knowledge: An Interpretation of Paradise Regained and Samson Agonistes*. Hamdon, Conn.: Archon Books 1965.
–. *The Art of Presence: The Poet and Paradise Lost*. Berkeley: U of California P 1977.
Stevens, Paul. *Imagination and the Presence of Shakespeare in Paradise Lost*. Madison: U of Wisconsin P 1985.
–. "'Leviticus Thinking' and the Rhetoric of Early Modern Colonialism." *Criticism* 35 (1993): 441–61.
Sundell, Roger H. "The Narrator as Interpreter in *Paradise Regained*." *Milton Studies* 2 (1970): 83–101.
Swaim, Kathleen. *Before and After the Fall*. Amherst: U of Massachusetts P 1986.
Tayler, Edward W. *Milton's Poetry: Its Development in Time*. Pittsburgh: Duquesne UP 1979.
Teskey, Gordon. "From Allegory to Dialectic: Imagining Error in Spenser and Milton." PMLA 101 (1986): 9–23.
Toliver, Harold E. "Complicity of Voice in *Paradise Lost*." MLQ 25 (1964): 153–70.
Turner, James. *One Flesh: Paradisal Marriage and Sexual Relations in the Age of Milton*. Toronto: Oxford UP 1987.
Turner, Victor. *The Forest of Symbols: Aspects of Ndembu Ritual*. Ithaca: Cornell UP 1967.
Tuttle, Edward F. "Borrowing Versus Semantic Shift: New World

Nomenclature in European Languages." In *First Images of America: The Impact of the New World on the Old*. Ed. Fredi Chiappelli et al. 2 vols. Berkeley: U of California P 1976.

Underdown, D.E. "The Taming of the Scold: The Enforcement of Patriarchal Authority in Early Modern England." In *Order and Disorder in Early Modern England*. Ed. Anthony Fletcher and John Stevenson. Cambridge: Cambridge UP 1985.

Van Den Berg, Sara. "Eve, Sin, and Witchcraft in *Paradise Lost*." MLQ 47 (1986): 347–65.

Waddington, Raymond B. "The Death of Adam: Vision and Voice in Books XI and XII of *Paradise Lost*." MP 70 (1972): 9–21.

Webber, Joan. *The Eloquent "I": Style and Self in Seventeenth-Century Prose*. Madison: U of Wisconsin P 1968.

Weber, Burton J. *Wedges and Wings: The Patterning of Paradise Regained*. Carbondale: Southern Illinois UP 1975.

–. "Point-of-View in *Paradise Lost*, and Critical Point of View." *English Studies in Canada* 10 (1983): 278–88.

Wedgwood, C.V. *Poetry and Politics under the Stuarts*. Ann Arbor: U of Michigan P 1964.

White, Hayden. *Metahistory: The Historical Imagination in Nineteenth-Century Europe*. Baltimore: Johns Hopkins UP 1973.

–. *Tropics of Discourse: Essays in Cultural Criticism*. Baltimore: Johns Hopkins UP 1978.

Wilding , Michael. *Dragon's Teeth: Literature in the English Revolution*. Oxford: Clarendon 1987.

Williams, Arnold. *The Common Expositor: An Account of the Commentaries on Genesis, 1527–1633*. Chapel Hill: U of North Carolina P 1948.

Williams, Raymond. *Keywords: A Vocabulary of Culture and Society*. New York: Oxford UP 1976.

Wittreich, Joseph Anthony. *The Romantics on Milton: Formal Essays and Critical Asides*. Cleveland: P of Case Western Reserve U 1970.

–. *Visionary Poetics: Milton's Tradition and His Legacy*. San Marino, Calif: Huntington Library 1979.

–. *Interpreting Samson Agonistes*. Princeton: Princeton UP 1986.

–. *Feminist Milton*. Ithaca: Cornell UP 1987.

–. "'John, John, I blush for thee!': Mapping Gender Discourses in *Paradise Lost*." In *Out of Bounds: Male Writers and Gender(ed) Criticism*. Ed. Laura Claridge and Elizabeth Langland. Amherst: U of Massachusetts P 1990.

Wolfe, Don M. *Milton in the Puritan Revolution*. New York: Humanities P 1963.

Yoon, Hye-Joon. "'The Fiend Who Came Thir Bane': Satan's Gift to *Paradise Lost*." *Milton Studies* 29 (1992): 3–19.

# Index

Abraham, 32; in *Paradise Lost*, 60, 131, 133
Addison, Joseph, 43, 163n3, 176n17
Aeneas, 56, 62, 68, 71, 73, 84; *see also* Virgil
Anderson, Benedict, 35, 171n1
Appelbaum, David, 43
Aristophanes, 95
Augustine, 20, 21, 98, 112, 181n4

Babel, 10, 13, 21, 23, 39, 78, 116, 131, 150, 155–9, 171n2; and Pentecost, 10, 22, 36, 51, 157, 166n17; *see also* Nimrod
Bacchus, 69; and Nimrod, 79–80; and Urania, 176n16
Bacon, Francis, 37, 42, 91–2
Bakhtin, M.M., 6, 7, 35, 36, 44, 46, 50–1, 71, 76, 82, 85, 175–6n11
Barbaros, 146, 183n13
Barthes, Roland, 7, 12, 37, 47, 48
*Be Merry and Wise*, 29
Bede, 20

Bellerophon, 70
Belsey, Catherine, 109
Belus, 20
Benjamin, Walter, 53, 107
Bennett, Joan S., 136, 173n18
Bible: 1 Chronicles, 33; Daniel, 151–2, 155; Deuteronomy, 157; Exodus, 157; Ezekiel, 33; Ezra, 23; Genesis 2, 119–20; Gen. 3, 102, 120; Gen. 8, 24; Gen. 10, 24; Gen. 10–11, 19–20; Gen. 10–11, 19–20; James, 91; Jeremiah, 147, 159; Judges, 148; 1 Kings, 33; Luke, 25, 157; Mark, 157; Matthew, 157; Numbers, 157; Proverbs, 167n3; Psalm 97, 157; Revelation, 47, 146, 149; Romans, 124
Birch, T., 44
Blackburne, Francis, 14, 44, 48, 65, 80, 163n2
Blake, William, 163n3
Bloom, Harold, 11, 70, 71
Boccaccio, 20
Bookchin, Murray, 113
Booth, Wayne, 81

Bouchard, Donald F., 4, 63, 64, 82–3
Brisman, Leslie, 44–5
Broadbent, John Barclay, 115
Brooks, Peter, 36, 37
Browne, Sir Thomas, 20, 42
Burke, Kenneth, 53–4, 165n10, 171n4
Butler, Samuel, 17, 44, 168nn11–12

Calliope, 104, 180n16
Calvin, Jean, 20, 22, 23, 168n9
Cartwright, Thomas, 31
Censorship, 7, 8, 12, 13, 18–19, 29, 30, 41, 47, 48, 74, 77, 79, 137, 140, 142, 149, 172–3nn10–13, 175n9, 176nn14–15, 187n14
Chambers, A.B., 93
*Character of the Rump*, 43, 183–4n17
Charles I, 40, 139, 146–7, 150, 152, 155; *Eikon Basilike*, 19, 139, 140, 152, 186n7
Charles II, 80, 96

Christopher, Georgia, 116, 184n18, 186n9
Cicero, 64
Circe, 90, 91, 97, 178n3
Clarke, John, 43, 44
Cleveland, John, 16
Coleridge, Samuel T., 82, 176n14, 177n20
Colonialism, 12, 41–2, 72, 74, 85, 98, 100, 111–35, 183n15; *see also* Empire
*Craftie Cromwell*, 95
Cromwell, Oliver, 25, 26, 28, 57–8, 95, 96
Crouch, John, 96
Culler, Jonathan D., 75
Cyr, Marc, 82, 165n9

Dante, 20, 38, 74, 94, 167–8n8, 171n2
Davies, Stevie, 23, 25, 101–2, 186n8
Derrida, Jacques, 7, 109
*Dignity of Kingship*, 29, 183–4n17
DiSalvo, Jackie, 65
Donne, John, 42
Dryden, John, 4, 43
Du Bartas, Guillaume de Saluste, 23, 24, 37, 38–9, 80

Eagleton, Terry, 53, 61, 180n19
Eco, Umberto, 8
Eden: censorship in, 117; ecology, 113–15; feminization of, 111, 181n1; language in, 115; violation of, 111–35; wilderness, 122, 145–6
Edwards, Thomas, 32
Eliot, T.S., 6–7, 52, 164–5n7
Elyot, Sir Thomas, 17
Empire, 14–34 *passim*, 74, 117, 147, 149–59, 182n10; *see also* Colonialism
Epic, multivocal, multigenre, 46; *see also Paradise Lost, Paradise Regained*
Episodes, 84, 176–7n19

Erasmus, Desiderius, 17
Evans, J. Martin, 117

Feminization of confusion/ tyranny, 11–12, 26, 80, 88–110, 116, 122–3, 178–9n6, 179nn7–10, 183n16
Ferry, Anne D., 5, 163–4n4
Filmer, Robert, 27
Fink, Z.S., 30
Fish, Stanley, 5, 175n7, 185n3, 187nn12, 17
Fokkelman, J.P., 22
Foucault, Michel, 37, 48, 53, 107
Fox, Margaret Fell, 102
Freud, Sigmund, 69, 70
Froula, Christine, 100

Gallagher, Philip, 93
Gardner, Helen, 163n4
Gender politics, 11–12, 87–110, 113–14, 123–7 *passim*, 177nn21 and 1–2, 180–1n20, 182n7, 184–5n23
Genette, Gérard, 37, 106
Gilbert, Allan, 63
Gildon, Charles, 50
Goldberg, Jonathan, 4, 5–6, 82
Goodwin, Thomas, 31
Greenblatt, Stephen, 168n14, 183n13
Greg, W.W., 95
Grossman, Marshall, 6, 72, 174n20, 184n19
Guillory, John, 114

Hall, Joseph, 10
Halley, Janet E., 100
Hamilton, Gary D., 49
Harrington, James, 28; *Censure*, 29
Helgerson, Richard, 166n16, 171n1
Hill, Christopher, 18–19, 48, 49, 58, 136, 172–3n10, 174n2
History: constructions/ interventions, 10, 12, 36,

51–61, 125–35; continuum, 52, 53, 54, 59, 107, 130, 137, 173n14; conversation, 54, 55, 113, 160, 173n15; cycle, 143, 150–1, 154; effective history, 48, 53; historiography, 55, 107; misreading, 71–2; and monarchy, 10, 140, 148–9, 185n2, 185–6n4; *see also* Memory, Narrative, Providence, Typology
Hobbes, Thomas, 39–40, 43, 53
Hollander, John, 70
Howard, Jean E., 165n12, 166n13
Hunton, Philip, 138–9

Iconoclasm, 129–30, 131, 149–154, 164n6
Image, definitions of, 164n6; *see also* Voice: images of
Intentionalism, 8, 49; and New Historicism, 165–6n12

James I, 16, 49
Jameson, Fredric, 58, 166–7n21, 173–4n18, 185n1
Jerome, 20
Johnson, Barbara, 98
Johnson, Samuel, 4, 44, 84
Jonson, Ben, 39
Josephus, Flavius, 20, 24, 155, 183n14

Kendrick, Christopher, 49, 61
Kermode, Frank, 37, 64
Kerrigan, William, 4, 5, 176n16, 180n20
Kingship, 9, 15, 17, 19, 20, 72–4, 79, 97, 170n25; *see also Paradise Regained*: kingship
Kress, Gunther, and Terry Threadgold, 8, 46
Kristeva, Julia, 99

Lacan, Jacques, 89; imaginary/symbolic sphere/order, 100, 102, 107, 108, 178n6
LaCapra, Dominick, 54–6
Language: evolution of 115; indirection, 44–51, 91–4 *passim*, 167n4; linguistic confusion, 4, 10, 22, 23, 35–51, 117–23, 145–6, 171n2, 171–2n6, 172–3nn10–13, 181n4
Lawry, Jon S., 65
L'Estrange, Roger, 29, 123, 135
Lewalski, Barbara K., 4, 6, 74, 75, 76, 179–80n15
Loewenstein, David, 164n6, 184n21
London, Bette, 85
Love, Harold, 172n9, 173n13
Luther, Martin, 20, 24, 167n5, 168n9
Lydgate, John, 20

McColley, Diane Kelsey, 103, 113–15 *passim*, 179–80n15, 182n7
Madsen, William G., 65, 67–8
Markley, Robert, 42
Martz, Louis Lohr, 5
Marvell, Andrew, 111
Mascia-Lees, Frances E., 85
Masson, David, 11, 135
Memory, 53, 104
*Mercurius Pragmaticus*, 95
Millenarianism, 29, 57
Milner, Andrew, 61, 136
Milton, John:
– letters: to Benedetto Buonmattei, 36; to a Friend, 28; to Monk, 28
– works: "Adam unparadiz'd," 59; *An Apology against a Pamphlet*, 8, 25–6, 82; *Animadversions*, 152–3; *Areopagitica*, 8, 24, 33, 47–8, 79, 128, 131, 142, 148, 160; *Art of Logic*, 22, 39, 43; *Christian Doctrine*, 67, 98; *Colasterion*, 87–8, 177n2; *Comus*, 145, 182n6; *A Defence of the People of England*, 17–18, 19, 30, 146, 147, 155, 158; *Doctrine and Discipline of Divorce*, 87, 123; *Eikonoklastes*, 10, 13, 19, 25, 80, 137, 139–41, 149, 152, 155; *Of Civil Power*, 149; *Of Education*, 34; *Of Reformation*, 19; *Of True Religion*, 159; "On the New Forces of Conscience," 26; "The Passion," 140–1; *Prolusions*, 91; *Ready and Easie Way*, 18, 24–5, 26, 28, 29, 30, 33, 80, 135, 157; *Reason of Church-Government*, 11, 33, 47, 51, 148; *Samson Agonistes*, 21, 73, 141; *A Second Defence*, 56–7, 190n36; Sonnet 12, 26; *Tenure of Kings*, 34, 140, 146; *Tetrachordon*, 87; *see also Paradise Lost*, *Paradise Regained*
Mink, Louis, 104
Moi, Toril, 109
Monk, George, 28, 29
Mulder, John R., 164n4
Multigenre, 46–7, 172n8
Muse, invocation of, 71, 79–84, 104, 176n16
Mustazza, Leonard, 132

Narcissus, 89–90, 99–100; narcissism, 90, 97, 99, 102, 103, 106
Narrative: accommodation 62–9; continuum, 52, 75, 76; definition of, 174nn19–20; design and emplotment, 36, 51, 52, 55–6, 59, 125–35 *passim*, 166n18; focalization, 13, 55, 116, 130, 167n22; narrator, 163n1; and story, 106; *see also* History, Memory, Poet-narrator
Nebuchadnezzar: *see Paradise Regained*
Neville, Henry, 95
Nietzsche, Friedrich, 52, 53, 60, 173n14
Nimrod, 4, 9, 10, 14–34, 43, 50, 60, 69, 70, 79–80, 94, 112, 117, 133, 150, 157, 167n6, 181n4; *see also* Babel, Tyranny
Norris, Christopher, 7
Nye, Philip, 31
Nyquist, Mary, 106, 179nn11, 13, 179–80n15, 180nn17–18

Odysseus, 84, 90, 97
Ong, Walter, 75
Orpheus, 79, 80, 104, 180n16
Ovid, 89–90, 99–100, 178n3; *see also* Sandys, George

*Paradise Lost*:
– narrators/genesis stories: Adam, 104–10; Eve, 97–104; Michael, 127–35; Raphael, 63–9; 174n1; Satan, 69–78, 78–86 *passim*, 92–4; Sin, 88–97
– other characters: Abdiel, 56, 86, 131; Beelzebub, 71, 118–19; Cain and Abel, 60, 131; Death, 89–94 *passim*; Enoch, 60, 131; God, 21, 43, 58–9, 86; Isaac, 133; Moses, 60, 134; Mulciber, 18, 33, 96; Muse, 71, 79–84, 104, 176n16; Noah, 60, 131; Pharaoh, 60, 133; Son, 43, 86, 170n25; Uriel, 146; *see also* Poet-narrator
– politics, 9, 11, 13, 14–34, 65, 72, 73–4, 79–80, 94–7, 117, 118–19, 127–8, 134

*Paradise Regained*: censorship, 137, 140, 142, 149, 187n14; debate, 12, 136–7, 138, 141, 146, 150, 159, 187n13; Eliah/Elijah, 131, 146; empire, 147, 149–59; fishermen (Andrew, Simon), 138, 144, 187n16; Herod, 155–6; iconoclasm, 138, 149–54; John, 47, 142, 143, 145, 146; kingship, 138–42, 143, 144–5, 148, 151, 153, 158, 186nn7–8; Mary, 14, 138, 144–5; poet-narrator, 145–6, 147, 150–1, 187–8n17; politics, 138–42, 146–7, 148–9, 152–9, 185n1; prophecy, 142–5 *passim*, 149–54, 185n2; 185–6n4; quietism, 136–7, 156; soliloquy, 83, 143–4, 148; tyranny, 138–42 *passim*, 146–7, 150, 151–2, 186n8
— Christ: authority of, 137, 142; evasive language, 138, 146, 148, 153, 156–7; humanity, 141, 154, 156–9, 187n11, 190n35; identity-formation, 142, 145, 156–7; as prophet, 136, 137, 151–2; political role/king, 136–7, 141, 144–5
— history: as cycle, 143, 150–1, 154; and monarchy, 140, 148–9, 185n2, 185–6n4; as process, 138, 144, 154
— Nebuchadnezzar: Book of Daniel, 151–2, 155; and Charles 147, 152, 155; and Satan 146, 154
— Satan: authority of, 146–7, 155; censor, 137, 138, 142, 149; as false prophet, 154; wildness of speech, 146, 154, 157, 158

— voice: negating, 138–42, 186n8; populace/miscellaneous rabble, 10, 25, 150, 155, 157, 188n21
Pareus, David, 47
Parker, Henry, 139
Patterson, Annabel, 49, 167n4, 173nn12, 13
Pearson, A.F. Scott, 31
Pechter, Edward, 9
Peck, Francis, 44
Plato, 17, 64, 65, 178n6; Platonists, 68
Poet-narrator: *Paradise Lost*, 5, 62–3, 68, 69–78 *passim*, 78–86; *in propria persona*, 82; *see also Paradise Regained*
Politics: *see Paradise Lost*, *Paradise Regained*, Republicanism
Prophecy, 12, 13, 28–9, 47, 127–35; *see also Paradise Regained*
Providence, 11, 12, 56–61, 132, 173–4n18
Puttenham, George, 38

Quietism, 13, 136–7, 156, 166–7n21
Quilligan, Maureen, 93
Quint, David, 49

Radzinowicz, Mary Ann, 167n21, 173n12
Rajan, Balachandra, 3, 64, 123, 183n16
Raleigh, Sir Walter, 17, 20, 27
Ramism, 75
Ray, John, 111
"The Rebellion," 15–16, 167n1
Reeve, L.J., 152
Republicanism, 9, 14, 15, 17, 25, 26, 28, 169n18
Richardson, Jonathan, 44
Ricoeur, Paul, 8, 55, 104, 173n16
Riggs, William, 5
Rollin, Roger, 163–4n4

Roudiez, Leon, 92, 178n16

Sackville, Thomas, 68, 73, 74
Said, Edward, 37, 45
Salmasius, 17, 18, 170n21
Sandys, George, 89–90, 91
Saussure, Ferdinand de, 7
Schmidt, A.V.C., 20
Schwartz, Regina M., 77, 176n13, 179n14
Scylla, 90–2
Shelley, Percy Bysshe, 163n3, 171n4
Sheppard, Samuel, 95
Silverman, Kaja, 99, 179n12
Soliloquy, 11, 51, 62–86, 97, 117, 120, 121, 143–5, 148, 175n5
Solomon, 33, 60, 156
Sowernam, Esther, 111, 118, 182n12, 183n14
Spenser, Edmund, 9, 20, 44, 89–91, 97, 145, 178n4
Sprat, Thomas, 40–1
Stavely, Keith W.F., 117
Steadman, John M., 4
Stein, Arnold, 136, 163n4
Stevens, Paul, 178n5, 183n16
Swaim, Kathleen, 4, 6, 64, 164n5

Teskey, Gordon, 4
Todorov, Tzvetan, 37
Toliver, Harold E., 50
Tooke, Andrew, 79–80
Turner, James, 98, 177–8n2, 181n3, 182n12
Typology, 65, 128, 134–5, 184n21
Tyranny, 10, 11, 14–34, 39, 59–60, 74, 85, 94, 133, 177n21; *see also* Babel, Nimrod, *Paradise Regained*

Underdown, D.E., 87

Van Den Berg, Sara, 103

Virgil, 71, 73, 74, 84, 94, 115, 123; *see also* Aeneas
Voice: appropriation, 165n9; conversation, 40, 45, 87–8, 107, 108, 118, 121, 125–6, 177–8n2, 183n14; definition, 6; dialogism 8, 13, 50, 138; dialogue, 172n7; evolution of, 3–9, 166n19, 174–5n4; images of voice, 6, 8, 11, 70, 79, 92, 93, 104, 164n5, 165n8; multivocality, 13, 81–2, 86, 138, 161; negating, 138–42, 186n8; of history, 55; populace, 9, 10, 15–17, 25–6, 28, 30, 31, 39, 150, 155, 157, 160, 169n17, 170nn21, 23, 188n21; ventriloquism 82, 85, 177n20; *see also* Narrative, Poet-narrator, Soliloquy
Voltaire, 43–4

Walton, Izaak, 17
Walwyn, William, 32, 141
Webber, Joan, 85
Weber, Burton, 4
Wedgwood, C.V., 40
Welsted, Leonard, 43
White, Hayden, 55, 72, 125, 166n18
Wilkins, John, 41, 42, 115
Wilson, Thomas, 38
Wittreich, Joseph Anthony, 37, 82, 184nn5, 23
Wolfe, Don M., 48
Wooton, David, 27

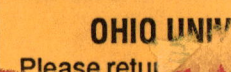